Education for Work

Multilingual Matters

Child Language Disability: Implications in an Educational Setting
    KAY MOGFORD and JANE SADLER (eds)
Community Languages: A Handbook
    BARBARA M. HORVATH and PAUL VAUGHAN
Deaf-ability – Not Disability
    WENDY McCRACKEN and HILARY SUTHERLAND
Emerging Partnerships: Current Research in Language and Literacy
    DAVID WRAY (ed.)
ESL: A Handbook for Teachers and Administrators in International Schools
    EDNA MURPHY (ed.)
Every Child's Language
    (Open Univ. Pack)
Gender in Education
    EILEEN M. BYRNE (ed.)
Language Policy Across the Curriculum
    DAVID CORSON
The Management of Change
    PAMELA LOMAX (ed.)
Managing Staff Development in Schools
    PAMELA LOMAX (ed.)
Oral Language Across the Curriculum
    DAVID CORSON
Parents on Dyslexia
    S. van der STOEL (ed.)
Performance Indicators
    CAROL T. FITZ-GIBBON (ed.)
Story as Vehicle
    EDIE GARVIE
TVEI
    COLIN McCABE
TVEI at the Change of Life
    D. HOPKINS (ed.)

Please contact us for the latest book information:
Multilingual Matters Ltd,
Bank House, 8a Hill Road,
Clevedon, Avon BS21 7HH,
England.

Education for Work

Background to Policy and Curriculum

Edited by
David Corson

MULTILINGUAL MATTERS LTD
Clevedon ● Philadelphia

The Open
University

To the Memory of Joan Sweetland

Library of Congress Cataloging in Publication Data

Education for Work: Background to Policy and Curriculum/Edited by David Corson.
p. cm.
Reprint. Originally published: Palmerston North, New Zealand: Dunmore Press, 1988
Includes bibliographical references and index.
1. Working Class–Education. 2. Education and State. 3. Education–Curricula.
I. Corson, David.
LC5015.E2   1991
371.96   dc

British Library Cataloguing in Publication Data

Education for Work: Background to Policy and Curriculum.
1. Education related to work. 2. Work related to education.
I. Corson, David.
370

ISBN 1-85359-124-6 (pbk)

Multilingual Matters Ltd

UK: Frankfurt Lodge, Clevedon Hall, Victoria Road, Clevedon, Avon BS21 7SJ.
USA: 1900 Frost Road, Suite 101, Bristol, PA 19007, USA.
Australia: P.O. Box 6025, 83 Gilles Street, Adelaide, SA 5000, Australia.

First published in 1988 by The Dunmore Press, P.O. Box 5115, Palmerston North, New Zealand, who retain the distribution rights for New Zealand and Australia.

Copyright © 1991 David Corson.
Reprinted 1993.

Cover design by Tauwira Turipa.
Printed and bound in Great Britain by the Longdunn Press, Bristol.

Contents

Foreword

The reader will find commentaries on the four Parts of this book in the Introductions at Chapters 1, 4, 7 and 14. This Foreword has two purposes: to indicate why *Education for Work* is confined in scope to education in English-speaking countries; and to acknowledge assistance and permissions that helped in the job of writing and compiling the book.

In the past, social scientists and educationists have tried to define 'the human condition' in general as a basis for policy making and curriculum planning in education (LeVine and White, 1986). We have tended to view those who lived in non-Western countries as lacking in development, especially the kind of development that wide processes of formal schooling were thought to provide. There has been a frequent attempt to translate the 'best from the West' to these countries, to supply what they are thought to lack, to open their horizons to advantages that they have not encountered. We know now from a range of studies, such as those undertaken by the Harvard Project on Human Potential, that these earlier views disregarded the multitude of benefits and advantages that do not fit into the categories of desired outcomes in Western educational thought; we know that non-Western peoples have visions of utopias growing from their traditions that are often very different from our own; and we know that they possess "distinctive and coherent images of well-being, public virtue and personal maturity that guide the education of children and motivate the activities of adults" (Levine and White, 1986 p. 12).

Knowledge of this kind places severe limitations on the scope of a book that looks at policy and curriculum practice across societies. It limits that scope inevitably to a tight consideration of Western education, ideas and values about work. More than this our scope is further limited by the practical constraints that language places on scholarship: a book that owes much to the works of Anglo-American scholars like Dewey, Popper and Russell has its perspectives narrowed by the cultural constraints within which those scholars themselves operated. We are certainly far enough advanced in our thinking to recognise that generalisations in the social sciences are much rarer than we had once thought; 'education for work', for example, can have many manifestations across societies and cultures. For all these reasons, then, this book is limited in its scope to 'education for work' in the English-speaking countries from which the authors of its eighteen chapters are drawn: the countries that make up North America, Britain and Australasia. For the book to be read in those countries will be enough; for it to be read beyond those countries will be a bonus.

Acknowledgments

The UNESCO Institute of Education in Hamburg provided the impetus for this book, in particular the former Executive Editor of UNESCO's *International Review of Education*, Paul Fisk. In bringing the manuscript into its final state I gratefully acknowledge the help of Michelle Cheetham, Gillian Hammond, Elaine Martin, Charmaine Keys and Alison Gunning. I am grateful to Ivan Snook for his scholarly comments on the chapters that introduce the four Parts of the book and for his support in other ways. Finally, I am indebted to the fourteen contributors of chapters for their unstinting commitment to the project. Some of the chapters have been reproduced with the permission of the original publishers:

Chapter 2 "Towards a humanistic conception of education [and work]" by Noam Chomsky in *Work, Technology and Education* edited by W. Feinberg and H. Rosemont. University of Illinois Press: Urbana (1975) pp. 204-219.

Chapter 3 "Education, schooling and the world of work" by Colin Wringe in *British Journal of Educational Studies* 29 (1981) pp. 123-137.

Chapter 11 "Social and technological change: diversity or commonality in post-school education" by Douglas Weir in *British Journal of Educational Studies* 32 (1984) pp. 118-124.

Chapter 12 "Youth unemployment: a review of the literature" by Adrian Furnham in *Journal of Adolescence* 8 (1985) pp. 109-124.

Chapter 16 extracted from "Education and the world of work" by William Taylor in *Education and the World of Work*. Australian College of Education: Melbourne (1980) pp. 107-125.

David Corson   February 1988
Massey University
Palmerston North
New Zealand

Part One

The Meaning and Value of Work to the Individual

1

Introduction: The Meaning and Place of Work

by David Corson

Cultural and Historical Influences

It is a risky business to make recommendations about policy in education and then try to apply those recommendations across cultures. This is why our concern here is with 'education for work' only in those cultures that are broadly alike in the knowledge, beliefs and experiences of their peoples; countries that are linguistically and culturally similar. Even this does not eliminate the problem, though, for 'work' itself means different things in different cultures. When we come to discuss the meaning of 'work' across cultures it is also a risky business to try to generalise about that meaning. Clearly 'work' means very different things to people depending on their cultural backgrounds and social history. Contrasts in meanings of this kind become marked when we compare agrarian cultures with the urban-industrial ones that are our concern in this book.

For example, in agrarian societies common economic and demographic conditions are portrayed in a widespread approval of 'child labour' and in a commitment to 'natural fertility' (LeVine and White, 1986); both of these conditions in turn affect the way that work is viewed in those societies. In urban-industrial societies, on the other hand, such as the English-speaking democracies that we are concerned with, the rise of wage labour and bureaucratic employment has come to provide an alternative to the agricultural and craft production that shaped people's expectations and views about work in earlier times. The workplace has become separated from the home; occupational roles have become distinct from kin-based roles and relationships; labour market values have penetrated into family decisions about the future of offspring; parents have come to see that children's job prospects are far removed from any form of socialisation that they can possibly receive within the family; and parents are not usually well placed to make the social connections necessary to put their children in touch with work that might suit and satisfy their wants and talents.

There was a brutal intermediate stage in the development of the contemporary view of work in urban-industrial societies, a stage reached in western Europe in the eighteenth and nineteenth centuries. Our views of work are still heavily coloured by events in that early modern period which saw a decline in the ability of parents to provide their offspring with genuine training for work. As a result the influence of parents over their children's lives weakened. This supervisory control was passed instead to the foremen and overseers of early capitalism, uncommitted to the workers by any ties of affection or blood but committed mainly to the success of the work in which their charges were engaged. This period gave birth to William Blake's 'dark, satanic mills' and his 'Spectre rising over Albion' which Jan Branson alludes to in Chapter 8 of this volume. The stage was set for the cruel periods of child labour and worker abuse that accompanied the onset of the Industrial Revolution, a set of events that fostered working class reform movements that are still very much with us in the form of trade unions and other labour organisations.

This change in the way that work was organised produced another set of satellite attributes that still influence our modern interpretations of work: almost universally work became a contractual arrangement organised along lines that were and are broadly bureaucratic. The workers of the late Industrial Revolution (and their descendants today) were asked not only to tender their skills in exchange for a wage but also to conform to a new code of social behaviour; this code involved a radical change in the ways they viewed themselves, their work and their relationship to it. Instead of having commitment to their work established for them as a result of skills learned and refined in the family or by their craft membership, workers very often had their loyalty shaped for them artificially by the bonds of a contract with their employer, either written or more commonly verbal. An arrangement of this kind, though, produces shallower loyalties to work itself; the meaning and value of work changed as a result. Workers instead found an outlet for the commitment, that could no longer be located in work, in the causes espoused by the trade and professional organisations that offered them membership by occupation type. They ceased to be bound as much by a sense of loyalty to any given form of employment in any particular locale; very often too they were not bound necessarily by a strong commitment to any particular standard of production or level of service in their work.

These and other changes in urban-industrial societies have produced changes in the way that work itself is viewed. We might argue that work has become a less 'natural' form of behaviour in developed societies than it is in agrarian ones, since it is directed towards ends that are themselves largely artificial: in the sense that the ends are fabricated by human beings themselves and not by the needs that we have as a biological species. This argument, though, that what is natural is somehow better, is not very helpful; it suggests that a move 'back to nature' is something to be prized and recommended. The reality, though, is that returning to a more natural approach to work and lifestyle is beyond the reach of the majority of people in urban-industrial societies and not remotely desired by them either. Work has a meaning for most people, at least in contemporary English-speaking societies, that is firmly set by the socialisation and enculturation processes that they have been through. For most people the meaning of 'work' is the way it is because it could be no other way. How can we approach and understand this meaning of 'work' in a way that will reveal the place of work in the lives of people in urban-industrial societies and establish, at the same time, some of the necessary connections between work and education?

Occupational and Recreational Work

One sociologist's definition contrasts 'work' with 'recreation'. Work is a means to an end, while recreation is an end in itself: "Work is a purposeful activity performed by men [and women] in producing goods or services of value, whether for remuneration or not" (Anderson, 1964 p. 133). This distinction between work and recreation, the one a means to an end and the other an end in itself, is an important one for my discussion. If we do accept it as a reasonable distinction and 'work', as a result, is characterised as a means to an end, then drastic implications might follow for 'education for work'. I believe, though, that we cannot accept this 'means to an end' interpretation of the meaning of 'work'. If we subscribe to the common view that 'the meaning of a word is its use in a language' then any reasonable and common instance of the word 'work' being used to describe an activity of recreation will suggest that the 'means to an end' and 'end in itself' distinction is not watertight.

Are there instances of recreational activities to which the English word 'work' can be appropriately applied? The recreational field of 'hobbies' suggests itself immediately. So many hobbies are conducted in workshops, using tools of work operated on workbenches. Do we refer to the activities themselves as work? The answer is that we commonly do refer to hobby activities as work without attaching any specialist sense to the meaning of the word 'work'. The philatelist, for example, might say 'I am at work on my collection'. Even those who play games or exercise for recreation describe their activities on occasions as work. Mountaineers or chess players might reflect on their activities, the former describing them as 'hard work scaling that cliff' and the latter as 'easy work disposing of our opponents'. Recreational activities, then, can be described as 'work', even when there are no overt goods or services of value produced. It is clear from this discussion that work can be both a means to an end and an end in itself.

Work becomes a means to an end when it is performed in an occupational role: as the work activity of a job. Let me use the term 'recreational work' to describe the form of work that is an end in itself; let me use 'occupational work' for that variety of work which is instrumental to some other goal (usually the remuneration of workers or the survival of themselves and their societies). Recreational work is voluntary in every respect, for it is of the nature of recreation that it ceases to exist for people compelled to pursue it. Recreational workers are free to choose the time, the venue, the duration, and the intensity of their work activity. If they are not reasonably free to choose these aspects of their work then they are not recreational workers, since their work is instrumental to some other goal (for example, placating the forces that impinge upon their freedom of choice).

On the other hand occupational workers may be less free to control these intruding aspects of their work since they are usually under contract to perform certain things. They are constrained to accept certain limiting conditions of time, venue, duration and intensity that might not be to their liking. These occupational workers may not be able to exclude these constraints from their interpretation of the meaning of the work they do. Their work is so influenced by these factors that the meaning of 'work' for them becomes an amalgam of interests, circumstances and forces which may seem to others to be separate from the work activity itself. This work is a less unalloyed form of work than is recreational work, unless occupational workers are able to separate the work from the constraints, either in practice or by some mental adjustment that allows them to perceive the 'work' and the 'constraints' as distinct.

Constrained and Unconstrained Occupational Work

Workers differ markedly in the degree of constraint under which they work. At one extreme, for example, galley slaves or assembly line workers are subject to influences of time, venue, intensity and duration that are quite outside their control. We might call these people 'constrained occupational workers' or 'labourers'. Moving along to the other extreme of the continuum there are, for instance, many professional persons or academic researchers who can afford to adopt a quite whimsical and licentious approach to matters of time, venue, intensity and duration. We might call these people 'unconstrained occupational workers'. The meaning of 'work' for this latter group of workers is much closer to the work activity itself than it is for the more constrained occupational workers who tend to perceive the contraints affecting their work as part of the work.

In fact the meaning of work for unconstrained occupational workers is very like the meaning of work for recreational workers, since recreational work is performed in an atmosphere relatively free from intruding constraints. The further along the continuum that workers move from unconstrained to constrained occupational work, the less like recreational workers they become.

Unconstrained occupational workers, like recreational workers, are more able to see work as an end in itself; they are able to see it as a desirable alternative to recreational work or even as a special form of recreational work activity. They are doubly rewarded by their work: even without its remuneration, it still represents 'meaningful work'. The more constrained occupational workers though are not encouraged to see work as much more than a means to an end. Their work has a meaning that is separate from themselves and from their non-work activities. The meaning that they place on work is unavoidably linked with the remuneration that they receive for it.

In a paper that is very relevant to our theme here, Robin Attfield (1984) contends that 'meaningful work' responds to an essential human need, offering most people their best chance in life of the necessary good of self-respect. He begins with the traditional accounts of work offered by Herbst (1973) and Arendt (1958); he shows that these accounts are very like an account which Escheté (1974) derives from Karl Marx to distinguish 'meaningful work' from 'labour' (categories similar to my unconstrained and constrained occupational work). Attfield concludes that Marx's' well-known premise is true : free and creative productive activity, of the type provided by meaningful work, is an essential human capacity. Attfield argues that because meaningful work in our culture and the self-respect that goes with it are usually linked with having employment, then we should recognise the value of work to the individual and accordingly plan for full employment as a high social priority. Many of the chapters that follow lend support to this view : it is a social value that this book embraces.

A fundamental value at stake in the 'education for work' debate is the individual's entitlement to freedom. In English-speaking societies we are accustomed to cherishing this value ahead of others; we are ready to allow a good deal of social inequality to exist in order to preserve individual's rights to freedom. Perhaps the leading 'apostle of freedom' in the twentieth century has been Bertrand Russell. His humanistic conception of Man remains a standard libertarian viewpoint; it leads directly to the libertarian educational theories with which he was associated; it also leads to libertarian concepts of social organisation that lay stress on a particular view of the nature of work. Noam Chomsky, writing in Chapter 2 as a social and educational theorist, supports the 'humanistic conception of education and work' advocated by Russell; he also extends this set of ideas to show that the view is coherent with the ideas of Kropotkin and Marx. In this chapter Chomsky points out the dangers of a form of schooling that does not educate for critical autonomy but seeks rather to train workers to labour uncritically and conform with authoritarian ideologies. He ranges widely over recent events in education and in societies; in particular he seizes on that central event in the mid-twentieth century that has been a catalyst for so much else, the Vietnam War, to argue against forms of training and indoctrination that control minds, restrict key freedoms and serve to bolster policies of oppression.

Chomsky sets this libertarian view, which sees work as a free and conscious activity that is necessary to life, against the common economist's stance: the 'contrasting and more prevalent view of the nature of work, namely that labour is a commodity to be sold on the market for maximal return, that it has no intrinsic value itself. Constrained occupational work, in which the constraints are tolerated in order to ensure an end-of-week wage, comes much closer to this view of the nature of work than does unconstrained occupational work. The latter, which is both an end in itself and a means to an end, is closer in nature to the libertarian view, which sees work as having value for its own sake: a necessary part of a normal healthy life.

The factors that motivate occupational work and determine its value for individuals include the level of remuneration for the work, the constraints that impinge upon the work activity itself, and the ability of workers to separate the meaning of the work activity itself from its constraints and its remuneration. If they see work as a commodity to be sold, then its remuneration is very important as a motive, and remuneration will be a part of the meaning of their work. They may embrace more strongly the constraints that impinge upon their work, thereby increasing their capacity to sell their work as a commodity. The constraints become an intricate part of the work activity.

On the other hand, if individuals are able to separate the work activity from its constraints and remuneration by approaching work more in the fashion of recreational workers, then they become more like craftsmen, they become more like the skilled workers of agrarian societies who love their labour for its own sake.

'My work means a lot to me' is the statement a craftsman might make. It is the sort of statement made by people who see value in their work. This is a different type of 'meaning' for work. It depends perhaps on workers seeing the other meaning of their work first (its point or significance) so that they make their own assessment of its value and place in their lives.

The attitudes of people to work reflect the way their culture values work. In many ancient cultures occupational work was not highly valued, while recreational work was valued. For the Hebrews and Ancient Greeks work was painful drudgery that brutalized the mind. Aristotle, for example, distinguished between 'work' and 'leisure' and regarded work as inferior to non-work. In his 'Politics' he argues that the many have to work to give the few the chance of leisure (and this has happened in many periods of history).

For the Roman ruling class in the first century AD, when up to ninety percent of the population of Italy were slaves or their descendants, occupational work of any kind, apart from warfare or statecraft, was despised. Since the Renaissance, though, attitudes to work in the Western world have changed. Luther, for example, saw work as "the base and key to life", an activity to be prized for its own sake.

The Renaissance view of work finds the reasons for work in the work itself. This contrasts with the so-called Protestant view of work, which places value on the religious rewards associated with the activity and warns against the powerful guilt that might arise if one were not to work (Best, 1973). Neither the Renaissance nor the Protestant view is now fashionable. The Renaissance view has declined with a recognition that the joy creative work can carry in practice seems limited to a small minority, and the Protestant view has declined with the decline in the search for religious rewards. The meaning (as value) of occupational work to modern individuals and their society needs expression in terms that go beyond the ideas of Renaissance and Protestant rhetoric. The humanistic conception of work that Chomsky presents in Chapter 2 seems much closer to the ideal that is shared by men and women in today's urban-industrial societies.

Why else is work of value to the modern individual? Occupational work remains very much a way of life. In earlier times, before there was a strict division of labour and a 'job register', people were defined as individuals according to the work activity that they performed: people took their identities and often their names from the distinguishing marks of their work; they lost their identities if their work lacked these marks or if they themselves lacked work. These marks of identity remain today. Cassirer observes that the mark of individuals is not their metaphysical or physical nature, but their work. Work is "the system of human activities which defines and determines the circle of humanity" (cited in Entwistle, 1970 p. 20). More than this, though, Attfield (1984) shows that work is a vital component of the human essence. For individuals work has a worthwhileness that takes ready precedence over the value of its products. Work defines their individuality; it distinguishes for others their preferred way of life, and it lays the important building blocks for self-esteem that are provided when individuals have distinguishing marks for their identity. Work is regarded by many as the central life activity; it has created human civilisation.

Social theorists and political figures though sometimes oversimplify matters: they wrongly argue that since human individuals appear to be driven by a need to spend much of their lives at work then they have a duty through that work to contribute to the societies to which they belong. They further argue that societies, then, have an overriding goal to meet in the education of their citizens: to equip them in their schooling with the means of contributing to material production in the service of those societies. Colin Wringe in Chapter 3 looks at earlier views that have been held by educational thinkers about the relationship that should exist between school and work. He bypasses the 'elitist' view, held in the days when the graduates of education were not expected to enter work, a view which therefore saw no connection between school and work. Wringe also looks at the 'liberal' view, which grows out of older positions: on this view any accidental link between education and work is a happy bonus, but schooling should not deliberately address the task of preparing students for adult social functions. Thirdly Wringe addresses the 'deschooler's position' on this question and sees it as a straightforward acknowledgement that schools work to convince most people that they do not measure up and that they should see their occupational future therefore as restricted to menial work. Finally he briefly examines Warnock's position: that any learning is 'education' if it contributes to the 'good life' made up of virtue, work and imagination. Using these views as a backdrop Wringe outlines the position that teachers seem obliged to adopt as professional persons: firstly, because of the commitment to truth that is part of every teacher's responsibility in the task of educating, certain things need to be communicated frankly to children about the world of work; he itemises these things. Secondly, he gives several reasons why preparation for work is a morally acceptable part of schooling, provided that the preparation is intended as education, not simply as training. Wringe, like Chomsky, sees the aim of training as the production of a conforming mind, while education's aim is the development of rational autonomy. He concludes by urging a change in the balance between education and training. In Chapter 4 I return to the education/ training issue, a theme central to this book.

Toward a Humanistic Conception of Education and Work

by Noam Chomsky

I had the very great personal honour to deliver some memorial lectures for Bertrand Russell at Trinity College, Cambridge (published as Chomsky 1971), and in the course of thinking about and preparing for them I had the pleasure of reading and rereading a fair amount of his work written over many years. Russell had quite a number of things to say on educational topics that are no less important today than when he first discussed them. He regularly took up - not only discussed but also tried to carry out - very interesting and provocative ideas in the field of educational theory and practice. He claimed throughout his years of interest in this area that the primary goal of education is to elicit and fortify whatever creative impulse Man may possess. And this conclusion, which he formulated in many different ways over a period of years, derives from a particular concept of human nature that he also expressed in many different forms. It grows from what he called a "humanistic conception," which regards a child as a gardener regards a young tree, that is as something with a certain intrinsic nature, which will develop into an admirable form, given proper soil and air and light.

Elsewhere he pointed out that "the soil and the freedom required for a man's growth are immeasurably more difficult to discover and to obtain ... And the full growth which may be hoped for cannot be defined or demonstrated; it is subtle and complex, it can only be felt by a delicate intuition and dimly apprehended by imagination and respect." Therefore he argued that education should be guided by the "spirit of reverence" for "something sacred, indefinable, unlimited, something individual and strangely precious, the growing principle of life, an embodied fragment of the dumb striving of the world." This is one view of the nature of education, based on a certain conception of human nature that Russell called the humanistic conception. According to this conception the child has an intrinsic nature, and central to it is a creative impulse. Pursuing that line of thinking, the goal of education should be to provide the soil and the freedom required for the growth of this creative impulse; to provide, in other words, a complex and challenging environment that the child can imaginatively explore and, in this way, quicken his intrinsic creative impulse and so enrich his life in ways that may be quite varied and unique. This approach is governed, as Russell said, by a spirit of reverence and humility: reverence for the precious, varied, individual, indeterminate growing principle of life; and humility with regard to aims and with regard to the degree of insight and understanding of the practitioners. Because he was well acquainted with modern science Russell was also well aware of how little we really know about the aims and purposes of human life. Therefore the purpose of education, from this point of view, cannot be to control the child's growth to a specific predetermined end, because any such end must be established by arbitrary authoritarian means; rather the purpose of education must be to permit the growing principle of life to take its own individual course, and to facilitate this process by sympathy, encouragement, and challenge, and by developing a rich and differentiated context and environment.

This humanistic conception of education clearly involves some factual assumptions about the intrinsic nature of Man, and, in particular, about the centrality to that intrinsic nature of a creative impulse. If these assumptions, when spelled out properly, prove to be incorrect, then these particular conclusions with regard to educational theory and practice will not have been demonstrated. On the other hand, if these assumptions are indeed correct much of contemporary educational practice is rationally as well as morally questionable.

The humanistic conception of Man leads to what might be called libertarian education theories. It also leads in a natural and direct way to libertarian concepts of social organization that incorporate closely related ideas concerning, for example, the central and essential concept of the nature of work. In this context Russell quoted a remark by Kropotkin that "... overwork is repulsive to human nature - not work. Overwork for supplying the few with luxury - not for the well-being of all. Work, labour is a physiological necessity, a necessity of expanding accumulated bodily energy, a necessity which is health and life itself" (Russell, 1919 p.100). Elaborating on this theme, Russell pointed out that "... if man had to be tempted to work instead of driven to it, the obvious interest of the community would be to make work pleasant," and social institutions would be organized to this end. They would provide the conditions, in other words, under which productive, creative work would be freely undertaken as a part of normal, healthy life. To place these particular remarks in an appropriate historical context, one who conceives of the "species character" of man as "free, conscious activity" and "productive life," in the words of the early Marx, will also seek to create the higher form of society that Marx envisioned in which labour has become not only a means of life, but also the highest want in life.

There is a contrasting and more prevalent view of the nature of work, namely, that labour is a commodity to be sold on the market for maximal return, that it has no intrinsic value in itself; its only value and immediate purpose is to afford the possibility to consume, for on this account humans are primarily concerned with maximizing consumption, not with producing creatively under conditions of freedom. They are unique and individual not by virtue of what they make, what they do for others, or how they transform nature; rather individuality is determined by material possessions and by consumption: I am what I am because of what I own and use up. Thus on this view the primary aim of life must be to maximize the accumulation of commodities, and work is undertaken almost solely for this aim. The underlying assumption, of course, is that work is repulsive to human nature - contrary to Kropotkin, Russell, Marx, and many others - and that leisure and possession, rather than creative labour, must be the goal of humankind.

Again the issue involves factual assumptions. On this conception of human nature the goal of education should be to train children and provide them with the skills and habits that will fit them in an optimal way for the productive mechanism, which is meaningless in itself from a human point of view but necessary to provide them with the opportunity to exercise their freedom as consumers, a freedom that can be enjoyed in the hours when they are free from the onerous burden of labour. Such an idea is, of course, repugnant to one who accepts Russell's humanistic conception of human nature, but it bears repeating that between these contrasting views of work and education there is a factual judgment involved with regard to intrinsic human nature.

This queston, in short, is whether creative work can be the highest want of life or whether labour is a burden, and idleness and consumption of commodities the highest want and goal of life.

It may be that the humanistic conception expressed by Russell, Kropotkin, Marx, and many others is wrong. I believe it is correct, but in either case there are direct consequences with regard to social organization as well as education. This possibility has been recognized by social critics who tried to elaborate the humanistic conception and draw appropriate conclusions from it. For example, Russell quoted a pamphlet of the National Guilds League, a British working-class radical socialist organization of the early part of the century, which tried to develop a point of view rather like the humanistic one outlined above. In the course of speaking about what Russell called the humanistic conception of Man, it admits that "there is a cant of the Middle Ages and a cant of 'joy in labour.'" But it goes on to declare that "it were better, perhaps, to risk that cant" than to accept a philosophy that makes "work a purely commercial activity, a soulless and joyless thing". Again, my personal bias is toward Russell and the "medieval cant," but I am not directly concerned to defend this position here so much as I want to suggest a connection between the concomitant view of human nature - specifically with regard to creativity and productive work - and certain questions concerning educational practice: namely, whether it should be oriented toward freedom and challenge or toward guidance, direction, and control.

This debate between the positions did not originate in the present century. To mention one case of considerable historical importance, Wilhelm von Humboldt, an extremely important and too-neglected thinker whose works have only been made readily available in the last few years, wrote about educational practice and its foundation in a certain concept of human nature, along the lines of the humanistic conception we have been considering. He said that "... to inquire and to create - these are the centres around which all human pursuits more or less directly revolve". "All moral culture," he wrote, "springs solely and immediately from the inner life of the soul and can only be stimulated in human nature, and never produced by external and artificial contrivance. ... Whatever does not spring from a man's free choice, or is only the result of instruction and guidance, does not enter into this very being, but remains alien to his true nature; he does not perform it with truly human energies, but merely with mechanical exactness". If a man acts in this way, he says, we may "admire what he does, but despise what he is" (Humboldt, 1969 pp. 76; 63; 28).

This view had implications for educational practice similar to Russell's, and, of course, related implications for social theory. Again, one who regards human nature in this light will proceed to search for social forms that will encourage the truly human action that grows from inner impulse. In this case, Humboldt writes, "... all peasants and craftsmen might be elevated into artists; that is, men who love their labour for its own sake, improve it by their own plastic genius and inventive skill, and thereby cultivate their intellect, ennoble their character, and exalt and refine their pleasures. And so, humanity would be ennobled by the very things which now, though beautiful in themselves, so often tend to degrade it" (Ibid. p. 27)

Humbolt was an important educational theorist as well as a practitioner. He was one of the founders of the modern university system and at the same time he was a great libertarian social thinker who directly inspired and in many ways anticipated John Stuart Mill. His rationalistic conception of human nature, emphasizing free creative action as the essence of that nature, was developed further in the libertarian social thought of the industrial period, specifically in nineteenth century libertarian socialist and anarchist social theory and their accompanying doctrines concerning educational practice.

Let me reiterate the point that these views involve questions of fact concerning human nature, and that there are certain conclusions that one may draw from these factual judgments with respect to educational theory and practice, social theory, and the activism which naturally flows from a conscientious commitment to the conclusions of that theory. Judgments about these matters are, in fact, very often determined not so much by evidence as by ideological commitment. This is not particularly surprising, though it is not too happy a state. It is not surprising because there is very little evidence that bears on these issues, yet we cannot avoid making judgments on them. We may, and commonly do, tacitly accept most of the judgments which prevail in a given society. In other words, we make these judgments rather mindlessly in conformity to prevailing ideology. It requires effort to make them thoughtfully, recognizing the inadequacy of the evidence. But there are no other alternatives.

In this kind of situation the null hypothesis would be the point of view that Bertrand Russell expressed. That is, in the absence of conflicting evidence, the proper course should be to approach these problems with the reverence and humility that Russell suggested in discussing his "humanistic conception". In the absence of compelling reasons to the contrary, one should be quite cautious about trying to control someone else's life and character and mode of thought. The acceptance or rejection of the null hypothesis has political and social as well as pedagogic consequences for the educator and teacher. There are, in other words, significant consequences to one's thinking or lack of thinking about these issues and a corresponding personal and professional responsibility.

To become somewhat more concrete, consider the matter of control of behaviour. In a certain sense this will be abhorrent to the person who accepts the humanistic conception of education. There is no doubt that control of behaviour can be carried out to some degree. Effective techniques of conditioning and control exist that have been investigated experimentally in great detail. But it would surely be a mistake to consider that these investigations have significantly advanced our understanding of learning processes. For example, there are numerous results on the effects of various schedulings of reinforcement on the frequency of simple responses. Have we learned that learning takes place through conditioning, by the application of such methods in a natural or contrived environment? Of course we have not learned anything of the sort. Learning involves the interplay of an innate endowment, innately determined maturational processes, and a process of interaction with the environment. The pattern of this interaction and the nature of the various factors is largely unknown, as any honest investigator will concede. In some domains - language is an example - such evidence as is available seems to indicate that the innate component is extremely significant and that, in considerable detail, the form and character of what is learned is determined by an innate schematism of mind. In fact, precisely those characteristics of language that make it an effective instrument for free thought and expression seem to have their origins in this innately determined structure. It is fairly clear that language cannot be seriously regarded as a system of habits and skills acquired through training. Rather it must be understood as an elaborate mental structure largely determined by innate properties of mind. This point of view may be right or wrong when it is spelled out in detail, but there is no inherent mystery about it. One could make it quite precise and quite explicit; it is in no sense mysterious. What is mysterious, perhaps, is the biological or neurophysiological basis for these (and other) mechanisms of mind, but that is another question entirely.

There is a point of confusion that might be mentioned here, a confusion that one finds among many linguists who have identified the free creative use of language with the system of rules that permit that free creative use, that is, with the recursive property of grammars that permits arbitrarily many utterances to be constructed. These two notions, although related, are not to be confused. To do so would be a category mistake, a confusion of performance and competence. There are rules that permit an indefinite range of possible expression. Such rules are an indispensable component in the creative use of language. But a computer that produced sentences randomly would not be acting creatively. There is an interplay, a complex relationship between constraints and rules and creative behaviour. If there is no system of rules, no system of constraints, no set of forms, then creative behaviour is quite unthinkable. Someone who is throwing paints at a wall in an arbitrary fashion is not acting creatively as an artist. Similarly some system of constraints and forms and principles and rules is presupposed as a basis for any kind of creative action. But creative action has to be understood in different terms, with this being only one fundamental component (Chomsky, 1971 pp. 3-51).

Returning to the question of what has been learned from the study of conditioning, it could not be true that these investigations have demonstrated that learning results from conditioning for the very simple reason that the fundamental problem of learning theory has barely been posed, let alone answered, within the theory of learning as it has developed over the years. There is an important conceptual gap in the theory of learning which makes it very difficult to pose this fundamental question and therefore casts a good deal of doubt on the significance of any results that are achieved, however interesting they may be in their own terms. The conceptual gap is basically this: the theory of learning is concerned with situation and action; that is, it is concerned with stimulus and response. But there really is no concept of "what is learned". The fundamental problem of learning theory, properly understood, is to determine how what is learned is related to the experience on the basis of which it is learned. We can study, if we like, the relation between stimulus and response, but it is very unlikely that such a study will contribute to solving the problem because that relationship is surely mediated by the system of knowledge and belief that has been acquired, by what has been learned.

Take again the case of language, which is perhaps the clearest example we can consider. Stimuli impinge upon the organism, which carries out certain "verbal behaviour". It is perfectly obvious that the person's behaviour as a speaker of a language is affected by what he or she knows as a speaker of this language, by the system of rules that is mentally represented in some fashion, which provides the framework within which the largely free, creative behaviour takes place. If we want to study learning of language, we are going to have to study the relationship between experience and what is learned, between experience and knowledge, experience and this internally represented system of rules. We can then go ahead to study behaviour, that is, interaction among many factors, including immediate stimuli, mediated through the already known system of rules. We can study the relationships between these factors and behaviour. But to try to study the relationship between stimuli and responses directly is a sure road to triviality.

We could not expect to find a direct connection between experience and action, omitting any reference to what is learned. Nor could we even pose the questions of learning theory - what is learned, what is known - with that concept missing. To pose the problem of learning theory in the first place, one must face the task of systematizing what it is a person knows or believes, or has acquired or learned at a certain stage in his or her development. (The same is true of animal learning, for that matter.) Later we can ask how that system of knowledge or belief arose from the various factors that enter into it - experience, maturational processes, and so on. But to avoid any concern for the nature of what is known and what is learned is simply to condemn the enterprise to barrenness in the first place.

When we pose the question of what is learned, the few tentative answers that seem plausible are remote from the tacit and generally unargued assumptions of many learning theorists. The belief that conditioning is an important feature of learning may conceivably be true, but at the moment it stands as a kind of dogma. And if, in fact, the humanistic conception of human nature, work, and education mentioned earlier is correct, then the theory of conditioning may be a dangerous and possibly pernicious dogma. Recall again Humboldt's remark that "whatever does not spring from a man's free choice, or is only the result of instruction and guidance, does not enter into his very being but remains alien to his true nature; he does not perform it with truly human energies, but merely with mechanical exactness" (Humboldt, 1969 p. 28). The fact that this observation was made by a profound social critic does not make it correct, of course, but there is not any scientific evidence to suggest that it is false. Indeed, I think that our own experience and the insights that arise from it - which are not to be discounted in areas where scientific evidence is so sparse - lend a certain credibility to this view. At an experimental level there is some evidence that voluntary, self-willed action plays a very significant role in learning and acquiring knowledge. The work supports the observations and guesses concerning the intrinsic, self-willed character of anything of real human significance that is acquired by a child in the course of learning - or an adult as well, for that matter.

What about the concomitant idea that knowledge is acquired in small incremental steps? Consider a teaching program for geometry. Again there are inherent dangers in any such approach. Perhaps the dangers are even greater if the approach begins to work. To educate mathematicians, you do not train them to face problems which are just on the border of what they have already learned to do. Rather, they must learn to deal with new situations, to take imaginative leaps, to act in a creative fashion. If they are going to be good mathematicians, they must have a good imagination and use it frequently. We really do not understand what is involved in taking such imaginative, creative leaps in mathematics, or in any other domain. But it is plausible to suppose that that ability to undertake these essentially creative efforts is acquired through the experience of coming to grips with interesting, complex problems that are challenging and which attract one's attention but are not at all closely related in any incremental fashion to the skills that one has achieved and acquired. Programs that work quite successfully in teaching some fixed domain through small incremental steps may precisely deprive persons of the opportunity to develop these poorly understood abilities that enable them to act in a normal human fashion, occasionally with genius; and perhaps much the same is true of normal human behaviour.

The schools have taken quite a beating in recent decades and I do not want to join in the pummelling. Personally, I do not really agree with the more radical critics like Paul Goodman or Ivan Illich who imply that the solution to the problem of the schools is virtually to eliminate them. (On the humanistic conception of education, it is important to provide the richest and most challenging of environments for children so that the creative impulse will have maximum utilization, and a well-planned school should be able to provide just that environment). But I think one cannot discount a good deal of what Goodman and Illich say. A close friend of mine came from Europe at age 15 and went to an American high school in New York. He was struck immediately by the fact that if he came to school three minutes late he had to go to the principal's office to be properly chastised, but if he did not do his work in a particularly intelligent fashion or if he was not creative or original, then people might not be too happy about it but at least he did not have to go to the principal's office. And quite generally, punctuality and obedience were very highly valued and were the values that definitely had to be instilled. As to originality or achievement, well that was nice too, but it obviously was not of paramount importance.

An approach to education which emphasizes such values as punctuality and obedience is very well suited for training factory workers as tools of production. It is not suited at all to the humanistic conception of creative and independent individuals, which brings us back again to those assumptions concerning human nature and the social forces and educational practices that give due regard to intrinsic human capacities.

The consideration of assumptions of this kind is particularly important in a rich and a powerful country with immense potential for good and for evil. The early experiences of citizens of the United States are a matter of enormous human significance. It is a cliché to say that the responsibility of the teacher to the student, like that of the parent to the child, is beyond calculation, but it is further amplified to the extent that this child can affect history. Here in the United States we are clearly dealing with that situation. One of the worst forms of control, developed to very dangerous extremes in totalitarian states, is indoctrination of children. We very rightly deplore it elsewhere. We rarely recognize it at home. I do not pretend to be well-versed in this matter but I do have several children in school and I look over their shoulders occasionally. Some of the kinds of indoctrination that face them are, to state it frankly, frightening. I went through an issue of the *Weekly Reader*, a children's newspaper, which discussed the problem of American prisoners in North Vietnam. It said, "A war is going on in Vietnam. The war has been going for many years. North Vietnam and South Vietnam are fighting each other. Americans are fighting on the side of South Vietnam. Many Americans have been taken prisoner by North Vietnam". Then it talked about some American children. "The children sent their letters to the president of North Vietnam. The children asked him to set American prisoners of war free and to let the men come home to the United States". There is also a teachers' edition which goes along with the paper, which explains how the teacher is supposed to elicit the appropriate answers (1971).

Look at what the *Weekly Reader* was telling these impressionable young children: first that there was a war between North Vietnam and South Vietnam. That is of course totally false. Anybody in the government knows that that was false. They know perfectly well that it began as a war between the United States and the peasant societies of Indochina, in particular South Vietnam. It never was a war between the North and the South. If you ask when the first regular units of the North Vietnamese Army were discovered in South Vietnam, you get the curious answer that it was in late April, 1965 - one battalion of 400 men, approximately two and a half months after the regular bombardment of North Vietnam and South Vietnam, approximately eight months after the first bombing of strategic targets - at a time when there were 35,000 American troops deployed. In fact U.S. military forces had been engaged in direct actions for four or five years. So it is hardly a war between North Vietnam and South Vietnam.

Second, the impression that the *Weekly Reader* tries to convey is that the pilots were captured while defending South Vietnam from North Vietnam. There is not a word about what the pilots were doing when they were captured. What they were doing, of course, was destroying everything in North Vietnam outside of the central population centres, a fact which is still (1975) not admitted in the United States. There is also not a word about prisoners captured by the United States and South Vietnam; for example, those who were dropped to their death from helicopters or those who were tortured or those who found their way to the tiger cages in Con Son island. And there is no particular explanation in the *Weekly Reader* as to why prisoners should be released while the United States continued to drop 70,000 tons of bombs on Indochina as it did during the month in which this article appeared, January 1971: (for a fuller, non-*Weekly Reader* account, see Chomsky, 1969a).

But worst of all there is not a word about what the United States soldiers have been doing in South Vietnam and in Laos. These countries, of course, have borne the main brunt of the American agression in Indochina, not North Vietnam. Now this kind of distortion, which we see in the *Weekly Reader*, continues to pound on children through most of their adult lives as well. The corruption of the media in this respect is extreme.

Children have to be spared indoctrination but they also have to be trained to resist it in later life. This is a very serious problem in our society and every other society. Let me give another example. I have a daughter in junior high school, and in looking at her history book on the topic of the countries of the communist bloc, I came across the following: "In no case did a revolution merely happen. The shift to Communism was skillfully brought about by groups of dedicated, Moscow-trained revolutionaries". In China and Cuba, for example? This is certainly nonsense, but it is pernicious nonsense, and when it is drilled into people constantly, day after day, week after week, throughout their lives, the effects are overwhelming.

This section of the book goes on to discuss peaceful coexistence. It says, "We all believe first in the existence of different systems of government and society, and second in the right of every people to settle independently all the political and social problems of their country. We have always had respect for the sovereignty of other nations and have adhered to the principle of non-interference in internal affairs. And we strongly believe in and practise the policy of trying to settle all international questions by negotiations". Then the book turns to the leaders of the Soviet Union. It says that "they claim they want to end the Cold War," and so on. Before this can happen, the book continues, "we have to learn to trust each other"; but "Such actions as those the Soviet Union has taken in North Korea, in North Vietnam and in Cuba, in which Soviet-trained communists have taken over the reins of government have given the United States ample cause to doubt the sincerity of Mr Krushchev's pronouncements about peaceful co-existence" (Kohn and Drummond, 1963).

There was often good reason to doubt the sincerity of Mr Krushchev's pronouncements, but on the basis of Soviet actions in North Vietnam, such doubt would be difficult to defend, particularly since this book was written in 1963 when there were no Soviet actions in Indochina. There were, however, plenty of American actions: in that year a substantial part of the population of South Vietnam was forcibly removed by the U.S.-imposed regime to what we would call "concentration camps" if any other country had built them.

Let me give a third example, also from the text book of one of my own daughters - this one in the fourth grade. It is a social science reader called *Exploring New England*. The book has a protagonist, a young boy named Robert who is told about the marvels of colonial times. In the course of the narrative the extermination of the Pequot tribe by Captain John Mason is described as follows: "His little army attacked in the morning before it was light and took the Pequots by surprise. The soldiers broke down the stockade with their axes, rushed inside, and set fire to the wigwams. They killed nearly all the braves, squaws, and children, and burned their corn and other food. There were no Pequots left to make more trouble. When the other Indian tribes saw what good fighters the white men were, they kept the peace for many years. 'I wish I were a man and had been there,' thought Robert". That is the last that Robert hears or speaks about this matter. Nowhere does he express or hear any second thoughts (Clifford, 1961).

The example and precedent set by Mason was not forgotten by later soldiers. It was, for example, cited by General Leonard Wood while justifying the Army's killing of 600 Moro men, women and children in the Philippines in 1906: "The renegades had from 3 to 6 months supply on the mountain, with an abundance of water. There was nothing to do but take the place .... I believe that some of our hard-praying ancestors dealt with the Pequot Indians in a somewhat similar manner, and on a great deal less provocation" (O'Connor, 1969 p. 295). The analogy is actually fairly accurate; like the Pequots, the native Moros were armed with bows, spears, and rocks (against Wood's machine guns, bombs, and howitzers).

I think it is very important to consider such passages and to take them seriously - I do not know how prevalent they are - especially in the light of the My Lai Massacre in Vietnam or the many incidents like it.

Even more important, perhaps, than direct and gross indoctrination is the general pattern of authoritarianism that one finds in the schools, and the associated pattern of the technocratic, problem-solving mode of thought combined with a great awe of expertise - quite natural in an advanced industrial society. In some areas of our lives this latter pattern has reached dimensions that can really only be described as pathological. To take only one dangerous example, the domain of counterinsurgency theory has been developed into an effective technique of mystification during recent years. The idea is to formulate the problems of repression of popular movements in purely technical terms. Thus, two experts in counterinsurgency writing in *Foreign Affairs* explain to us that all the dilemmas of counterinsurgency are "practical and as neutral in an ethical sense as the laws of physics" (Tanham and Duncanson, 1969 pp. 113-122). In short, the situation is a very simple one. We have the goal of establishing the rule of certain social groups in the society that is selected for the experiment in counterinsurgency. A number of methods are available, ranging from rural development and commodity import programmes to B52s and crop destruction. And the policy maker faces the task of combining these methods in such a manner as to maximize the probability of success. Quite obviously, only a hysteric or a self-flagellating moralist could see an ethical problem in this situation; it is just like an experiment in physics.

Academic terminology can be put to very mischievous use in this connection, and it often is. For example, driving people into government-controlled cities by fire power and chemical destruction is called "urbanization," which is then taken as a key index of the modernization of the society. We carry out what are called "experiments with population control measures". We should learn, one RAND Corporation theorist tells us, to disregard such mystical notions as attitudes; rather we should control behaviour by appropriate arrangements for positive and negative reinforcements such as "confiscation of chickens, razing of houses, or destruction of villages". Or consider, for example, "the offer of food in exchange for certain services ..... If this has in the past been a strong stimulus, it can probably we weakened by increasing local agricultural production. If it has been a weak or neutral stimulus, it can probably be strengthened by burning crops". This is from a publication of the *American Institute for Research*, 1967 (see also Chomsky, 1969b). Whatever such experts may be, they are not scientists, and the concept of "science" suggested by such pronouncements is not one that Russell - or any other honest commentator - could endorse.

Christopher Lasch once pointed out that one of the dominant values of modern intellectuals is their acute sense of themselves as professionals with a vested interest in technical solutions to political problems. The schools to a large extent are training professionals, and they are training the general population to accept the values and the ideological structures that are developed by professionals. All of this is particularly important in a "post-industrial" or advanced industrial society where the intelligentsia are increasingly associated with the exercise of power. This is, of course, not a criticism of professionalism or of technology or science, but rather of the subversion of intellectual values as part of a new coercive ideology that seeks to remove decision-making even further from popular control by exploiting the aura of science and technology, by pretending that social planning is much too complex for the ordinary person and must therefore be the domain of experts who claim to be value-free technicians, but who in fact quite generally accept without question the most vulgar forms of official ideology as a basis for their planning.

If you have read serious social science journals or foreign policy journals over the last few years, you have seen that it is very common to counterpose the "emotional approach" of certain people with the "rational response" of others. For example, the people who worry about the slaughter of peasant populations - these people are overcome by emotion. On the other hand, those who talk about arranging inputs to realize a certain outcome are "reasonable" commentators. This is an interesting development, the counterposing of emotion to reason, because it departs significantly from the Western intellectual tradition. For example, David Hume wrote that "Reason is and ought to be the slave of the passions". And Russell, commenting on the observation, noted that every reasonable person subscribes to this dictum. He surely would be an "unreasonable" commentator by the standards of today. Reason is concerned with the choice of the right means to an end that you wish to achieve, taking emotional and moral factors into consideration. Unfortunately too many modern technocrats, who often pose as scientists and scholars, are really divorcing themselves from traditional science and scholarship and excluding themselves from the company of reasonable persons in the name of a kind of reason that is perverted beyond recognition.

All of these are matters that require the most careful attention of teachers. We have to learn to adopt the questioning and iconoclastic approach that is highly valued and carefully nurtured in the physical sciences, where an imaginative worker will very often hold up his or her basic assumptions to searching analysis. We have to adopt this approach as teachers, and also as citizens who must be social critics, recognizing that in the domain of social criticism the normal attitudes of a scientist are feared and deplored as a form of subversion or as dangerous radicalism.

I have been discussing the negative potential of American power. There is also a positive side, one that should make the work of teachers particularly demanding but highly exciting. The United States has a real potential for revolutionary social change to a libertarian democratic society of the form that probably cannot be achieved anywhere else in the world. As compared with other societies, libertarian instincts are reasonably strong in the United States. There is also very little class prejudice as compared with most other societies. But most of all, in an advanced industrial society the rational and human use of resources and technology provides the possibility to free people from the role of tools of production in the industrial process. It provides the possibility, perhaps for the first time in modern history, to free human beings from the activities that, as Adam Smith pointed out, turn them into imbeciles through the burden of specialized labour. This, then, is the real challenge of the twentieth century in the United States: to create social forms that will realize the humanistic conception of Man. And it is the responsibility of teachers, of citizens, and of ourselves, to liberate the creative impulse and to free our minds and the minds of those with whom we deal from the constraints of authoritarian ideologies so that this challenge can be faced in a serious and an open-minded way.

3

Education, Schooling and the World of Work

by Colin Wringe

That an understanding of and preparation for the so-called world of work is an important educational aim has in recent years become not simply an established orthodoxy but something resembling official policy under both major British political parties.

Among other things it has been claimed that young people ought to be taught 'how industry creates national wealth' (DES, 1979 p. 6) and that they 'need to reach maturity with a basic understanding of the economy and the activities, especially manufacturing industries, which are necessary for the creation of Britain's national wealth' (DES, 1977 p. 35). It has been urged that steps should be taken to correct the situation whereby 'many of our best trained students ... have no desire to join industry, but prefer to stay in academic life or find their way into the Civil Service' (Callaghan, 1976 p. 1) and held that 'one of the goals of education from the nursery school to adult education' is to 'equip the child to the best of their (sic) ability for a lively and constructive place in society and to fit them to do a job of work'. It has also been suggested that efforts should be made to meet complaints from industry that new recruits from schools sometimes do not have the basic tools to do the job that is required (Ibid).

To remedy this it is suggested that 'industry and commerce should be involved in curriculum planning at national and local level' (DES, 1977 p. 34) and that consideration should be given to the appointment of people with experience in management and trades unions as governors of schools (Ibid).

From the above quotations it will be evident that in certain undeniably influential quarters the intention is that changes should take place in the content of what is taught at all levels - from the nursery school onwards - that would result in pupils making not only a more effective but also a more willing contribution to the production of goods. Such proposals may have much to be said in their favour, but ought scarcely to become part of the stock of received educational wisdom without examination.

Previous Positions

Debate concerning the relationship that ought to exist between school and work is not new and it is helpful to take brief account of a number of positions which are or have been widely held on this question before proceeding to our own discussion of it.

1. *Elitist and 'progressive' positions.* Little need be said of conceptions of education in which preparation for work played no part for the simple reason that work was expected to play no part in pupils' subsequent lives. By contrast, the view was widely canvassed in the fifties and sixties that education should be pragmatic, concerned with problem solving (Kilpatrick, 1963), shorn of 'inert ideas' and, in the case of some children at least, 'practical' and 'realistic' (Whitehead, 1962). The views with which we are concerned in this paper are not to be regarded as simply continuous with those of the 'progressive' educators of the fifties and sixties. Those writers were certainly prepared to see up-to-date, practical, including vocational, interests as a way into the education of young people left untouched by what was currently on offer. But their overriding concern remained the child-centred and morally unimpeachable one of bringing pupils to an understanding of themselves and of the world about them. If the 1963 Newsom Report led to a crop of curricula centred on the building trades and projects dismantling old cars this was in no way part of an overt drive to improve performance in the national housing programme or increase profits in the motor industry.

2. *Modern versions of 'liberal' education.* Some writers draw a sharp distinction between their own particular concepts of education which they see as the essential and proper function of the school and the preparation for adult roles. Peters, for example, concedes that training and education may have to proceed side by side in schools set up for what he terms 'mass education', but suggests that if performance of the school's 'instrumental function' is to be regarded as anything more than a necessary evil this is only because it may provide a powerful incentive in the cause of education and induce children to get started on activities whose intrinsic attractions may only become evident later (1966 p. 85). Oakeshott, with even less hesitation, scathingly attacks the notion of preparing pupils for their future roles as a usurper of education's prerogative, something foisted on people in consequence of 'the emergent doctrine that rulers have the right to instruct their subjects and that subjects (particularly the poor) have a duty to contribute to the well-being

of the "nation"' (1971 p. 62). Education and vocational preparation are seen by him as irreconcilably different. If occasionally the qualities of educated persons happen to be valuable in the performance of social functions, that is our good fortune and not something education is or should be designed to produce (op. cit. p. 40).

3. *The deschoolers' position.* In the view of certain deschoolers and other radical educationists, talk of 'education,' 'worthwhile activities', 'an intellectual inheritance of great splendour and worth' (Oakeshott p. 51) and so on is sheer ideology. For them, schooling is all too obviously about preparation for adult life not, as the naive suppose, in imparting useful skills but in legitimating social inequality by convincing the majority that they are not good enough for anything but the most menial occupations (see for example Holt 1979; Harris 1977).

4. *Mary Warnock's position.* Finally, account must be taken of a view of the relationship between education and work recently put forward by Mary Warnock (1977). This view merits consideration if only because of its compatibility with the quasi-official views set out at the start of this paper, and because it is likely to be accepted by simple souls as a statement of sober common sense. This is the view that any learning can count as education if it contributes to the 'good life' compounded of the three elements of virtue, work and imagination. In such a scheme, preparation for work is not only a legitimate but a necessary element.

Education, Work and the Teacher's Commitment to Truth

The main purpose of our present enquiry is to determine the attitude teachers should take to the advocacy of learning aimed at improving pupils' understanding of, commitment to, and efficiency at work. It is unlikely that we shall progress far with such an enquiry without some examination of the moral attitude we are to have towards work itself. Before proceeding to such an examination, however, it may be helpful to deal with a number of important but, I hope, relatively uncontroversial points. It may later be necessary to say something at length about what is to be understood by education, but for the present it is simply assumed that this presupposes some commitment on the part of the teacher to imparting truth about the world and contributing to pupils' understanding of their position in it. This is a wide brief, but it does rule out any systematic indoctrination or deception of one's pupils, even if this is thought to be in the public interest.

1. 'Knowing more about' industry fairly clearly is a proper educational aim. This can be accepted even by the radical who believes the present exploitative relationship between capital and labour to be possible only because the true nature of the situation is concealed from the masses. Knowledge of 'how industry works' is knowledge of the human and social world, of other minds, of other people's

lives and experience. It is part of individuals' understanding of the world and their relationship to it, for someone who does not understand the extent to which he or she is materially supported by manufacture is in error about his or her situation. Whatever we may think about the way industry is run, many productive processes are examples of human achievement and ingenuity and many productive enterprises manifestly embody standards of efficiency, economy, prudence, imagination and management of the rules of cause and effect. There are therefore grounds for arguing that a disinterested study of the manufacturing industry forms a proper part of the individual's education in the modern world.

As a corollary to this, however, if study of the world of work is an essential part of the child's education it follows that it must be carried out, not with amateurish good will and enthusiasm, but to proper professional and educational standards as regards the selection of material, economy of presentation and academic regard for accuracy, integrity and truthfulness. A series of talks on the importance and benevolence of industry by representatives of the local chamber of commerce will not meet the bill.

2. We say that importance was attached to ensuring that more, and especially abler pupils undertook a career in industry. Clearly, if it is the case that many such pupils take up other occupations because they are simply uninformed about industry, or because they are taken in by the gentlemanly ideology that trade is unworthy, then it would be a highly desirable part of the educational process to correct this false understanding. What must at least be considered as a possibility, however, is that those with sufficient ability to be in a position to choose, have perfectly valid reasons for electing to follow the careers they do. These reasons may be prudential, connected with the uncongenial nature of industrial work, material insecurity or the difficulties of reconciling success in industry with an acceptable family and personal life. There may also be good reasons of a more idealistic kind for finding public service or the liberal professions more attractive than the pursuit of profit, either for oneself or for one's employers. Possibly industry in a free economy cannot afford to be less than ruthless, whatever the cost in other values. If this is true, the benefits of ruthlessness may have to be weighed against whatever advantages are supposed to flow from attracting some of the recruits industry now complains of losing.

Careers education is obviously highly desirable if it is what it claims to be, i.e. careers *education*, the skilled, professional activity of seeking and passing on to one's pupils accurate, comprehensive information, duly evaluated and interpreted for their benefit. Clearly, however, it would be both educationally and morally unacceptable for schools to 'sell' industry to their pupils, or present it in a falsely attractive light.

3. Needless to say, any commitment to truth on the teacher's part must make the function of the school as described by what I have called the 'deschoolers' position' unacceptable. If it were the case that schools were necessarily instrumental in communicating the falsehood - on the assumption that a falsehood it is - that some are fit for menial tasks only, then it is difficult to see how there could be any defensible alternative to the abolition of schools, whatever the cost in social unrest or lost production. That schools do, in fact, promote this belief may just possibly be shown empirically. The claim that while schools exist they must necessarily do so, however, is not an empirical claim at all. There seems no ground for holding that schools cannot in principle ever be organized to convey a different message, despite the resistance changes necessary to this end would be likely to encounter. It should be added that nothing contained in the sources quoted at the beginning of this paper advocates anything likely to produce a greater crop of educational failures in the interests of the manufacturing industry. On the contrary, the claim seems to be that educators are already producing far too many citizens capable of menial tasks only.

The Morality of Work

In the previous section it was suggested that whatever moral status was ascribed to work itself, certain kinds of learning in relation to the world of work were fairly clearly morally and educationally acceptable, while certain others were not. In general, however, the rightness of encouraging or even obliging the young to spend time learning things that will enable them to work more efficiently or more willingly will depend on our views of the morality of work itself. It might be thought that the moral status of work and even the appropriateness of calling preparation for it 'education' would depend to some extent on the nature of the work in question. Mary Warnock, however, holds that work - she says any kind of work - is a necessary part of the good life and preparation for it 'education' properly so-called. Her reasons are that the worker resembles the Nietzchean superman impressing his will on the world, and that it is better to support oneself by one's own efforts than to depend on the 'charity' of others (1977 pp. 144-155)!

In the present section it will be argued that our view of the morality of work is sometimes confused not only by a rather obvious ambiguity but also by a number of contingent evils with which some kinds of work are often associated. It will be held that some kinds of work are not at all constitutive of the good life and are at best a necessary evil. To undertake one's share of this evil, and consequently to undertake such learning as will enable one to do so, however, may be a universal obligation as well, possibly, as being in itself an educative experience.

Some activities which are described as work are undoubtedly worthwhile in one way or another. When artists, philanthropists, political idealists, reformers and others speak of their work they often refer to something which is a kind of self-chosen activity - even though they may think of it as an obligation imposed from without. Their work may be worthwhile, either intrinsically, as in the case of creative or interpretive artists, or because of the end it is supposed to achieve. Sometimes the persons in question may refer to it as 'their' work, or as work which only they can do.

But work does not have to be as sublime or spectacular as this to be worthwhile. Many relatively mundane jobs can be challenging and varied and involve standards of logic, efficiency, integrity, judgment and so on. Many trades, crafts and subordinate occupations may be such that each situation provides its own challenges and problems to be solved within the standards of a craft or the parameters of a particular role.

Work of these kinds presents little difficulty for the claim that it may form part of a version of the good life and that some kind of preparation for doing it may be educational. But this can scarcely blind us to the fact that much work does not resemble any of the categories of worthwhile work mentioned above. Much work is tedious and repetitive offering no opportunity for the exercise of skill, variation or personal style. It may be concerned with the mass production of objects of no social or aesthetic value - even of objects which are socially harmful. Many jobs in the tobacco, confectionery and armament industries must fall into this category. Only extrinsic reasons can be imagined for doing them. One needs the money, or is glad of the chance to be out of the house.

It is this kind of work whose moral status might be judged if we are to assess the recommendation that the young should invest time and effort in preparing for it. And here in passing it should be noted that the fact that a particular kind of work requires training and preparation is not in itself a guarantee that the work itself will be worthwhile. A task may be intricate and depend on knowledge not widely disseminated, being perhaps of limited scope and of no general interest. The necessary facts and knacks may take time and effort to acquire, but once they are acquired the tasks in which they are applied may cease to provide challenge or variety.

Those who perform such work may endure long and exhausting hours so that waking life is a continous round of toil, possibly in foul and disagreeable conditions. They may be subject to extreme poverty or work in conditions harmful to physical health. The Victorian matchgirl, overworked, undernourished, exploited, gaping with phossy jaw bears little resemblance to Mrs Warnock's picture of the Nietzschean superman imposing his will on the universe. There is also the question of the worker's alienation from the product of his labour. It is not proposed to dwell on the evils of exploitation, but for the purposes of discussing the morality of certain kinds of work and the preparation of workers to perform it more willingly and efficiently there may seem to be significant differences between work that benefits the worker and the community to which he or she belongs, and work which in the first instance benefits a distant or impersonal employer who has, perhaps, neither desert nor need, or whose interests may even be opposed to those of the worker and his or her community. Clearly someone who saw a society organized in this way as an overriding evil could not approve educational recommendations that bolstered the system by making the worker more efficient.

Nevertheless, though both poverty and exploitation raise highly important questions of social justice, these questions may be distinguished from that of the moral status of toil itself. It is undeniably possible to conceive of workers whose work is uninteresting but whose material conditions are acceptable. It is also possible to imagine that tedious processes of mass production may need to continue even when factories are not privately owned.

But the defender of toil may be assailed not only by social reformers and Marxist revolutionaries but also by those who urge that the good life consists in a return to nature and renunciation of many of the things which work currently serves to produce.

Doubtless this view has much to recommend it. As noted above, many manufactured items may have neither aesthetic nor social worth. It is also conceded that labour in the pursuit of affluence may be carried to excess, so that it displaces other aspirations in the individual. It may be counter-productive in squandering resources, and destructive of the environment upon which some aspects of the good life may depend.

Once again, however, these may be regarded as in principle avoidable aspects of industrial production. On the other side of the argument it must be recognized as a contingent fact about human beings that work - someone's work - is actually necessary to produce what we need to survive. It is also hard to deny that for many life is nearer the good life because of the various means of transport, communication, health, study and even comfort and convenience which work produces. This being so, the moral problem posed by tedious and intrinsically unrewarding work is not to be solved by simply saying 'We'd be better off without it'.

The Morality of Toil and the Division of Labour

Since all depend for survival and an acceptable way of life on the products of toil it may seem that in an ideal world - in which toil were nevertheless a necessity

- all should bear their part of it. Barring incapacity there seems manifest justice in the dictum that those who will not work should not benefit from the work of others. If training is necessary before anyone can work in a socially efficient way, then it seems quite legitimate to require all to undergo such training.

There are, of course, further questions as to whether those with particular talents are entitled to buy off their obligation to do their part of the chores and engage only in work of a more absorbing and satisfying kind. It may also be asked whether a truly moral person would wish to do this, or whether society would be justified in preventing him or her if the resulting sense of injustice aroused in others were likely to lead to social strife. But since 'toil or starve' is an option at which the human race as a whole cannot baulk, it may also be the case that some experience of toil should play a part in everyone's education if all are truly to understand the nature of such work and the part it plays in human existence.

We may now seem to be in a position to make some coherent claims about the relationship between the good life, toil, and the legitimacy of schooling the young to perform it. Firstly, toil, regular, serious toil cannot itself be a necessary part of the good life, for those who have more intrinsically satisfying ways of earning a living appear to get along very well without it. At best it would seem a necessary evil, for time spent in toil could be spent in more intrinsically worthwhile pursuits, including more satisfying forms of work. But if toil is not of itself a necessary part of a satisfying life, the facts of human existence are such that preparedness to undertake it may be regarded as a necessary part of a life that is just. It would also seem to follow that, if certain kinds of work are a necessary evil rather than themselves part of the good life, the lives of those engaged in such work must contain something else. Artists, philanthropists and reformers may live for their work. For many others, by contrast, the promise of fulfilment through labour is fraudulent. It may be that all must work to live, but it would be unacceptable if some were to live or be taught to live only to work.

Secondly, if toil is a necessary evil, training which enables it to be completed more efficiently and reduces the amount of time to be spent on it or enables it to be replaced by a more challenging or worthwhile form of work seems morally desirable. Despite the fact, therefore, that there may be some aspects of the world of work as currently organized that are to be criticized, it would seem that to train someone to work more efficiently is not of itself necessarily to lend support to an evil state of affairs.

This, however, is to show only that preparation for work may be a morally acceptable part of someone's schooling. It does not show that it may count as part of his or her education.

Education and Training

Education and training are frequently equated by laymen and contrasted by philosophers (Peters, 1966 pp. 32-35). The relationship between them is not simple, however and needs to be explored if we are to understand fully the implications of concurring or declining to concur in any shift of the balance between them. In this final section an attempt will be made to show that there are important features common to both concepts. In some respects to train is necessarily to educate and vice versa, so that at times the two activities may take place concurrently. Against this it will be argued that some aspects of the two concepts are incompatible, and that the aims of educator and trainer must sometimes be in conflict.

Regrettably, perhaps, such an undertaking requires some analysis of both education and training. The latter poses rather less problems. Clearly training entails the transmission of both knowledge and skills which will enable the learner to engage in a certain occupation or group of occupations more successfully. It may also have implications for attitudes, commitments and habitual responses to certain situations (Peters, 1966 p. 33).

No particularly original understanding of the concept of education is proposed. Broadly interpreted, the term may include some socialization into acceptable modes of behaviour, but is here held to be fundamentally concerned with knowledge and understanding of ourselves, of the world about us and of the relationship between the two. If it is suggested that the world about us is known through the familiar categories of logical, empirical, aesthetic, moral and other forms of knowledge (Hirst, 1965), that is quite in accordance with the view I propose. This is the knowledge the individual needs for the general conduct of his or her life, for one cannot choose how to lead one's life without knowing who and what one is, what the world contains, what is possible, what is valuable, and so on.

Two objections to such a view of education are to be met. Firstly, to define education in this way is somewhat stipulative. Some may deny that 'education' is properly or exclusively used in this way and wish to employ it differently. So be it. Nevertheless, it is possible to conceive of an activity which consists of passing on knowledge of the kind described. This activity may be regarded as an important one without the benefit of which the life one leads is not one's own, in the sense of not being what one chooses, but becomes instead the unexamined life sometimes said to be not worth living. It is with this activity - under whatever name - that I am concerned and it is the implications for this activity that I wish to explore when it is urged that more attention should be given in schools to imparting the kind of knowledge that will make children into better workers.

Secondly, it might be objected that the view of education I have set out is rather far-fetched and does not relate to the lives of ordinary people. Autonomy, rationality, choice and so on, it might be argued, are concepts that belong to the culture of an elite, if indeed they are not altogether illusory.

Now, this view that "I choose, you are influenced, he/she is socially or psychologically determined" can, I think, be met only by flat denial. Within certain limits - which for some people may admittedly be narrower than for others - people just do seem to choose such things as where they live, what jobs they will, or at least will not do, how they will spend their time and money, who, or indeed whether, they will marry, how they will decorate their houses and so on. All these things are constitutive of the lives people lead, and in all these areas educated and informed choices may be distinguished from those that are not.

Education and Training - Compatibility

That there should be some overlap between education and training is not surprising. Knowledge of the world is relevant both to the way one lives one's life and to the way one does one's job. In the obvious sense it is knowledge of the same world. It is often with the same non-negotiable features of the world that we are concerned. The second kind of knowledge is a limited segment of the first. In our work we use knowledge of a highly specific part of the world to make decisions of a highly specific kind. In one respect, therefore, vocational training rests on and grows out of one's general education. Identical learnings may seem to form part of both. The elementary science one learns as part of one's coming to understand the physical universe may also be essential knowledge to the professional engineer and many things may have to be included in a programme of vocational training if they have not already been learned as part of one's general education. The line of demarcation between the two may depend on the state of society. Learning to read may be part of the specifically voactional training of a clerk, or it may be considered part of everyone's general educational achievement which courses of secretarial training presuppose, but take for granted. Nor is it always clear where vocational training begins and general education leaves off. A joiner without certain minimal mathematical, aesthetic and social understanding or certain moral responses to the idea of safe and reliable workmanship could be worse than useless to his employers or clients, however impeccable his knowledge of cutting tools and the properties of wood. If the recommendations quoted at the beginning of this paper were to be interpreted as a demand for more basic vocational knowledge, e.g. for joiners with more knowledge of cutting tools and wood and less time spent on social, personal and aesthetic development, the result might be quite literally counterproductive.

If education is, if not actually to train, then at least to provide with some of the knowledge one needs in one's work, it is also true that in some respects to train may be to educate. This, however, should not be given quite the naive interpretation it sometimes receives. It may be that if training is undertaken in a liberal and liberalizing way, this will provide a way into the education of some who would otherwise remain outside the citadel. But this may be no more than a pious hope. In any case such a contribution of vocational learning to an individual's education would be purely contingent.

What can more confidently be argued is that the learning of any occupation imposes its own discipline, in that the learner is obliged to come to terms with part of the real world, however circumscribed that part may be. In learning particular skills the trainee learns to act thus and not otherwise in the light of features of the material or social world, rather than simply to respond to the instructions of an authority, or the impulse of individual whims.

Education and Training - Incompatibility

Despite the degree of overlap and mutual entailment between education, which relates to the way people live their lives, and training which relates to the way they do their work, it should not be thought that teachers are currently being asked simply to do better the job they see themselves as doing already, or make adjustments of no great moment. Despite the common ground between education and training attention must be drawn to differences which must in consistency result in divergence and conflict in practice.

Firstly and perhaps most obviously, education and training differ in the relationship in which they stand to the major choices an individual makes in the course of his or her life. As we know, it is possible to be trained as a chef or a toolmaker, but not educated as this or that (Peters, 1966 p. 34). For this there is good reason, namely that education throws further light on the life-choices one has to make. It precisely does not determine them or presuppose that they have been made already. Training, e.g. as a chef, by contrast, does not typically help one decide whether to be a chef or not. Doubtless some future chefs, like some future teachers, are confirmed in their choice of a career in the course of their training, while others are confirmed in their worst fears and are glad of the chance to change to some other occupation before it is too late. But this is not the point of training as a chef. The point is to make people into better chefs once their choice of an occupation has been made.

One may consider the well-worn contrast between the teaching of pottery as part of an educational programme and as part of a training course for future potters.

In the first case the aim would presumably be to introduce a pupil to the disciplines, satisfactions and values involved in practising a craft, possibly enabling the pupil to choose this or broadly similar activities as part of his or her way of life, or to understand the lives and point of view of those who do. The training of potters, on the other hand, being intended first and foremost to increase the quality and quantity of pots in the world must necessarily be more narrowly concerned with an exhaustive mastery of particular processes. To subject people to such training is not to give them a taste for craftmanship which they can either pursue or leave as they choose, but to invest so much of their time and effort in this learning as to render the latter course not only unlikely but, under normal circumstances, irrational. The range of their choices is not thereby widened but narrowed.

Education and training also differ in respect of the intentions of those who undertake them and this must frequently result in differences in practice. We should not, perhaps, make unduly crude distinctions between the intrinsically valuable purposes of the educator and the utilitarian purposes of the trainer. It may well be that learning to operate a lathe can equally well be seen as a means of earning more money, or as a means of becoming a toolmaker, that is, learning a craft with its own inherent standards (Peters, 1977 pp. 51-53). The recommendations giving rise to the present chapter, however, have been made in the context of anxiety about production and profits in British industry, and this concern, it is suggested, is unambiguously utilitarian.

The intentions of the educator cannot be utilitarian for the reason that when we equip someone with certain pieces of knowledge and understanding, or put someone in a position to take account of values not previously considered, we cannot actually tell how that person will choose to act in consequence. Strictly, there can be no behavioural objectives in education. At most there can be objectives to be spelled out in terms of potential choices and courses of action made available to the pupil. Training, on the other hand, which does not in fact result in more efficient work-oriented behaviour has failed, and would certainly not meet the recommendations with which we are concerned, however considered the trainees' rejection of the industrial way of life, or however enterprising their investigation of the alternatives.

The different intentions of trainers and educators may even result in differences in practice when ostensibly the same thing is being taught. In an educational context a learner's observations in the course of operating a lathe might lead on to questions about causes and explanations about the molecular structure of metals. In a training situation a more likely response to such observations would be 'Just keep your hand steady and your eye on the cutting edge'. And the point is that in the context of a course of training of limited duration this might be a thoroughly appropriate response and not in any way indicate that the trainer was an unreflective or narrow individual. Stress on what is vocationally useful must inevitably and quite rationally mean a move from knowledge-that to knowledge-how, from understanding principles and an awareness of uncertainties and alternatives, to practical tips and rules of thumb where this is all that will be required for the trainees to perform their future work more efficiently. In contrast to education, in which a multiplicity of ends are proposed in relation to which the individual may regulate his or her conduct, training necessarily presupposes a single criterion of value: the efficient achievement of a particular end, however broadly that end may be conceived.

Thirdly, as we say, training may relate not only to someone's knowledge and skills, but may also imply possession of certain attitudes, habitual responses and commitments. To be trained for an occupation, however lowly, is in a sense to be a professional, to have accepted the constraints and obligations not of seeking the good in general but of fulfilling the expectations of a certain socially definable role. Not only certain lapses, but also certain quite natural hesitations become unthinkable in a trained person. This applies not only in such obviously brutal occupations as those of the trained soldier and slaughterhouseman, but also in many others. The nurse who demurs to inflict temporary pain, the teacher who feels uneasy about correcting children for fear of hurting their feelings, the advocate who scruples to present a client's case in as favourable a light as possible would all do their jobs less well and society would be the poorer. Yet precisely these would be the hesitations of educated persons of whom it is the mark to take the general view and consider a multiplicity of values. This is no doubt why we consider it important that the members of some occupations who hold power over the lives and fortunes of others should be educated and not just trained. This is not simply a renaming or even a broadening of their training, but an attempt to hold in check their crude efficiency in the pursuit of a single goal.

Now it may be thought that though there are some occupations in which the trained response is at variance with that of the normal, educated person, this is true of certain occupations only. This, however, is not the case, for to have become committed to acting with a view to achieving efficiently a certain kind of end is, in principle, to have abandoned the educated person's rational commitment to take cognizance of countervailing considerations and the multiplicity of values relevant to human action.

It will be recalled that at the time of the student unrest at the end of the 60s, it was frequently observed that students in disciplines more closely connected with the existing occupational structure - medical students, engineers and lawyers - were inclined to be less militant than others. It is not suggested that the production of social revolutionaries is the aim of education. Nevertheless, criticism rather than the conforming mind is characteristic of rational autonomy.

Possibly contingent factors, such as the social origins of students in different disciplines, were to some extent responsible for the differences observed. Nevertheless, teaching and learning which take place on the assumption that the learner will eventually enter a certain occupation would seem to imply some acceptance of, and commitment to, the existing occupational structure and belief in a degree of permanence in the *status quo* by both learner and teacher. For society to modify its educational aims and procedures in the way suggested by the various sources quoted at the start of this paper is for society as a whole to endorse this commitment. A policy of changing the balance between education and training especially training for entry into the manufacturing industry would therefore seem to merit the vigilance not only of educators but of all to whom the future of the next generation is of interest.

Part Two

Work, Education and Democracy

4

Introduction: Linking Education and Work

by David Corson

The Meaning of Education

My task in this chapter is not to provide an original analysis of the meaning of 'education'. This is a central issue of debate in the now well established philosophy of education which until recently centred mainly on the work of the British philosopher of education Richard Peters. I need only assemble some of the threads of meaning identified for 'education' within that school of enquiry in order to offer a description suited to our theme. Despite recent critiques of elements of Peters' work, his attempt to help us clarify the meaning of 'education' is of considerable value.

Initiation, Knowledge, and Understanding.

Most people would agree that it is difficult to conceive of education today without thinking about the transfer of knowledge and the acquisition of understanding. Nevertheless a more general use for 'education' still survives, a use that has little to do with knowledge and understanding. In English the word 'education' was originally used just to talk in a very general way about the bringing up of children and of animals. This older use survives, for example, when we talk about 'Spartan education': this is an instance of the older sense of the word being used since it is clear that acquiring knowledge and understanding, as we conceive of them, was not an important part of the training of a young Spartan (Peters, 1970 pp. 10-11). We also use education in this general way when we talk about our own forms of training, even when they have no close connection with knowledge and understanding.

The usual meaning of 'education' is not so limited. This meaning suggests passing on the ultimate values of a community so that people can make those values their own and use them in pursuing a worthwhile form of life. This view of Peter's, that education is 'initiation into a worthwhile form of life', is consistent with the views held about 'human interests' by social philosophers: both Dworkin (1983) and Rawls (1972) argue that the highest order 'interest' that humans have lies in having as good a life as possible, a life that has in it as much as what a life should have. In our culture knowledge and understanding are highly valued, both for their own sake and for what they contribute to technology and to our quality of life generally. For us the basic requirement in being 'educated' is that one have knowledge and understanding. More than this our concept of an educated person is of someone who lives a life engaging in a variety of pursuits and projects for their own sake and whose pursuit of them and the general conduct of his or her life is transformed by some degree of all-round understanding and sensitivity (Peters, 1970 p. 14). The first requirement for those charged with providing education, then, is: how do we organise our processes of schooling to provide students with initiation into some worthwhile form of life?

Education as initiation into a worthwhile form of life demands a careful selection of aims from the many available aims that educators can pursue. The choice of aims will depend on those features of a worthwhile form of life that educators think it most important to foster. Teachers need to appreciate what any worthwhile form of life might be for themselves and they need a breadth of vision sufficient to appreciate what any worthwhile form of life might be for others. Teachers especially need to be richly initiated into knowledge and understanding themselves if they are going to arrange processes of schooling aimed at fostering the initiation of others. Like all educated persons, they need to be more than just 'knowledgeable'; they need to possess knowledge that is built into the way that they look at their task. For instance, a knowledge of the stages of intellectual growth, that children from all cultures seem to go through, is a meaningless acquisition if teachers cannot use that knowledge in the design of syllabuses and in the application of pedagogies for children of different ages. What does it mean to have knowledge of something if it is not brought to bear when interpreting something else relevant to it? This is not a knowledge consistent with being educated. It is something less than the knowledge of an educated person, as having percepts is less than having concepts - something akin to the outcomes of training as practised on animals and sometimes on humans; but not education.

Education and Training

The distinction between 'education' and 'training' is a very useful one for our purposes here; by examining it we can bring the meaning of 'education' more fully into focus. We use 'training' in a narrow way and in a wider way too. In the narrow sense we speak of training plants or animals, or even hair. What we mean here is 'giving the subject one disposition to act rather than other dispositions'. We very often associate this narrow use of 'training' with psychological conditioning in which subjects become instruments to the will of the trainer. We also use 'training' in a wider way, as in training a philosopher, training an observer or training the mind. Even in these uses there is still the sense of imparting routine manoeuvres and skills, without rationale.

In agrarian cultures people may not need a distinction like the one that we make between 'education' and 'training'. Similarly in English-speaking cultures, until the Industrial Revolution and the introduction of compulsory schooling in the nineteenth century, the two words were used almost interchangeably. Peters recalls 'education' being used of animals and birds trained by human beings, such as hounds and falcons, and even silkworms (1970 p. 11). As mentioned, this older use for 'education' still survives when we talk, for instance, of Spartan education or of our own forms of training that do not have close links with knowledge and understanding. Today though we would not readily speak of educating animals and never of educating plants: we do continue to speak of training animals and plants though. The reasons for this change are easy to follow: with the coming of industrialism greater value was placed on literacy, numeracy, knowledge and skill; with special institutions developed to pass on these things education came to be associated very closely with the many processes of instruction that went on in such special institutions. Peters says that the development of the concept of an 'educated person' in the nineteenth century (characterised as an all-round developed person, morally, intellectually and spiritually) caused us to tighten up the concept of 'education' because of its association with the development of such a person: "we distinguish between educating people and training them because for us education is no longer compatible with any narrowly conceived enterprise" (Peters, 1973 p. 54).

There is no such thing as a general sort of training. 'Training' is specific in a way that 'education' is not. Training is directed towards some end beyond the task of training, while education means nothing less than initiation into a worthwhile form of life: "We do not speak of people being educated as cooks, in engineering, or for anything specific such as farming" (Peters, 1973 pp. 42-43).

What is the connection then between 'education' and 'training'? Certainly training is often used as an ingredient of education. I think we can conclude with Wringe that education, as initiation into a worthwhile form of life, will usually include training of some sort as a subordinate activity (for example, training in the skills of literacy and numeracy). We can say, therefore, that training is part of the experience of an educated person; we can even say of this sort of training that its aims are instrumental in reaching that worthwhile form of life into which education initiates. But we can never conclude that education always requires training; even training in the skills of literacy and numeracy can be bypassed by children appropriately motivated to teach themselves. Nor can we conclude that training is coextensive with education. Being educated demands much more than being highly trained; it involves the possession of a body of knowledge along with a conceptual scheme to raise that knowledge above the level of a collection of disjointed facts. This means some understanding of principles for the organising of facts. We need to understand the reasons behind things, an understanding that training on its own not just fails to supply, but which it can obscure.

If we want to connect educational processes with work, then, we are not going to manage it through some vast processes of training. The connection of education with work is a plain one: any process of schooling designed by people who view education as initiation into some worthwhile form of life will show regard for work as a component of that worthwhile form of life, because work is a part of the normal and necessary range of human activities. In exercising a minimum skill men and women are 'at work'. It behoves those responsible for framing educational processes to ask: what are the curricular processes that will reveal work as a component of a worthwhile form of life and that will prepare children for initiation into that work component of a worthwhile form of life?

Work, Education and Democracy

Because human work is very often performed in social contexts where issues of power and control, profit and loss, and even life and death are important ones, it is impossible to separate the 'education for work' debate from wider political issues. There is much at stake when we are deciding what processes of schooling are suitable in this area: there are those in societies who plainly stand to gain or lose in important ways depending on the decisions that we make. Obviously students themselves possess important rights of control over their lives that can be lost if educators choose badly in deciding the kind of curriculum that is appropriate: the right to freedom of action; the right to freedom of expression. At the same time those who employ the graduates of our schools have much to win or lose depending on our decisions. For example, consider the capitalist or mixed economy societies that are the social and educational contexts for this book: we might argue that private enterprise organisations, their owners and their shareholders, would benefit greatly if adolescent children were to be given a form of schooling that stresses training in the job skills that are most needed by those same private enterprise organisations.

The question recurs in educational debate: can schools be servants of technocratic efficiency within societies while still properly serving educational aims? The strident cries of would-be educational reformers of mid-seventeenth century England sound very familiar today. Beverley Southgate assembles some of these

(1987 p. 13): theory must be replaced by practice; the function of education is to prepare "everyone for industry and employment" (John Dury, in 1649); nothing is to be taught that is not socially "useful". "Let all children be fitted for common trades": less "vocational" education can then be pursued by those with time and money for such luxuries (John Newton, in 1668). For young men should "not be idly trained up in notions, speculations and verbal disputes, but may learn to inure their hands to labour, and put their fingers to the furnaces" (John Webster, in 1654). Clearly it is 'training' that these early theorists wanted; some early version of schooling for technocratic efficiency, not education.

Even allowing that education must remain the goal of schooling and that training has only a subordinate place, people still believe it possible to design a form of schooling that is 'education' but where training is deliberately given priority in order to equip children with the job skills needed for technocratic efficiency in societies. Gary McCulloch, in Chapter 9 of this volume, discusses policies in education directed very much to this end; he examines two cases: the 'secondary technical schools' policy established in Britain in the 1940s and abandoned in the 1960s; and the 'city technology colleges' introduced there in 1987 in direct response to government policy.

Similar demands that schools produce efficient workers, coming recently from politically diverse governments in Canada, the United States, Australia and New Zealand, raise anew the question: are schools the servants of technocratic efficiency? The most important and serious debate on this question took place in the first two decades of the twentieth century in the United States. Because of the character of that debate, and the importance for education of one of its participants, it provides the standard rehearsal of the issues at stake. In Chapter 5 Arthur Wirth reviews this 'vocational-liberal studies controversy', a documented debate that took place between the first modern philosopher of education, John Dewey, on one side and the 'social efficiency philosophers' on the other. In drawing on Dewey's work, Wirth is presenting for us the ideas of the central theorist in the 'education for work' debate. Indeed so influential were Dewey's ideas in the early 1900s that the Bolshevik revolutionaries in the Soviet Union used his theorising as their model for progressive education and continued to do so up to a decade after the October revolution, until their infant democratic institutions were washed away by dictatorship. I suggest that it is important to read Wirth's chapter not simply as history, interesting though the events are to historians of education; what the reader needs to extract from this chapter is a grasp of the enduring and recurrent issues about 'education for work' that arise in societies; issues that seem to be resurrected by politicians every decade or so, especially when unemployment is a visible social problem. The reader can also extract some standard educational responses to the demands in this area that governments often unreasonably make of schools.

As Wirth points out, Dewey did not win the 'vocational-liberal studies' debate. In Chapter 6 Robert Sherman argues that Dewey's defeat has had lasting consequences for democratic societies; he suggests that we have not come very far since Dewey first assembled the arguments; and he recommends a return to the Deweyan position: educators have to work within the scientific, industrial, corporate reality and use education to understand, transform and transcend inequities and oppressive influences within that reality. Also in this chapter Sherman discusses a form of schooling in the United States that was given prominence in the early 1970s: 'career education', where training and "fitting" students to a function was emphasised while the development of their critical faculties was not. Sherman uses his discussion of career education as the subject matter for his treatment of the wider issues. His conclusion is rather different from Wirth's: Sherman sees a prior need for educational reform coupled with social renewal if we are to create lifestyles that balance technology with humanistic concerns.

5 Issues In The Vocational-Liberal Studies Controversy (1900-1917)

John Dewey vs The Social Efficiency Philosophers

by Arthur G Wirth

> The question is whether or not our beautiful, libertarian, pluralist and populist experiment is viable in modern conditions.
> (Paul Goodman, *People or Personnel* and *Like a Conquered Province* (New York: Alfred A. Knopf, Vintage Books, 1968) p. 274)

By looking at the set of forces in contention in the vocational education movement (1900-1917), we can see more than how technology acts as a pressure for institutional change. We can see something about the conflict of the two Americas we, in fact, have become in the hundred years since the Civil War: the America which defines its aspirations in terms of the blind drive for an increase in material goods, and that other America which Paul Goodman has described as the "libertarian, pluralist and populist experiment".

To be blunt and to oversimplify, the choice then and now is whether schools are to become servants of technocratic efficiency needs, or whether they can act to help men and woman humanize life under technology.

In the liberal-vocational studies debate the technocratic drives of what Paul Goodman calls the Empty Society of mindless productivity showed in the social efficiency philosophy of David Snedden and Charles Prosser. On the other hand, John Dewey tried to define an approach that would combine democratic and humanistic values with science and industry. This chapter aims to compare the two philosophical models which grew out of that debate.

The Social Efficiency Philosophers

Beginning in the late 90s the National Association of Manufacturers became a powerful force advocating the addition of a vocational component to the school system. The Association had formed as a result of the 1893 depression. Its members soon identified as the cause of their problems a serious overproduction which had accompanied frenzied post-Civil War industrial expansion. Catastrophe, they felt, would be their lot if they limited themselves to the demands of the domestic market. New opportunities lay overseas in Latin America and Asia. Their salvation lay in entering the international economic arena. As they ventured out they found tough competition from aggressive German businessmen. Soon they sent emissaries to Germany to assess the source of German effectiveness. Their analysts reported that one critical source of German advantage was the existence of a powerful set of carefully-designed skill-training programs. There were, for example, twenty-one different schools for the building trades alone; there were *Werkmeisterschulen* for foremen and research-oriented *Technische Hochschulen* for engineers at the top. This finely-graded set of training programs was neatly meshed to the hierarchical skill needs of the technological system. It was administered by the Ministry of Commerce rather than Education so that it would be run by practical men rather than fuzzy-minded educators. American manufacturers became convinced that they could compete successfully only if the American school system introduced a set of separate vocational schools patterned after the German model.

David Snedden and Charles Prosser in their work and writings developed the theoretical rationale for the technocratic model. It was marked by a conservative social philosophy, a methodology of specific training operations based on principles of S-R psychology, and a curriculum designed according to a job analysis of the needs of industry, and by a preference for a separately-administered set of vocational schools.

Snedden shared the basic faith of Herbert Spencer and the conservative Social Darwinists that the emergence of scientific-corporate capitalism was the cosmic instrument for progress. He accepted the basic proposition of the manufacturers that what was good for business was good for America. In order to help more Americans enjoy progress, the task of education was to aid the economy to function as efficiently as possible - "To make each child a better socius," a more fit member of a complex society.

His social philosophy was reflected in his recommendation for the teaching of history. The job was to define the kind of citizen we wanted for the well-functioning society, then extrapolate the specific forms of training which would produce this type. The history teacher, he said, has a heavy obligation to present the opinions of the controlling majority - or withdraw from teaching. If a teacher held minority views he should suppress them and express the position of the majority.

Sneddon worked from an assumption about the nature of social life which he borrowed from his sociology teacher Franklin Giddings:

> Society, like the material world...passes from homogeneity and indefiniteness

of non-organization to the heterogeneity and definiteness of organization. The process of selection *is based upon the differences growing out of the unequal conditions of both heredity and nurture to which man is born.* Inequality - physical, mental, and moral - is an inevitable characteristic of the social population. (Giddings, 1896 p.9).

Snedden put the same idea in his own words in the 1920s when he likened the good society to a winning "team group." A team is made stronger by specialization of functions. Some, like the officers on a submarine crew, would be trained to lead and coordinate; others would be trained for their special functions in the ranks (Snedden, 1924).

Snedden argued that the ultimate aim of education was "the greatest degree of efficiency." We could afford to permit the universities to continue to provide inadequate education for the professionals and the leadership class, he said; but we could not tolerate the failure of lower schools to provide for "those who do duty in the ranks...who will follow, not lead." Efficiency for "the rank and file" meant "not only training for culture's sake, but that utilitarian training which looks to individual efficiency in the world of work." Training in the trades and business, Snedden said, was a legitimate obligation of public education. The "old educator" relied on Greek, Latin, and mathematics. This curriculum, more than poverty or the lure of employment, was what drove children from school. The "new education," he predicted, would be an elective program that included both a variety of child interests and a regimen designed to fit the child to his place in society. It would lead the child "toward the realities of present life"; and when the child was properly "fitted," he would possess "such an intelligent understanding or authority as (to) make the exercise of arbitrary authority unnecessary" (Drost, 1967 pp.42-45).

Fortunately, as Snedden saw it, human beings fall into ability levels which parallel the hierarchical work requirements of modern society. New scientific testing instruments combined with vocational guidance would make it possible for schools to do what Charles Eliot had suggested in 1907 - differentiate children into programs according to their "probable destinies" based on heredity plus economic and social factors. The new junior high schools would perform the task of sorting students into differentiated courses: prevocational offerings in commercial subjects, industrial arts, and agricultural or household arts for those "who most incline to them or have need of them" (Snedden, 1908 p. 753).

Frederick Fish, President of AT and T and Chairman of the Massachusetts Board of Education, was impressed by the vision of his Commissioner of Education. In 1910 Fish echoed Snedden in calling the schools to revise their values by providing training to meet "the practical needs of life" for "the rank and file" (Fish, 1910 pp.367-368).

The Snedden-Fish regime was prepared to act as well as talk. Snedden appointed his Teachers College colleague Charles Prosser to develop a system of vocational schools for the major industrial centres of the state.

By 1912, when Prosser became Executive Secretary of The National Society for the Promotion of Industrial Education (N.S.P.I.E.), he had clarified his goal: to reject the impractical manual training of the general educators and replace it with "real vocational education," by which he meant training for useful employment - train the person to get a job, train him so he could hold it and advance to a better job (Prosser and Quigley, 1950).

Prosser insisted that all vocational content must be specific and that its source was to be found "in the experience of those who have mastered the occupation." Throughout his long career, Prosser repeated endlessly the arguments of his position. Traditional scholastic education, he maintained, aimed to prepare the citizen for the worthy use of leisure time. Traditional schoolmen, committed to the task of fostering "leisure culture," operated from the discredited psychological tradition of faculty psychology and formal discipline. There were several clear reasons why new programs of vocational training could not be entrusted to such men. "Culturists" were cut off from the practical world of work, and their outmoded theory of learning made them incapable of managing genuine skill-training programs. "Vocational education," Prosser argued, "only functions in proportion as it will enable an individual actually to do a job... Vocational education must establish habits: habits of correct thinking and of correct doing. Hence, its fundamental theory must be that of habit psychology" (Ibid. pp.215-20). The new scientific psychology pioneered by Edward Thorndike, said Prosser, assumed that the mind is a habit-forming machine. There was an obvious fit between this psychological theory and vocational education when the latter was conceived as "essentially a matter of establishing certain habits through repetitive training both in thinking and doing" (Ibid. p.216). In contrast to the theory of general mind-training, Thorndike's theory taught that "all habits of doing and thinking are developed in specific situations." Prosser deduced correlatively that the content of vocational training should be determined by "the actual functioning content" of a given occupation. "If you want to train a youth to be an efficient plumber, you must select the actual experiences in the practice of the plumbing trade that he should have and see that he gets these in a real instead of a pseudo way" (Ibid. p.228). Furthermore, general studies like mathematics or science should be broken into short units which would bear "directly on specific needs of workers in the performance of specific tasks or operations." They should, when possible, be taught by the craftsman-teacher skilled in the task, rather than by general mathematics or science teachers.

A prototype of the plan favoured by Prosser was established in the short unit courses which he developed while Director of the Dunwoody Institute in Minneapolis. "In garment making, one unit might deal with kimonos, one with underwear, and another with house dresses" (Ibid. p.291). At the Dunwoody Institute, units were programmed in great detail to lead students step-by-step through the skill development cycle. Students punched in on time clocks, and instructors behaved like shop foremen rather than public school teachers. A no-nonsense attitude prevailed. If students were not punctual, orderly, and efficient, they were asked to leave.

If this brief description of Dunwoody conveys a feeling of Prosser's orientation, some of the features he wrote into the Smith-Hughes Act can readily be understood. Approved programs had to meet the criterion of "fitting for useful employment" persons over fourteen but under college age who were preparing for work on farms, in trades, in industrial pursuits, and the like. Federal funds were given only for support of vocational training classes. General education costs were to be borne by the states and local school districts. At least fifty percent of subsidized instruction had to be devoted to "practical work on a useful or productive basis." Funds for the training of teachers were restricted to those who "have had adequate vocational experience or contact in the line of work for which they are preparing" (Smith Hughes Act, 1917 pp.929-936).

Since his rationale excluded general educators from the management of vocational training, Prosser fought as long as possible for a separately-administered type of vocational education. In the final politicking prior to 1917, he had to make some concessions; but, in the main, he created a framework which permitted vocational programs to stand apart. The Smith-Hughes Act did establish a Federal Board for Vocational Education, separate from the United States Office of Education and responsible only to Congress. The seven-member Board consisted of the Secretaries of Labor, Commerce, and Agriculture and three citizens representing labor, agriculture, and manufacturing. The Commissioner of Education was added to allay the anxieties of the N.E.A. (Barlow, 1967 pp.114-115).

Prosser was immediately appointed Executive Director of the Federal Board and served in that office in its first two crucial years. He established the initial tone of administration. States were given the option of setting up separate boards, or of administering vocational education under the aegis of their general boards of education. In actuality, both the language of Smith-Hughes and the administrative style of Dr Prosser assured that vocational education would function as a separate aspect of education within the states. The genius of Charles Prosser lay in his capacity to create well-tooled manpower training programs. Somewhere in a technological society that task must be done.

Dewey's Position

Snedden, Prosser and Dewey were part of a general reform movement which assumed that traditional schooling would have to give way to approaches more relevant to new social-economic conditions. On the surface there were points of agreement. They all condemned "sterile, bookish education." All were convinced that city schools were isolated from the life-concerns of urban children. All three wanted to broaden the curriculum to include studies appropriate to a technological era. Just below the surface, however, there were profound differences. Dewey was quite aware of the disagreements, but Snedden was hurt and bewildered when Dewey lashed out at him for his advocacy of separate vocational schools. Snedden expressed his sense of betrayal in a letter to *The New Republic* in which he said that those who had been seeking sound vocational education had become accustomed to opposition from the academic brethren. "But to find Dr Dewey apparently giving aid and comfort to opponents of a broader, richer, and more effective program of education...is discouraging" (Snedden, 1915 p.40).

If Snedden expected Dewey to relent, he was in for disappointment. Dewey replied sharply that his differences with Snedden were profoundly social and political as well as educational.

> The kind of vocational education which I am interested in is not one which will "adapt" workers to the existing industrial regime; I am not sufficiently in love with the regime for that. It seems to me that the business of all who would not be educational time-servers is to strive for a kind of vocational education which will first alter the existing industrial system, and ultimately transform it (Dewey, 1915 p.42).

Furthermore, Dewey charged that Snedden had failed to meet the heart of his argument on pedagogical matters: "I argued that a separation of trade education and general education of youth has the inevitable tendency to make both kinds of training narrower and less significant than the schooling in which the traditional education is reorganized to utilize the subject matter - active, scientific, and social of the present day environment."

Dewey was right - the differences were profoundly social and political as well as educational. Snedden and Prosser, operating from Social Darwinist assumptions, viewed individuals as isolated units with varying capacities and potentials; if each pursued his own advantage, a rough sorting out would take place which would coincide with the skill and status needs of a hierarchically-organized work world. The schools could aid the process by scientific counselling. Differentiated skill-training programs, designed in terms of emerging needs of industry and business, would provide the kind of trained manpower required by the corporate system. The emerging American industrial democracy would provide opportunity for everyone to have an equal chance to run for the prizes - and all could have a share in an ever-growing material prosperity. If that was not what the "American dream" was all about, then what was it? Snedden and Prosser were simply mystified by those who were so astigmatic as to look at the new scene and come away with doubts and misgivings - or with fear and trembling.

Dewey, of course, had a very different conception of the nature of the person and the problems of democratic traditions in the technological society. He rejected the image of isolated individuals moved by the play of natural forces in the marketplace. He operated from the social psychology position of his colleague George H. Mead - with its self-other concept of personality. The self was seen as emerging from both the patterning of culture plus the value choices of the individual. The premise held that, if you wanted persons with qualities capable of sustaining democratic values, they had to be nourished in communities marked by such values. The problem as Dewey saw it was whether democratic values of meaningful participation and respect for persons could be sustained under urban-corporate conditions. People were beginning to repeat the rhetoric of democratic values while living in daily contradiction of them. This produced individuals wasted by neurotic conflicts, incapable of sustaining meaningful freedoms.

The task of overcoming the contradictions, as Dewey defined it, was to develop strategies for bringing qualities of the democratic ethos into institutions being transformed by science, technology and corporatism. Dewey rejected elitist answers. His general strategy was to seek means by which the qualities of mind, required to reform institutions, could be made available across the entire popula-tion.

In his design the schools were assigned a critical role: they could help the young gain insights as to how human experience was being transformed by science, technology, and economic corporatism; they could teach the hypothetical mode of thought required to handle complex problems; the schools themselves could be turned into communities where the young in living and learning would experience the life qualities exemplified in the creative work of scientists and artists. By spending the years of childhood and youth in such learning communities, the young might become the kind of persons who could change institutional life styles so they would serve to liberate persons rather than manipulate them as functionaries.

While Dewey and the progressives no doubt had exaggerated hopes for schools as agents of reform it is not true that Dewey expected the school to do it single-handedly. The meliorist philosophy assumed that institutional reform would have to go on across the board. For example, the critical, evaluative quality would manifest itself in muckraking journalism and scholarship; the formation of unions would counter the helplessness of individual workers and create union bases of power and criticism to make changes in the quality of work-life and product (a hope at odds with the later myopic quality of some unions who became content to collaborate with employers in simply milking consumers).

The move would be in the direction of creating persons capable of producing "the planning society" in which each institution would be evaluated by whether modes of operating contributed to the growth of persons. This was to take the place of an exploitative economic system which let all consequences flow from a senseless pursuit of profits.

With concerns like these why would Dewey get seriously involved with the vocational education movement? The importance Dewey attached to the relation of vocational to liberal studies is evidenced by a generally-overlooked passage in *Democracy and Education*: "At the present time the conflict of philosophic theories focuses in the discussion of the proper place and function of vocational factors in education ... *significant differences in fundamental philosophical conceptions find their chief issue in connection with this point*" (Dewey, 1916a p.358).

I shall note only several examples of Dewey's complex argument that new integrations of technological or vocational studies with liberal studies could serve to revitalize school learning and eventually aid in social transformation.

First, he worked from a premise rooted in the new sociology and economics, namely, that the basic mode employed in producing life-necessities had a pervasive effect on all social institutions and on qualities of selfhood. Thus, when there were shifts from a hunting-and-gathering to a pastoral or to agricultural economies, then modes of governing, defending and educating would change. New expressions in the arts, religion and philosophy were inevitable. As men entered the twentieth century they were well into one of the great transition periods - with expansion of scientific thought and technique as the great change factor. A distinctive feature of Dewey's philosophy was his conviction that human renewal might be engendered from within the very culture of science, which also posed major threats.

Pedagogically Dewey placed the occupations at the heart of the program of his Laboratory School. Children, for example, could get the feeling of how science and technology had affected such a basic process as the turning of raw wool into clothing by first trying the process by hand and then observing factory methods. They could study also what the social and human effects were when people moved from handicraft to corporate industrial modes of production. The doing and the intellectualizing phases of such projects should be conducted so that children would get the feel of the scientific mode of inquiry that underlay the process - the hypothetical style of holding ideas, and reporting and testing them in a climate of openness.

Secondly, he argued that chances to take part in the "doing" aspects of such studies would offer an alternative to the ancient tradition of equating education with lesson-saying in classrooms. In his Laboratory School children worked at weaving, cooking, constructing, gardening. Studies in the sciences, history, language, mathematics and the arts were related to these activities. As students grew older, activities and studies could be extended to the out-of-school community. Thus Dewey developed an interest in the Gary Plan, where children combined science study with experiences in the school steam plant or in the steel mills of the town. Dewey was drawn, too, to the polytechnical education concepts in the U.S.S.R. in the 20s and the reforms of rural education in the *"escuelas de accion"* of the Mexican Revolution. Currently such programs as the New Jersey Technology for Children Project, the work of the Center for Technological Education in the San Francisco Bay Area, the Parkway Plan in Philadelphia, and the University Without Walls experiments would contain features related to Dewey's rationale.

Thirdly, there was the valuational aspect. In *Individualism Old and New* and elsewhere he made his economic critique in which he argued that the single-minded pursuits of profit in a laissez-faire economy involved a tragic misuse of the power of science and technology. Children and the young had to be educated so as to learn how to examine the consequences of technology. He stated the criterion they should learn to employ in an often-quoted statement in *Reconstruction in Philosophy*:

> All social institutions have a meaning, a purpose. That purpose is to set free and to develop the capacities of human individuals without respect to race, sex, class or economic status ... (The) test of their value is the extent to which they educate every individual into the full stature of his possibility. Democracy has many meanings, but if it has a moral meaning, it is found in resolving that *the supreme test of all political institutions and industrial arrangements shall be the contribution they make to the all-around growth of every member of a society* (Dewey 1950, p.147).

The goal was to develop a populace who would take that criterion seriously and apply it to all institutions.

With a rationale like this Dewey joined those who resisted the pressures for a dual system in the vocational education movement. The only defensible approach, Dewey argued, was to incorporate a new kind of industrial education - as part of general education reform - whose aim would be to cultivate "industrial intelligence" throughout the population.

A general education designed to promote industrial intelligence would provide a genuine alternative to German dualism:

Instead of trying to split schools into two kinds, one of a trade type for children whom it is assumed are to be employees and one of a liberal type for the children of the well-to-do, it will aim at such a reorganization of existing schools as will give all pupils a genuine respect for useful work, an ability to render service, and a contempt for social parasites whether they are called tramps or leaders of "society"... It will indeed make much of developing motor and manual skill, but not of a routine or automatic type. It will rather utilize active and manual pursuits as the means of developing constructive, inventive and creative power of mind. It will select the materials and the technique of the trades not for the sake of producing skilled workers for hire in definite trades, but for the sake of securing industrial intelligence - a knowledge of the conditions and processes of present manufacturing, transportation and commerce so that the individual may be able to make his own choices and his own adjustments, and be master, so far as in him lies, of his own economic fate. It will be recognised that, for this purpose, a broad acquaintance with science and skill in the laboratory control of materials and processes is more important than skill in trade operations. It will remember that the future employee is a consumer as well as a producer, that the whole tendency of society, so far as it is intelligent and wholesome, is to an increase of the hours of leisure, and that an education which does nothing to enable individuals to consume wisely and to utilize leisure wisely is a fraud on democracy. So far as method is concerned, such a conception of industrial education will prize freedom more than docility; initiative more than automatic skill; insight and understanding more than capacity to recite lessons or to execute tasks under the direction of others (Dewey, 1940 pp. 131-132).

Neither Congress nor the people were of a mind to heed such talk. By 1917, the urgent need to increase military production provided the special motivation required to spur federal action. Congress and the President gave Charles Prosser and his colleagues the measure for which they had worked so long and hard.

As we reach the last decade of the twentieth century a major challenge for all societies is to create life styles which will overcome the divorce of technology from humanistic concerns. If we make it, educational reform and social renewal will go on together. The emergence of educational experiments aimed at providing humanizing experiences with technology will be one kind of sign. The flourishing of bland, well-engineered school efforts to serve narrow technocratic efficiency needs will be a counter-indication. The inner conflict, over which kind of society Americans want to create with the power of science and technology, continues - only the stakes are getting higher.

6 Vocational Education and Democracy

by Robert R Sherman

The debate over vocational education, which took place in the first twenty years of this century, has current parallels and applications. For all practical purposes, the debate was won by the social efficiency advocates. Professor Wirth has noted that there was little inclination to heed Dewey's theory, and the need for increased military production during World War I provided the special motivation for a federal program based on the social efficiency theme. "Practical needs" won out over "theory." But the victory has had consequences to the present day. It has continued to define the shape of democracy and the role of education in a democracy.

An obvious example is the operation of schools. Much current criticism has this as its focus and resembles similar criticism in the debate over vocational education. For example, there is (and was) the belief that education is impractical. Much of what is learned in schools is said to be unrelated to the way the world actually runs, and schools do not prepare students for what they will do in life. Thus, education is said to lack "relevance." The remedy advocated for this is that schools should insure that students are able to perform in a work society. This is to say that education should be held "accountable" for what it produces. If public schooling cannot produce graduates who can "do something," other forms of education should be tried. So there is suggested today such plans as "voucher systems" and contracts with business corporations to operate the schools.

A consequence of this thinking, if not an assumption, is that education should "serve" society by providing manpower and by helping it operate efficiently. The purpose of the school, so the thinking goes, is to sort, shape, and certify students for the needs of commercial and governmental enterprises. The way to do this is to run the schools as a business; the business approach will insure the wise expenditure of resources and will utilize for education the same setting and logic on which work, to be entered shortly, is organized. Thus, what is to be learned and how depends not on philosophic purpose, psychological and sociological knowledge, and educational experimentation, but on commercial needs and business management techniques.

It seems to be of little consequence that these recommendations have been tried before and have not proven their worth. A thoroughly convincing critique has been made of the business efficiency movement in education (Callahan, 1962). It shows that the demands for such things as relevance, practicality, scientific management, separate schools, teacher ratings, accountability, and so on, all are related to the belief that education should be run as and for the benefit of business and the depressing results that have come from acting on that belief. Yet, still it is thought that whatever is wrong with education can be changed by making it more practical and efficient.

We must not be trapped by words. At a time of high costs and competition for resources, no one will get far by denying that education, unlike other activities, should be efficient and practical. Cutbacks in educational programs and services are making this point with force today. But what "efficiency" and "practicality" are taken to mean makes a difference. Of course education should be run with a minimum of waste and with the idea that it will make a difference in the conduct and quality of life. But it does not follow from this that the purpose of schooling is to sort, shape, and certify workers for the economic system and that it should operate by following business management techniques.

It has been noted previously that the view that education should service a practical social interest narrows the vision of what education and democracy can be and provides an inadequate base for response to forces affecting society today. This would be true for any practical interest to be served. The point needs explanation. Not all demands for relevance or practicality today are motivated by the belief that students should be educated to operate effectively in a business society. Some critics hold that the schools serve that function too well and that the quality of life is diminished because of it. Thus it is suggested that schooling actively should resist the business interest; the school should act politically to remake society in some other image.

The usual response to this criticism is that the schools should not be politicized to serve a special interest. But it is mystifying that so many who give that response do not see its logical implications for prescribing the sorting, shaping, and certifying functions that schools have practised for so long. Those functions serve the special interests of business more than anything else. It has been argued that some interests should be preferred (Calvin Coolidge once said, "The business of America is business"), but such a view has practical political and educational problems of its own. For example, determining what shall be preferred and how change will be encouraged and carried out are points at the heart of this debate. The only real way out of the dilemma of determining which interest the schools should serve is to insist that they should not aim for any particular or practical result.

That should not be taken to mean that education can be unrelated to the social scene or that it should be practised on the level of high abstraction. It is to say that in addition to better logic (and for those who believe ends and means must be consistent, better logic is important), the problem of deciding whose interests will be served in a democracy is a false issue. Insofar as possible, all interests need to and should be served. In order to do this, of course, the school must be a general, not a special, agency. Thus students should not be expected to have a "proper" interest before they can be educated, or submit to an undemocratic authority in the name of discipline, or be satisfied with a limited perception and availability of opportunities when they finish.

We have not come very far since John Dewey first put some of these views in perspective. For example there was in the early 1970s a new push toward the kind of education thought to be inadequate by Dewey. Commissioner Sidney P. Marland, Jr, of the US Office of Education, put his prestige and authority behind "career education" (Marland, 1971a; 1971b; 1971c; Schwartz, 1970; 1971a; 1971b; 1971c). Vocational education, Marland says, has not insured that everyone who receives a diploma is qualified for immediate employment or higher education. Businessmen complain that graduates are not prepared with business skills or even basic skills. These failings come from having followed not vocational education, but a general education that is "ill-conceived and unproductive," a "fallacious compromise between the true academic liberal arts and true vocational offerings." Furthermore, general education is "discriminatory" in the same sense that racial and ethnic considerations are discriminatory, because those who receive it lose out in the job market. Youngsters thus are the unfortunate "inmates" of general education, and all educators must share the "guilt" of the system's failure to equip young people to get and hold decent jobs.

What is needed, according to Marland, is a plan for career education. This should blend academic and vocational curricula, and by school leaving age such an education should have prepared a student for higher education or useful and rewarding employment. Throughout Marland's discussions, however, the attention mainly is on employment. The US Office of Education, he says, will act to improve the preparation of the young for work. Career education will "fit a person to a function efficiently," as well as make him aware of why he is doing what he is doing. Such an education will be "relevant." The smallest child should get an "indoctrination" to the world of work, "to the real world" (the term may not be Marland's;

Schwartz, 1971c). Career education should begin as a general concept and gradually become more specific, so that somewhere halfway through high school "entry level skills" are gained and in the last years of high school work skills are acquired.

With such views it should not be surprising to find Marland advocating an alliance with business to produce the individuals described above. His language is that of business: boards of education serve one "stockholder" -the child, but parents and taxpayers also are called "stockholders." Marland's appointment as Commissioner was opposed by teacher and labour organizations because of his ties with an industrial-educational complex "greedy for a share of the educational dollar." (The words are George Meany's. Prior to his appointment as Commissioner, Marland was president of an institute involved in "performance contracting" under government grant.) (Schwartz, 1970). He believes a new partnership is needed in education between schools and industry, and prior to his confirmation he vowed to name a "businessman with management background" as deputy commissioner for management in the Office of Education

Later Marland advocated that "public relations professionals," with one foot in education and the other in communications ("the world of the non-specialist public"), be employed to bring rationality to the debate over education by interpreting the need for reform and the realities of whatever change is possible. Educators cannot gauge these things accurately, he said. Marland claims to be aware of the risk of anti-intellectualism he runs with these views, but he thinks that career education, which would "shore up and rationalize the Protestant work ethic," (again the term may not be Marland's: Schwartz, 1971 c) would make grade and high schools more realistic and provide the implicit motivation for academic learning undergirding the career mode. For all students, career education should provide a solid understanding of the free enterprise system and the opportunities and obligations it holds for us.

We have been through all this before. There is no indication in the views expressed that Marland is aware that business, industry, and technology are the primary forces that have changed society. His suggestion that students be educated for careers sounds good, but it would feed those forces rather than enable one to cope with them. The emphasis on "fitting" to a function, "shoring up" the work ethic, and understanding the "opportunities and obligations" of the free enterprise system suggests that criticism and reformulation of the system is not envisioned. The case is not one-sided, of course. Marland says career education is intended for individual fulfilment, that it should not preclude one who trains for and enters work from going on to higher education later, and that it seeks to erase the snobbery associated with working with one's hands. All of these are good. But a close attention to his plan suggests more defects than merits.

Another defect is that career education seems to be just another attempt to use the schools to "solve" social problems. It has taken a long time to realize what Dewey knew long ago, namely, that education is not done directly. It follows from this that education cannot be successful in direct intervention into social problems. Considerable empirical evidence is claimed to confirm that conclusion today. Recent leaders in the federal government have not tired of making this point repeatedly when assessing attempts to eradicate, for example, poverty and racism through education. Yet the same people continue to advocate a kind of vocational education that has the same intent. These observations should not be taken to diminish the urgency of dealing with social problems or to suggest that education has no bearing on them. The point is that many officials are inconsistent in their thinking about the matters. It is common to hear that other institutions than education are vital in dealing with social problems, but the advice is as little understood as it is followed. The point is that education cannot be relied on as some magic to repair the lives of those wasted by other forces. This is as true for career as for any other kind of education.

Marland believes it would be a bold new approach to turn some career education programmes over to industry. Three models can be tried - the school-based, home-based, and business - or employer-based; but the last is the "most radical," he says, because it calls for an alternative system of education. It would be voluntary for students and by contract with the school system. (Presumably students who did not learn could cause the business to lose its contract, a result different from dismissing students at Dunwoody Institute!) One wonders if Marland simply has jumped on the "alternatives in education" bandwagon. It seems incredible to call an old idea for operating the schools along business lines "radical" or to be enthusiastic about its possibilities in light of past criticisms and current appraisals of such attempts (Callahan, 1962). Marland testified before a congressional committee in 1969 that "no sound evidence has been offered to demonstrate that improved circumstances for teachers have brought improved education for children" (Schwartz, 1970). He does not seem inclined to apply a similar test to the business operation of schooling.

Another old risk is evident in the career education proposals. It is the separation of the intellectual from the practical. The claim is made that career education is designed to bridge this gap, to make learning and work continuous throughout life. But some of the language used and proposals made by career education advocates gives another impression. Advocates talk about "combining" vocational training, education in academic fundamentals, and work experience; and Marland has been quoted as saying that vocational-technical study should, among other things, "recognize excellence in areas not primarily intellectual". These are mild expressions, certainly, and there can be no quarrel with the desire to mark the dignity of work. But they do show a separation of the intellectual and the practical of the kind that John Dewey opposed. Perhaps as a gesture toward bridging the gap, Marland says that, whatever their goals, students most likely will not want either vocational-technical training or academic learning, but rather a combination of the two. The idea seems to be wishful thinking if viewed in light of the pressures within which such choices usually have to be made.

A more serious expression of the dichotomy between the intellectual and practical comes in the current widespread denigration of schooling and the time spent in formal education. Marland seems to have jumped on the "alternatives in education" bandwagon in order to justify the involvement of industry in education. But he criticizes also the pervasiveness of education in American society. For example, he asks whether or not we are producing too many Ph.D.'s and if the dream for higher education has become a "fetish," a national "totem," surviving long after its gods have died. He suggests that we have lost sight of what education is for, but he does not say directly what that is. But it is clear from the ideas examined here that education properly is "for" the job market, so that when there no longer is a need in that area (Marland never tires of telling that eight out of ten persons will not need credentials for work in the future), it follows that educational offerings, opportunities, and aspirations should be trimmed. This educational "vision" clearly is different from Dewey's. It ties education to narrow practical interests and emphasizes that in most things throughout life it is unnecessary.

The same point can be made with equal force about the "alternatives in education" and "deschooling" movements in general. One must not be misled by the freedom implied in "alternatives" or by the claim that these movements simply express an educational "pluralism" basic to democratic and progressive thought. Nor is it the intent here to deny that much is wrong with the operations and uses of education today and that many, and some drastic things should be tried in order to correct the problems. The point, however, is that glib movements toward "alternatives" and "deschooling" run risks of the kind opposed by Dewey in the vocational education debate. Such movements make wider vision and social unity more difficult to realize. The movements reflect a belief, claimed here to be erroneous, that the proper purposes and uses of education are limited and that a more general conception of education has little utility. This belief is a dim vision for a democratic society to aspire to, and acting on it would produce results (e.g., intellectual and moral separations) that were the basis of invidious (and undemocratic) social distinctions made in the past.

Nor is it the case that a society trying to be democratic must accept because of a commitment to "pluralism" all attempts to use education as anyone pleases. A simple realization of how ends and means need to be consistent should make that clear. Some alternative educational systems may not work for the common good. The belief that "alternatives" are "experiments" with other forms of education must be considered also in light of the values and practices it seeks to test. In this regard it is instructive to note that Dewey insisted that his school in Chicago was a "laboratory," not a demonstration, practice, or training school, because its purpose was to test implications of democratic educational theory (Wirth, 1966). Finally, how are "alternatives" and "deschooling" helping individuals to become more able to deal with the industrial, technological, and corporate forces in their lives? Many persons try to ignore such forces by turning away from them, but their effects continue nevertheless. All these points are not presented to suggest that new "forms" of education should not be sought, but rather that the current "alternatives" and "deschooling" movements may have more theoretical defects than practical merits. The defects were anticipated in the debate over vocational education years ago.

The net effect of the beliefs and proposals analyzed above is that education and democracy are being undermined. In part this is due to their own failings, of course; but it is due more to the loss of vision we have for them. It is incredible that there is today such widespread advocacy of the view that education really is unnecessary. Most attempts to account for this situation have little merit. For example, it does not help to equivocate on the point by noting that the criticism really is of "schooling," not education. Nor is it necessary here to debate the meanings of education and democracy. A suggestion of these things has been given in the debate analyzed above. Rather, the point here is that we do not follow the best sense of what education can be and we have lost the belief that it can help to secure democracy.

It is evident from Professor Wirth's chapter that the main question raised in the debate over vocational education is whether or not democracy is viable under modern conditions. He begins by referring to Paul Goodman's expression of the issue; he observes that Dewey's belief that human renewal can emerge from the same scientific culture that poses threats is scorned today (though it still is shared by a few radicals); and he ends by noting that the conflict continues among Americans over the kind of society that should be created with science and technology. Many different criticisms are made of democracy, and its education, today. Some believe democracy is no longer viable because it has become just another tool of aggrandizement and oppression. It is morally bankrupt and beyond redemption. Others believe that all political systems stifle liberty. But the central issue raised in the debate over vocational education is whether the conditions of modern life, conceived and dominated by science, and not democracy itself, are so defective that a liberal and humane society no longer is possible.

Anyone can have an opinion about the matter, but it is impossible to determine a general answer conclusively. That is because the matter turns on one's view of the efficacy of human effort and whether or not the results of science, on balance, are good or bad. We can note, however, a few things that should be obvious by this time. One is that, whatever the circumstances of life, they are the only, and thus the proper, place for education to begin. As Dewey says about children, so it is with other things; we start with precisely the assortment of activities with which we do start. "Education must take the being as he is ..." (Dewey, 1916a). Wishing things were otherwise is not the way of education. Thus, we have to work within the scientific, industrial, corporate reality.

Secondly, making things otherwise by a direct attack on the conditions equally is beyond the ken of education. But this should not lead to pessimism; rather, it should give a better sense of what education can and must be. Obviously this is the crux of the debate. The social efficiency advocates did not aim high in the role they gave to education, and thus it is not surprising that their theory served special interests better than the general welfare. Dewey, on the other hand, saw clearly that the general welfare (more extensive and thoroughgoing liberty, both individual and social) depended on using education to understand and thus to transform and transcend the limitations and restrictions of special interests.

Some persons suggest today that the widespread achievement of material affluence has made Americans satisfied and no longer inclined to extend the democratic vision. Thus, in the same way the argument about science goes, these circumstances make democracy increasingly difficult to preserve. There can be no question that the circumstances bring new difficulties, but the general conclusion that they are incompatible with democracy is faulty. Examine the converse. Can it be suggested seriously that, if there were not science and material wealth, life in general would be more satisfactory? Is this not the age-old argument that in order to be creative and dynamic people must be in want? It is sobering to recall that these views have been held for millennia not by the masses of people but by small groups who themselves have not been in want. On the other hand, there is the view that science and material wealth probably have done more to spread freedom widely than any other thing.

The task for the philosopher today, through education, is to recreate and publicize the democratic vision and to indicate how intellectual and physical energies and resources can be directed to accomplishing that vision. Of this kind we need more education, not less. And if current education is bad, we need a better form - not the abolition of it. It should not be surprising that people are troubled about a way of life that is changing - about students who seem to lack motivation and are ill-prepared and a thousand other things. These problems may not have been common in their own lives; or, if they were, their existence long ago has been forgotten. A natural reaction is to try to suppress them. And too often education is used as an easy attempt to solve the problems. Thus, such practices as homogeneous grouping, sorting, authoritarian management, and similar things are tried because they promise to make life and education easier, even though they violate in many ways the democratic vision.

But the democratic educator cannot yield to these things. The dilemma of the democrat in the twentieth century is to find ways to preserve and extend democracy without sacrificing it for work, material goods, and order. Long ago Dewey noted this as the problem between individualism and socialism: to determine how this and that factory and field operation can contribute to the education release and growth of human capacities - as well as the production of material goods (Dewey, 1944). Professor Wirth has said (in his last paragraph) that "If we make it," if we "create life-styles which will overcome the divorce of technology from humanistic concerns .. educational reform and social renewal will go on together". But the case really is the other way around: if we continue educational reform and social renewal, then we will make it. The social efficiency advocates did not see the world "steady and whole" in this regard; they had little understanding and no vision, and therein lies the limitations of their social and educational theory.

Part Three

Key Policy Issues in Education for Work

7 Introduction: Policy in Social Context

by David Corson

Two Types of Policy

We can identify two clear meanings for the term 'policy' which have a wide general currency. Firstly there is policy in the limited sense: policies of this kind provide major guidelines for action by creating frameworks that provide direction yet allow discretion. This form of 'policy' anticipates action; it usually involves the creation of detailed policy documents and is the kind of policy that we are able to state, and must state, with a considerable degree of explicitness. Secondly there is a broader sense for policy: a course of action or inaction towards the accomplishment of some intended or desired end; this kind of policy may embrace both what is actually intended (including 'policy' in the limited sense) and what occurs as a result of the intention. These ideas are developed elsewhere (Corson, 1986).

Our concern in Part Three is with policy in the second sense: matters of broad social policy reflecting changes in community values that are often referred to in policy documents but rarely made clear. Policies of this type affect societies in general; in education they address the large systems in which schools are set. Later, in Part Four, we deal with policy in the limited sense: the policies that are formulated in educational institutions and embedded in documents to provide a framework for the operation of a school and its curriculum.

The Problem of Utopian Policies

People who are asked to translate large-scale social policies into action within specific settings often have difficulties in understanding both the policies and their task. The reasons for these difficulties are not hard to discover if we reflect for a moment on how large-scale social policies come into being. Frequently important changes in social and cultural values (such as changed attitudes to gender in our own culture) receive their first public recognition and widespread articulation in the policies and promises of politicians or political parties. These policies and promises are reactions to climates of opinion that politicians try to be sensitive to. In their public statements, soliciting the support of their constituencies, politicians often offer a vague expression of belief or purpose; usually this is accompanied by an even vaguer statement of a course of action or inaction intended to lead towards the accomplishment of some intended or desired end, an end that recognises and responds as explicitly as possible to the original changes in social values. If a government receives a mandate for these policies and promises, social policy action of some kind will often result.

What policy-makers in education are often charged to do is to respond, in a concrete way, to these vague changes in social values and the political promises that are based upon them. As a result policy-makers are regularly confronted with difficult social policy dilemmas of the kind addressed in the chapters of Part Three: the need to educate for full employment while acknowledging the reality of high rates of unemployment; the need to preserve some semblance of equality of educational opportunity while providing an adequately diverse range of post-compulsory education provisions; the need to prepare young people for the possibility of unemployment without destroying their employability; the need to instill a 'female' aspect into education for the workplace without producing counter-productive male resentment; the need to address the training needs for work that lay-persons in the community advocate while still meeting educational criteria.

The responses of politicians and bureaucrats to these key issues, that reflect changes in social and cultural values, are very often impetuous and utopian ones. Often politicians have neither the time nor the background to implement fully considered and sensitive policies; their planning will rarely offer realistic agenda to transform the original visions into cultural action; in trying to achieve their aims in planning, politicians and bureaucrats will often unknowingly trample on some other set of important values or sensitivities. What politicians and bureaucrats often deliver for implementation is holistic and utopian.

Holistic planning, in which a decision is taken at the moment of planning that a complete reconstruction of some kind is possible and desirable, is fraught with risks. My purpose here is simply to draw attention to these risks while offering an alternative approach. Holistic planning may be very appropriate for simple organisations where policies can speak unambiguously to participants: in these circumstances policy makers can reasonably advocate a trial of their policies and expect some measure of success if the policies themselves seem reasonable. In the case of social or educational systems of structural and ideological complexity, however, the diversity of views, values, ends and sensitivities that relate to any broad policy make the design of coherent holistic policies very difficult to attain.

These ideas are at the base of Karl Popper's advice (1961) on the process of social policy formulation. Let me make it clear that my borrowing of Popper's ideas in this and other areas implies no blanket acceptance of Popper's personal political positions (which are difficult to categorise in any case since at various times in his life Popper has embraced Marxist, social democrat, libertarian and liberal points of view [1976]). It is Popper's opposition to totalitarianism in any form, whether political, cultural or intellectual, and his well-known theory of knowledge itself that are relevant to my purpose here.

Popper's explicit criticism of social policy planning relates to vast social and political programmes, such as the 'Five Year Plans' in the early decades of the Soviet Union or more recently 'The Great Leap Forward' in the People's Republic of China. Today we have ample evidence that these grand schemes and many others like them in every country have not only fallen well short of their objectives but have produced social costs and private agonies out of all proportion to their limited achievements. In the 1980s the so-called monetarist economic policies applied by governments of all political shades, in North America, Australasia and Britain, offer evidence for this claim. The past approaches to 'education for work' by governments in English-speaking countries, that are discussed in the pages of this book, may have been more humane in their results than these huge programmes; yet they are still widely regarded by their critics as sacrificing too much of importance in order to gain too little. An alternative approach to social policy derives from the following points:

1. Popper's view of what is possible in social reform grows from his theory of knowledge: all knowledge is the product of our conjectures in response to problems and our trial and error refutations of parts of those conjectures (Popper, 1963; 1972);

2. Our conjectures are our theories about the world, about what is possible, to which we apply ingenious and imaginative test statements in order to eliminate error from them;

3. A social policy, for Popper, is a conjecture about what is possible: its value depends upon how susceptible it is to refutation; this means that its formulation, or the formulation of its stages, must be unambiguous;

4. Any policy that is not a refutable theory in the sense of being testable against experience (either the policy as a whole or parts of it) is a holistic or utopian policy and in principle is beyond the rational control of its authors.

In changing any social institution a policy maker's approach for Popper should be a 'piecemeal' one [he uses this term in a different way from the pejorative use that is often applied to it]; social change requires small adjustments in the direction of reform and improvement. He explicitly contrasts the piecemeal reformer with the holistic or utopian social engineer who attempts revolutionary changes that are impossible to control from the outset: the greater the changes attempted by the utopianist, the greater will be their unintended, uncontrollable and severe repercussions upon the values, aims and sensitivities of the participants in the planned reconstruction. An alternative may well be found in what Harman (1980) briefly proposes: the policy innovator needs to be able to design features likely to invigorate rather than disturb. He quotes Bardach who warns that "designs for disruptive change are relatively easy to conceive, whereas their counterparts require more sophisticated analysis and more disciplined imagination" (Harman, 1980 p. 148).

Some Policy Problems and Tentative Solutions

"Educational policy in non-Keynesian and monetarist times" says Peter Musgrave "must be complex, taking account of a wide range of factors". This is nowhere more clearly the case than "when thinking about the transition from school to work. The more narrowly the problem is conceived, the smaller will be the range of practical suggestions made" and "the more likely these cures will be to increase rather than to lower the level of alienation amongst students" (1986 p. 301). I think that we can firmly conclude that some overriding policy decisions need to be taken beyond the level of the school if we are to deal with the range of 'education for work' issues confronting societies: grassroots solutions on their own will not suffice; some clear policy lead from outside the schools is needed. My starting point is to recognise that Musgrave's 'problem' is not one but many problems. By addressing some of these many problems in turn and offering tentative solutions to them, I hope that some good might result. In later chapters of Part Three other key problems for social policy are discussed along with suggestions for their resolution.

Problem 1: student alienation from secondary education and their growing rejection of the things that schools offer, including education for work.

We now know that this is a widespread problem, perhaps the most serious problem for contemporary education. The Chief Inspector for the Inner London Education Authority sees ILEA's present secondary school system exerting on many pupils "a destruction of their dignity which is so massive and pervasive that few subsequently recover from it" (Hargreaves, 1982 p. 7). Nor is it just the notorious inner-urban settings of London, New York, Sydney or Toronto that offer up examples of this alienation. The evidence from many settings is public and compelling (see Fensham et al., 1986). A solution to this problem in large societies, where reforms are difficult to implement, may be discovered in the examples of structuring patterns for schooling that are practised in three smaller social settings: Tasmania, Canberra and New Zealand. A trial application in larger social settings of one or a blend of the following structuring patterns may reduce student alienation and suggest ways of re-applying similar intersectoral patterns more generally in those larger settings.

Firstly, in Canberra, a system-wide change from six-year high schools to a 4 + 2 system, with the last two years in secondary colleges, produced dramatic improvement in the attitude to school of the students in their final two years in the senior secondary colleges, with no detrimental change among the students in the new four year junior high schools (Anderson, Saltet and Vervoorn, 1980).

Secondly, in Tasmania, which provided the model for the Canberra innovation, academic senior secondary colleges have been the norm for two decades. These colleges provide a counter example in answer to the common criticism that senior high schools are institutions designed for children and inhabited by young adults. Although senior school retention rates in Tasmania remain the lowest of the six Australian states (for reasons of population decentralisation) the morale and commitment of students in senior colleges is very high, even in those colleges that have intakes of students widely mixed in social background and ability level. Further insights for policy in the 'education for work' area can be derived from a recent Tasmanian initiative to merge the work of the hand with the work of the mind by integrating the technical college system into one new organisation with these senior secondary colleges. This initiative foundered not on educational or social but on industrial grounds: those of long-standing influence in the two component systems felt their interests threatened by a policy that might well have provided a model for other similar social settings (Corson, 1986). In the 1970s in England's Leicestershire LEA a similar development operated with considerable success: community colleges were established there integrating technical, senior secondary and community education provisions. This venture has since suffered from severe funding cuts. Community colleges for post-compulsory students, however, are a common feature of North American education (OECD, 1985).

Thirdly, in New Zealand, the problem may even be avoided in many places through the unique inter-sectoral relationships that have prevailed there since the earliest days of the national education system. 'Intermediate Schools', provided in New Zealand for many children, may serve to reduce levels of adolescent alienation (although adolescent alienation is still common in areas where ethnic inequalities exist). These schools span what are in most other countries the last of the primary and the first of the secondary years of schooling, thereby reducing secondary education by one year. The arrangement is not without its critics; I doubt whether just two years of 'middle schooling' is justification enough for other unsettling effects that Intermediate Schools may promote; however both in New Zealand and elsewhere the creation of middle schools, catering for pupils variously in the eight to fourteen year age range, has been promoted partly to lessen the adolescent alienation that derives from long years of 'claustration' in a high school.

Problem 2: preparing all children for all the life transitions that confront them, including transition into work as part of a 'worthwhile form of life'

Part of the difficulty here is that 'transition to work' cannot provide an unambiguous aim for schooling: this is not an endpoint that schooling can genuinely be directed towards when unemployment is a common destination for many school graduates; nor can it ever be a discrete aim for education, a point made by many contributors to this book. Several of the chapters that follow in Part Three address this problem in detail; Part Four of course, by considering the curriculum of schools, is devoted to suggesting solutions. There are three initiatives at system level that I recommend as partial solutions: a core curriculum; a gradual restructuring of the wage bond; and the gradual introduction of work experience for all in secondary education.

A 'core curriculum' would aim to specify the combination of school subjects and some details of the minimum content that are necessary to achieve the aims of education. It would do this for three overlapping reasons: firstly to initiate children into a worthwhile form of life; secondly to give them a chance to 'succeed' (in conventional terms) if they want to; and thirdly to prepare them to cope with the normal uncertainties of adult life including the risk and the hardship of unemployment. A large part of this initiation, as I have argued in Chapter 4, consists of initiation into work as part of a worthwhile form of life. A 'core curriculum' would recognise this fact by specifying the minimum criteria needed for entering occupational work. These criteria, however, need not necessarily include anything beyond the achievements that are already considered minimal for graduates from a successful secondary education and that can be generalised to most occupational or recreational work settings: literacy; numeracy; oracy; mastery of and unrestricted access to the mother tongue[s]; an acquaintance with the history of the culture and of related cultures; an understanding of the natural world; an acquaintance, based on extensive experience, with literature and the arts; and interpersonal skills including the application of those ethical ideas needed for everyday living.

It seems to me a futile undertaking to be much more specific in setting out a core curriculum than I have been above, unless it is mere curriculum content that is spelled out from which schools and teachers can choose what suits their own context. There is a counter-example, though, that is much more specific: the British Manpower Services Commission's heroic attempt to set out the 103 basic or core skills needed by young people to prepare for work (MSC, 1984). This list is not very helpful; it misleads rather than clarifies. Richard Pring (1986), for example, offers an alternative and very different list of possible skills, developed in the United States. He argues that any choice from the infinite range of skills available to us depends on the concepts and values through which we analyse what needs to be done; what constitutes a basic skill is hopelessly confused and to have non-educationists prescribing what skills should be taught in schools adds to the confusion. If these approaches to defining educational aims are given their head education will take a backseat role to training, rather than the reverse position that was advocated in Chapters 3 and 4.

A core curriculum has already been attempted in Australia (CDC, 1980); the notion received government approval in Britain in 1987 after a long debate; and, as part of wider changes to the level at which curriculum decisions are taken, a national curriculum is supported at system level in New Zealand (New Zealand Education Department, 1987). Clearly establishing a core curriculum is an important innovation; ensuring that all children have access to it is the real task.

My second response to this problem was the restructuring of the wage bond. Peter Musgrave (1986) advocates a policy guaranteeing a minimum wage for all those above the legal minimum school leaving age, whether in the workforce or not. Musgrave believes that advanced industrial societies can afford to pay a minimum income, that is not a dole. He believes that this policy would influence the willingness of adolescents to do without work and would modify their views of and needs from schools at a time when work is no longer available for all. Certainly the school would become a more desirable alternative for young adults if it were not perceived as the only alternative to the dole that it often represents at present. The transition from school to work might also become a less traumatic exercise. This proposal offers a less than optimal solution, however; the point of view advocated throughout this book, is for social and educational policies directed towards full employment.

The third point, work experience for all, can be better elaborated as a solution to the next two contingent problems.

Problems 3 and 4: relating students' learnings more securely to the world of work; and creating genuine relations between schools and society.
A ready solution to both these problems is the gradual adoption of education policies at the state level that support work experience for all adolescents. This seems the right course for educational systems to support on simple economic grounds: there is strong evidence now to suggest that while the costs of vocational programmes within schools are considerably higher than those of general education, their benefits to societies in simple economic terms are no more than comparable. Those planning in-school vocational programmes would be well advised to consult and

scrutinise that evidence (Hu, 1980; Grubb, 1985; Weisberg, 1983; Nystrom and Hennessy, 1985; Psacharopoulos, 1987): 'work experience for all' may well be the alternative way to go in English-speaking societies that are not as yet heavily committed to vocational education. Perhaps some small-scale trial of generalisable policies for work experience could be the place to start.

The advent of comprehensive secondary schooling in English-speaking countries has rarely been accompanied by more than narrow interpretations of 'comprehensiveness' (Poole, 1983). Elsewhere educational history has created very different approaches: in Denmark and France the curriculum during the years of compulsory schooling incorporates work-related studies (Watts, 1983); in West Germany young people who have completed their full-time general education enter a dual system that combines practical education, in a firm or a separate training establishment, with a general education aimed particularly at 'studies in work'; in Swedish comprehensive schools work experience is incorporated for all throughout the secondary years in order to relate pupils' learnings more pointedly and securely to the wider world of work, and to forge new relationships between schools and societies (Blackburn, 1986).

The possibility of concurrent part-time work and part-time schooling offers another partial solution to both these problems. Peter Musgrave cites the educational grounds outlined by Karl Marx in *Das Kapital* to support this idea for restructuring the labour force; the proposal has further value on economic grounds in times of high unemployment.

The central educational reason for introducing widespread work experience schemes, though, follows from recognition that schools do have an obligation to prepare children for work and other adult roles as part of their initiation into a worthwhile form of life. Acquiring knowledge and understandings about these roles is best accomplished while actually engaged in them, rather than through the artificial and vicarious practices often used in schools before young people have had much involvement or experience in the roles.

Problem 5: narrowing the cultural distance between policy makers and the implementers of policy at the school level.

This problem relates to the relative absence of knowledge and cultural experience that is genuinely shared between those who lay down 'education for work' policies and those who are asked to take action in implementing them. Even the task of understanding this complex problem is a difficult one; offering solutions may depend on reaching that understanding first.

In understanding the difficulties that confront the implementers of large scale policies we can find relevance in the work of Thomas Greenfied (1978). There are grave dangers in uncritically applying to policies the rational or conventional approach to understanding educational organisations, which adopts a broad systems perspective: seeing organisations as social systems. The role of the policy maker on this account is to generalise, abstract, universalise and so come to understand ultimate social reality and plan for it. Organisations are seen as phenomenal entities engaged in goal-seeking behaviour; they are instruments of social and cultural order. In following this systems approach policy makers set themselves the tasks of identifying social structures and showing how they work or fail to work in achieving ends. Any pathology in the body of an organisation that policy addresses can be cured in principle by identifying its aetiology and by then rearranging the organisation's structures, which means making planned alterations in its hierarchical arrangements: tinkering with the structures.

In opposition to the conventional systems approach is the significant movement of theorists, including Greenfield, who question how much of importance we can really know about educational organisations. This question responds to another more enduring debate which questions what schools ought to be doing; the former debate is of course dependent on the latter at many points, and it informs my own interest in linking educational administration (as means) more closely with curriculum planning (as ends). Theories about educational organisations are seen as very limited in what they can tell us. To observe an organisation is to see it according to our pre-conceived beliefs about what reality is and what is significant in our experience of reality. Our judgments are affected by the beliefs and values we hold, so that an objective interpretation of an educational institution is difficult to reach. On this account organisations consist of the accumulation of the realities and meaningful actions of involved individuals: they are areas of belief, not of knowledge, and their problems are not structural, they are ideological. Effective cures for the pathologies of organisations, on this account, are to be found in assessing the intentions of participants and in attempting to change some of those intentions after examining values problems within the organisation, rather than in attempting first to fiddle with the organisation's structures. (In Chapter 14 I try to put these ideas to work: the task for education for work at the school level is mainly to change teachers' conceptions of what they do, which does not necessarily mean changing curriculum content very much).

This latter view about organisations seems closer to what practitioners now believe about schools and school systems. A central point in this view is that there is not much that we can know about organisations without finding out about the values, inclinations and motives of the people within them. Policy makers are restricted therefore in what they can really achieve: the very possibility of constructing effective large-scale policies, as mentioned above, is constrained by the number and diversity of views of organisational reality that are possessed by planned participants in the given policy.

Presthus' study (1962) examined the ways in which individuals in organisations accommodate to bureaucratic pressure of the type that policies regularly bring: some uncritically adopt the values of the organisation's policy and become 'upward mobiles'; some reject the organisation's values of success and power and become 'indifferents'; and some cannot make the accommodations necessary to achieve security within the organisation, even while not willing to become indifferent to it, and become 'ambivalent'. There may be other responses. A policy that fails to address the organisational realities of participating individuals, their values and ends, risks pushing people into a range of undesirable accommodation modes. Policies in 'education for work' face twin problems: addressing the changes in social values that they set out to address; and convincing implementers that the aims of the policies themselves deserve loyalty, commitment and genuine efforts at mutual adaptation in the direction of the policy's broad intentions.

What I am suggesting may be clearer if I give an example: Consider the solutions suggested as responses to Problem 1 above. Before implementation of these structural solutions, the prospective changes need to be carefully negotiated; they need to be carefully trialled on a small-scale; and they need to be explicitly documented as part of a corporate plan, that is subject to public scrutiny, alongside and integrated with wider policy initiatives.

Perhaps the only starting point in solving this problem is for widespread collaboration to occur between people at system level and people at institutional level. "In the context of the contemporary nation state" say LeVine and White "neither official policy nor grassroots voluntarism alone can be relied upon to realize desired potentials; they must work together convergently and synergistically" (1986 p. 217). Culture becomes a critical term in all this: policy makers and implementers need to share cultural models of life, education and social performance if the possibilities for their collaboration are to be enhanced. Problems can then be explained and understood; small-scale and tentative solutions can be tried out; and some hope of mutual adaptation can be envisaged. Finding an ideological basis for collaboration of this kind is one of the key problems addressed in the chapters that follow in Part Three.

Key Policy Issues in Education for Work

A central problem in reducing the distance between policy makers and policy implementers relates to matters of gender, education and work. Most policy makers in education are male, while many policy implementers are female; most work contexts and most work tasks themselves have their historical origins in life ideals that are exclusively male, while nearly half the workers in contemporary societies are female. The links between gender and the labour market receive detailed analysis in the literature (for example: Walby, 1987; Brenner and Ramas, 1984). The evidence clearly argues for change; part of that change can be brought about by a meticulous reorientation of educational policy to lessen the impact on students of the following curriculum and pedagogical processes: that prepare female students for 'female' jobs (see Wanda Korndorffer's field study findings in Chapter 18); that integrate assertive boys into the 'official' life of schools but exclude assertive girls (see Jim Walker's comments in Chapter 15); that encourage boys to be resentful of girls who have career interests in traditionally male-dominated occupations; that allow harassment on gender grounds in the workplace to be perceived by young people as a part of the 'normal' social intercourse that accompanies life 'at work'; that encourage boys and girls to see their future responsibilities in the care of dependants as limited by traditional gender-specific roles; or that encourage girls to see their life options as very different from the options available to boys. These and other factors in gender inequality, both at school and at work, need to be firmly acknowledged by policy makers before they engage in any act of policy creation, so that recommendations insensitive to these factors are not randomly included in documents. An official and agreed document, providing a 'policy on gender equality' for the entire system, should be routinely consulted and available at all stages in the policy-making process.

In Chapter 8 Jan Branson gives an example of the method of arriving at policy that is set out in this chapter: she attempts to discover what the real problem is and then poses solutions to it. She begins by tracing the history of recent feminist theory. There have been some significant changes in perspective here: there is, in certain schools of feminist thought, a move away from earlier views that saw the priority for women as a process of winning greater control in male-dominated societies or succeeding in male-dominated jobs. Instead a new perspective has arisen that attends to a more subtle and perhaps more important need that is deemed to precede these other needs: changing that society and those workplaces so as to include more of the 'female'.

Branson acknowledges that structural arrangements, guaranteeing equality of opportunity in the workplace for women and a measure of affirmative action, have their place. She also applauds attempts to eliminate biases in educational content and organisation. Taking her lead, though, from recent idealist movements in feminist theory she examines the more subtle processes of discrimination that are at work through and beyond education; she asks about the role that the traditionally 'female' part of humanity might play in the development of a non-exploitative society. Fastening on the nature of the 'difference' that is implied by gender she addresses the massive contradiction that girls experience within the school and the workplace.

Branson's recommendations for an 'education for work' policy that recognises this contradiction are radical and long-term: she sees a very different relationship between education and work evolving which will involve very different societies as well. Some examples will illustrate the imbalance that she sees between the 'male' and the 'female' within education itself: the dominance of the maths and sciences, which are the subjects of ordered calculation, over the greater subjectivity of literature, arts and humanities; the stress on competitive assessment, rather than the sharing of knowledge for communal enlightenment; intensive and excessive specialization in the final years of schooling; strict entry requirements to science-based professional faculties; and the existence of artificial barriers that are too sharply drawn between family, school and work. She is anxious to see an end to the view that certain human attributes and values are 'male' or 'female'; the starting point for this is for the 'female' to be reintegrated into all aspects of our lives. Her chapter suggests changes through education that might be socially 'transforming' in the way that Dewey suggested, a point which Robert Sherman addresses in Chapter 6.

In Chapter 9 Gary McCulloch is concerned with a very different set of policy issues. His theme is one that runs throughout this book: the tension in 'education for work' policies between addressing the needs of 'work', that are perceived as important by parents, employers and increasingly by politicians, while addressing the need to meet accepted educational criteria at the same time. This problem, he believes, has lessened the impact that vocational progammes have had, notably in England and Wales. He examines, firstly, technical and vocational schooling as practised in Britain from the 1940s to its demise in the 1960s; and secondly the Technical and Vocational Education Initiative (TVEI) of the 1980s. The failure of the secondary technical schools to live up to the ideals set for them is put down to their inability to offer much that was really different from other forms of schooling; they provided neither a particularly reputable form of education nor an effective training ground for the world of work. The TVEI's difficulties are due to its apparent disregard of the needs of education in favour of those of work and the economy. McCulloch looks ahead to another emerging British policy in education for work: the development of 'city technology colleges'. He foresees the now familiar tension between education and work affecting this new enterprise; he recommends that any new policy in this area should attend to the errors of the past and learn from them.

In introducing Part One of this book I went to some lengths to draw a distinction between recreation and work, only to draw them together again immediately to show that recreational work is closely linked with certain kinds of occupational work. There is a common view that, because occupational work is becoming scarcer, there will be an increased demand by people for leisure in the future; perhaps education, then, should be addressed more directly to initiating people into leisure as part of a worthwhile form of life? An answer to this follows from that earlier discussion: if we understand the way that recreation and unconstrained work are related as 'ends in themselves', then this suggests that in preparing people for 'work' of this kind education is also preparing them for leisure, since pursuing leisure and pursuing recreation are similar and overlapping activities.

In Chapter 10 Harold Entwistle argues against the common assumption that leisure can compensate for alienation at work and that one task of education in a world of alienating work is to meet the need to initiate students into a variety of leisure pursuits. One reason offered against this approach to schooling is that it quite simply represents an attempt at blatant social control: it is another form of the 'bread and circuses' used by the emperors of Ancient Rome, the 'bread' was a form of dole that the emperors were able to dispense by keeping personal control over the empire's corn supply, and the 'circuses' were regular entertainments or leisure activities provided free of charge on as many as half the days of the year. Another reason that Entwistle advances against the 'education for leisure' supporters is that this policy is based on the false assumption that we can redeem people from the dehumanising effects of heavily constrained occupational work by teaching them how to make constructive use of their spare time. He arrives at a conclusion that is taken up in many places in this volume: it is a mistake to conceive of work, play, recreation, home life, political activity and social service as discontinuous. Work, especially, cannot be divorced from the rest of life; it is, as Dewey, Russell and Marx suggested, the central life activity: it has created human civilisation. From all this it follows that leisure and work are inseparable. Education directed toward preparing children for a working life and a leisure life of quality must be conceived in the widest possible terms to include the moral, the political and the aesthetic dimensions. A liberal education is one that frees learners from whatever constraints might hinder their development as persons. The traditional, liberal, humanistic curriculum suitably up-dated provides the answer in harnessing technological innovation to the task of humanising work and leisure.

In the contemporary 'education for work' debate we return to the British experience again and again for good reason: in no other English-speaking country have the ravages of unemployment been as severe; and nowhere else has the range of policy responses been as diverse. In Chapter 11 Douglas Weir examines the impact of social and technological change on the forms of schooling needed by post-compulsory school adolescents. Using the plain language of a person dealing with the problems of 'education for work' on a daily basis, he sets out two policy problems for us: how can we provide fairly for children with different educational destinations and aspirations; and how should we educate for technological change? He takes as his starting point, in answering the first question, the assumption that we need vocational education for all. After making some informed predictions about the future of work, he decides on a curriculum that provides an education developing the broad 'skills' of decision-making, flexibility and problem-solving [goals, it seems to me, of any considered form of education]; he believes that an experience-based curriculum, based on these criteria, will escape the pitfalls of current attempts to match training capacity to manpower needs. The second part of Weir's chapter builds on the first to suggest how we should approach the challenge of information technology: the task is not one of instructing in the use of today's technology, which we know from experience will be obsolete tomorrow; it is to identify the underlying skills that can be taught to all and incorporate these skills as part of a common core of knowledge. From this conclusion Weir offers a solution to his first problem: we provide for children with different life destinations and aspirations by giving to all a common basic competence and a common stock of knowledge and understanding that includes the small common core of new technology skills.

Teachers are repelled by the idea of 'educating for unemployment'. Harold Entwistle in his chapter makes a nice logical point that an activity of that kind does not make much sense in any case. Nevertheless, in practice, it seems brutal for education systems to ignore the social reality of unemployment and to remain insensitive to the likelihood that it will affect many school graduates, interfering with their initiation into a worthwhile form of life or even any hope of such a thing. Some form of planned preparation for the realities of unemployment should be included as part of every school's curriculum. Policy decisions in this area are probably best made at the school level itself, where people know their local needs and have some idea about how best to respond to them. Yet without some coordination, without funding and without a few ideas provided at the system level it is unlikely that busy teachers and school administrators will give more than cursory attention to this problem. Adrian Furnham's chapter reviews studies on youth unemployment from North America, Australasia and Britain. He draws no overt conclusions for education policy; my point in including his chapter is to give some guidance in curriculum content and underline the suggestion that school systems do need to give attention to this question as a priority policy matter. Furnham's review covers six themes: problems of psychological adjustment among unemployed school leavers; their attributions of blame for their own unemployment and for unemployment generally; education about the problems and prospects of unemployment; job choice, willingness to work, and work experience in the young; changes in values as a result of unemployment; and training in the skills needed to go for job interviews. His conclusion that the reactions of the young to unemployment are often different from those of adults is an important one for teachers and parents to grasp at a time when adolescent suicide is on the increase: being able to see the world through the eyes of the young must be very nearly the first requirement of a good teacher.

Better than policies for unemployment are policies for full employment. A tenet of this book, supported or implied in some way by most contributors, is that full employment should be a social aim for humane and civilised societies. Education policies are only a part of broad social policies that might be used in achieving full employment. Ian Shirley, in Chapter 13, ends Part Three by reviewing alternative sets of social policies adopted by urban-industrial countries in response to the global economic upheavals of the 1970s and 1980s. He begins by giving a very clear summary of events preceding this 'crisis of capitalism'. Relevant to our concerns in this volume the most interesting aspect of the crisis has been the way that different institutions and policies introduced in similar countries have resulted in markedly different rates of unemployment. Some countries, such as Canada, Britain, Belgium, Holland and Denmark plunged into massive unemployment; other countries, such as Austria, Sweden, Norway, Japan and Switzerland were able to minimise their rates of unemployment. Shirley summarises the five roads to success in the latter countries that helped them to avoid high unemployment. He sets these factors within two alternative developmental paths: the path offered by policies emanating from what he calls the 'New Right'; and the path offered under the rubric of 'Left Revisionism'. He discusses these two orientations to social policy, extracting their dominant features. The New Right approach employs restrictive monetary policies, the dismantling of social services, tax reductions, privatisation and deregulation; the Left Revisionist approach introduces a policy for full employment, manifests a conservative concern for order and stability, and incorporates a degree of state interventionism in monetary policy. It is clear from present evidence that the Left Revisionist approach is more successful over time in providing full employment for its citizens. Shirley concludes by urging us not to see education policy too narrowly: he disagrees with the New Right's conception of education as a commodity, divorced from other aspects of life, to be purchased by the individual and used instrumentally and individually. He urges us to see education policy for work as part of a wider set of social policies linking work, income and power in societies.

Gender, Education and Work

by Jan Branson

Gender, education, work. The first encompasses the other two but together they do not form a coherent whole. They are but aspects of the wider socio-cultural process. Education and work are inextricably linked in the Western consciousness for not only is access to the world of work assumed to lie through education but compulsory schooling is an ideological practice which engineers society's consent for the operation of a ruthless, dehumanised labour market in which access to privileged employment is governed by the possession of cultural skills and qualities governed by gender and ethnicity which cannot be gained at school. Equality of opportunity, success through individually-based intelligence and aptitude, achievement through free and equal competition, these are the ideologies of education which blind people to the structured inequalities fundamental to capitalist production, inequalities based on class, gender, ethnicity and the distinction between the disabled and the able-bodied, categories of experience which overlap in the complexities of individual identity and cultural experience.

This chapter looks critically at the interrelationships between gender, education and work in the light of recent feminist theory. It is not your conventional 'review of the literature' or 'state of the art' paper. It does not review the interrelationships as though 'gender', 'education', and 'work' were unproblematic, observable, measurable. Current theorizing on gender seriously questions the deepest of our assumptions about the nature of knowledge and the mode of its transmission. As the discussion that follows stresses, to understand gender, education and work we must be prepared to place in doubt all that we take for granted.

First a note on feminist theory. Feminist theory involves, on the one hand, the search for explanations of gender construction and of the discriminatory practices based in gender distinctions, and on the other speculation on the means by which sexism can be confronted and destroyed, involving either the achievement of equality or the non-discriminatory coexistence of gender differences. Much feminist theory eschews disciplinary labels and is concerned rather with a transdisciplinary search for understanding which is not bound by male-dominated views of the nature and organisation of knowledge. Also, feminist theory is by no means theorising for its own sake. The women's movement has at all times steered clear of a dilettantish preoccupation with ideas *per se*. The history of feminist theory is the history of a praxis, of a constant and creative interaction between theory and practice. So the current and complex theoretical debates about the cultural construction of gender, the theorising about sexual 'difference', about the psychological aspects of gender construction, and the literary theory concerned with the construction of meaning, are all integral to the overtly political women's movement. The theories are complex because the issue of gender is complex. Simplistic determinist theories and their associated practice have not destroyed sexism. There is no simple solution. Women fought for the vote. They got it, but the vote did not result in an equal society. So too, as we shall comment on further below, the movement concentrated much of its attention on the provision of equal access to education and then on equal access to all aspects of the curriculum, in the hope that this would result in the equal distribution of qualifications among boys and girls at the end of school (which to a large extent has been the case) and that this in turn would lead to the non-sexist distribution of school leavers through tertiary education and the workplace. But the workplace and the tertiary sector remain thoroughly biased in gender terms. Legislation outlawing discriminatory employment and work practices did not correct the imbalance. What became apparent with the passage of a wide range of anti-discriminatory legislation, was that purposeful discrimination by men against women, while real and extensive, reaching its most extreme expression in sexual violence, was but the tip of the iceberg and that there was a need to concentrate on the bulk of discriminatory forces that lurked below the surface, below the threshold of consciousness. This is the search that has dominated feminist theorising for the past decade, theorising which this chapter places within the context of gender, education and work.

Before proceeding to discuss gender in education and work the terms themselves need to be confronted as controversial concepts, concepts that will be examined in the context of a particular view of society and culture. The perspective taken here, like Bourdieu's 'theory of practice', avoids the voluntarism and astructuralism of phenomenology, and the tendencies towards dehumanised atemporality characteristic of much structuralism, structural functionalism and some versions of Marxist analysis, by viewing the individual as thoroughly social and cultural but at the same time unique and creative; structurally constrained but calculatedly strategic in thought and action; innovative but in a culturally restricted mode; pursuing individual objectives but thereby contributing to the formation and transformation (the 'reproduction') of on-going social structures.

> Men [and women] make their own history, but they do not make it just as they please; they do not make it under circumstances chosen by themselves, but under circumstances directly encountered, given and transmitted from the past. The tradition of all the dead generations weighs like a nightmare on the brain of the living (Marx, 1970 p.96).

'Gender' refers to the qualities 'male' and 'female' which, while directly associated with the biological distinction between man and woman, go far beyond mere biology to encompass all aspects of our lives as aspects of ideology and culture. In thought and practice the ideology of gender is the basis for the evaluation of people, actions and qualities. Styles of behaviour, personality types, occupations, teaching subjects, the public and the private aspects of our lives are all cultural expressions of gender. All are evaluated as 'male' or 'female', evaluated not just labeled for they stand in unequal opposition to one another. 'Male' is high, 'female' is low. So as people strategically orient themselves towards the people and tasks that constitute their particular experience of society and culture they do so in terms of the existing ideologies and, through their interpretations of ideology, act as agents of the creation and transformation of social structures, of relationships structured in terms of class, of gender, of ethnicity. These structured inequalities give rise to different, unequal life experiences which in turn differentially orient children and adults in their desires, their aspirations, their abilities and their achievements. They participate in ideological practice. The learning of gender-based evaluations is a constant process, at home, at school, at work, at leisure; the experiencing and exercising of prejudice at the hands of parents and siblings, teachers and fellow pupils, employers and fellow employees, performers and viewers.

'Education' must be understood as the constant process through which people internalise their culture, through which they learn to conceptualise their environment and so orient their behaviour. It is a process which is never complete, contained but never static, bounded but undergoing constant transformation. The formal education system is but part of this process. Schooling is an overt rather than a covert attempt to mould aspects of individual development. As the horse is 'schooled' to develop the physical form and athletic skills to satisfy the standards of the judges of equestrian art, so too we school our children towards effective participation in the pre-defined competitions they must participate in beyond the school, according to standards which, unlike those of the dressage arena, are unstated and covertly acquired. For the purpose of this discussion we concentrate on formal education and on secondary schooling in particular. As such, 'education' is much more than an

aspect of the social process labeled by the sociologist, it is, as pointed out already, a thoroughly ideological concept and practice. It is the embodiment of the most fundamental contradictions of capitalist society, between, on the one hand, the claimed orientation towards equality of opportunity, freedom to pursue individual interests and the achievement of individual potential, and, on the other, the actual practice of an intensely unequal world, involving for the majority the performance of codified tasks essential to the profit making and personal enhancement of others.

'*Work*' is what we orient ourselves towards in childhood and adolescence and what we must compensate for when forced to leave it in retirement. In ideological terms it is the most meaningful stage of our lives. If we do not 'work' we are assumed lazy, parasitic, disabled, still in childhood, still being educated for work, resting in our dotage after fulfilment in work, or a housewife. 'Work' is public work, labour that secures financial reward in the public world. It is the realm of *homo oeconomicus*, the entrepreneur, the worker, the breadwinner. It is ideally - and that means for a select few with privileged access to the means of production - an arena for the exercising of individual interest through rational calculation. It is a ruthless place, not tolerant of weakness, irrationality, emotion or disability. It is 'male' in opposition to the 'female' private world. It is what Blake chillingly described as 'The Spectre [which] like a hoar-frost and a mildew, rose over Albion' (Blake, 1934 p.398), over pre-industrial England and beyond with the birth of capitalism[1]. For the purposes of this discussion we both recognise and transcend work as ideology. Here we will include in our discussion of work all activities pursued to contribute to subsistence and support a lifestyle. As such, work may be private or public, paid or unpaid, but is distinct from leisure which involves the expenditure of funds and energy *on* lifestyle.

So we are all born into an economically and culturally biased environment, biased in class, gender and ethnic terms. The child proceeds through early experience in a family of some kind, an experience measured against ideal images of what a family ought to be like (television is full of them), to the combined experiences of 'family' and school. At school, the combined pressures of curriculum, peer group and the demands and examples of teachers mould further, through the creative, culturally variable and conditioned response of the student, the development of the child as a future adult participant in productive work. The orientations, expectations and potential achievements of the student are a dynamic and complex interweaving of personal, ideological, cultural and social structural factors. The students come to the school already equipped with views of themselves

---

[1] Blake's 'Spectre' is 'the masculine principle which may divide from a being when his feminine portion ... separates to assume independent life ... it is brutal, obsessive and selfish, and must be reintegrated.' (Ostriker, 1977 p.1054-5)

and others learned through experience in the home, the community and the media. Teachers, their peers and the curriculum choices available channel and develop these views further. There are no abstract 'opportunities' available, conditioned only by 'intelligence', 'aptitude', 'motivation' and the 'facilities' available at the school. These qualities are mediated through the socialised, enculturated individual. The experience of gender as a factor influencing one's view of oneself and others, as an identification imposed on the individual and reacted to by the individual, is the central focus of this chapter. That discriminations on the basis of gender occur in the orientation of students towards curriculum and labour market, as well as in their treatment by teachers, is clearly established. That female students become the subtle agents of their own oppression through their views of themselves and of what is relevant for them as they orient themselves towards particular subjects, peer group behaviours and future occupations, is now being acknowledged[2]. But why does this discrimination occur and what, from a feminist perspective, should be done about it? These are the basic questions behind the discussion that follows.

Gender and Education

As Lyn Yates has pointed out, prior to the mid 1970s gender was invisible as a problem for research in education:

> This happened by omission (failing to distinguish results by sex, or to note the sex composition of the sample, or to include girls in the sample) and by treating any evidence of difference as self-explanatory and appropriate outcomes of biology or different social roles (Yates, 1987a p.291).

The ideologies of gender were rarely questioned, especially by established academics. This is not to say that the early 1970s saw no challenges to the status quo in education. Quite the contrary. The repercussions of the Paris uprisings of 1968 were not only felt in the universities but in the schools as well. Many teachers responded with enthusiasm to the spate of subversive educational literature that came in the wake of 1968. Illich, Freire, Holt, and a host of others were the prophets of a new society through revolution in education[3]. Relevant, democratised curricula and open, creative classrooms were the order of the day. But while the educational radicals were fervent in their opposition to capitalism and class-based discrimination, any confrontation with sexism was too personal, too close to the bone to be

---

[2]   For a comprehensive review of the relevant literature see Yates, 1987b.
[3]   See for example Illich, 1971, Illich et al, 1972 and Postman & Weingartner, 1971.

taken on board. But just as the black power, socialist and peace movements radicalised their women members by their chauvinistic refusal to take the women's movement seriously, so too were many female teachers radicalised. Convinced of the revolutionary power of education they set about attacking sexism in education with fervour.

By the end of the 1970s sexism in education was an issue directly confronting governments, teachers, pupils, academics and the community. Curriculum content, achievement patterns and general levels of privilege and disadvantage came in for attention, documented in the main by investigation conducted by teachers' organisations and government enquiries (Yates, 1987b p.245) plus a few feminist academics. A new educational problem had to be dealt with. Historians and sociologists began to document past and present discrimination until by the 1980s sexism in education was an established fact demanding positive remedial action. Research on women was suddenly the order of the day. The facts of gender-based discrimination poured in.

So the debates began to concentrate not on whether gender bias existed in education but on how to do something about it. The range of issues confronted in this search for solutions has been thoroughly documented by Yates (1987a p.292ff and 1987b). On the whole, research concentrated on the investigation of the operation of gender within the environment of the school. Changes looked for, and proposed, were also essentially within the context of formal schooling. The links from and back into the world outside the school were and remain to a large extent ignored or assumed. There has been, as Yates makes clear, much asserted and assumed about the connections between school and society but far less careful theorising about the relationship. The assumed goal was an untheorised equality.

But there was plenty of action. Feminist teachers were quick to respond to the call for the reform of gender bias. Curriculum content and classroom dynamics were, as they had been in the early 1970s, the prime focus for action. Equal access to information was the dominant concern. *Girls must have equal confidence* - hence the debates over single-sex versus coeducational schooling, the calls for more female teachers and for equal attention to girls in class. *Girls must have equal access to the whole curriculum* - to maths, physics, chemistry, metalwork, woodwork. *Textbooks must be rewritten* to rid them of gender bias and incorporate examples relevant to girls. *The gender-biased language used in the classroom must be reformed.* All these calls for reform were in response to demonstrated biases in the education system, research had made this clear, but it was *assumed* that it was the bias in educational content and organisation that generated the inequalities experienced in and beyond the school. That reform of the education system was, and is, needed is undeniable but what few social theorists realised was that the reforms in question were not grounded in a coherent theory of the relationship between schooling and society, of the relationship between family and education and education and work.

Education and Work

The government enquiries which followed close on the revelations about the sexist nature of schooling were evidence of the anxiety felt by those who promote our ideologies of equality of opportunity, individuality and competitive achievement through intelligence, when the very embodiment of those ideologies, the school, is brought into disrepute. The schools are represented to society at large by the economy, the polity, the media and the schools themselves as preparation for work, or at least as preparation for tertiary planning for work. In Australia this vocational orientation has been particularly marked (Branson & Miller, 1979 p.59ff). Technical schools for the vocational training of boys; academic high schools preparing boys for tertiary training; and domestic science schools preparing girls for nursing, elementary teaching and housework were an early and overt expression of the assumed role of education. Such overt streaming has been replaced by apparent comprehensive education for all, with opportunities for specialisation increasingly reduced (as current debates about the development of the new Victorian Certificate of Education make clear). But the assumed direct link between education and work remains as strong as ever with current changes rationalised as widening and therefore equalising access to tertiary education. Education as preparation for work, as the means by which individual aptitude can be realised and developed, remains the main rationale for school attendance and the main motivation for teachers.

When effective theorising of the relationship between education and work did not take place, the results were disturbing for educationalists and politicians alike. The work of Bowles and Gintis (1976) and Bourdieu and Passeron (1977) in particular, seriously challenged existing views, radical and conservative, of the role of formal education in the wider social process. In one way or another they demonstrated that the education system was neither an autonomous arena for the exercise of high ideals nor the determining factor in the shaping of the world of work. The education system was presented as shaped by the capitalist ideology, legitimising the alienated, individuated and fundamentally unequal relations of production. Reform of education alone appeared as at best cosmetic, the tail attempting to wag the dog.

While rejecting such hardline materialism, Bourdieu's view of education as a culturally conditioned experience which operated covertly to ensure the reproduction of classes, provided an understanding of the possible ways that education contributed not only to the construction of class, but as we will discuss further below, to the construction of gender. In neither Bowles & Gintis nor Bourdieu & Passeron was there any claim that the education system did not prepare people for the workforce. Rather they concentrated on the unequal distribution of school leavers through the labour market and on the determinants of that distribution. The basic components of the ideology of equality of opportunity - intelligence and aptitude (see also Bisseret, 1979), school success, competitiveness - were themselves seen to be culturally defined and determined rather than individual qualities, not to mention the aspirations and expectations that oriented students towards a curriculum imbued with cultural cues known only to a privileged proportion of the population, and towards a labour market biased towards those who possess class specific, gender specific and ethnically specific qualities. For Bowles & Gintis the mode of production shaped these processes while for Bourdieu social class extended far beyond the economic. He concentrated rather on the cultural production of classes for whom economic practices are but one expression of a wide range of practices involving economic capital and symbolic capital, physical violence and symbolic violence. The world of work itself is not in any way divorced from the overall field of socio-cultural practice (Bourdieu, 1977a p.176ff). There is no 'base', no 'superstructure'.

In the research of Bourdieu in particular, vital clues were provided to uncover the subtle processes of discrimination at work through and beyond education. Sub-cultural competence emerged in his research with Passeron as decisive both in the ability of students to respond to the curriculum and in their orientation towards schooling and work. This view of the link between education and the securing of qualifications for work was summed up in the following statement:

> By doing away with giving explicitly to everyone what it implicitly demands of everyone, the educational system demands of everyone alike that they have what it does not give. This consists mainly of linguistic and cultural competence and that relationship of familiarity with culture which can only be produced by family upbringing when it transmits the dominant culture (Bourdieu, 1977b p.494).

Thus for those who did not continue to seek comfort in faith in the ideology of education but took Bourdieu's work seriously, education could no longer be theorised about independent of the rest of the socio-cultural process. It became but one of many interlinking arenas for strategic action, one aspect of a broader educational process by which cultural codes were transmitted (see Miller & Branson, 1987).

In theorising the link between school and work both the Marxist materialism of

Bowles & Gintis and the theory of practice of Bourdieu presented school as an agent of inequality. As neither the source of occupational structures nor the source of cultural competence, the school could not be perceived as the prime focus for reform or revolution. It is little wonder that those imbued with the ideology of equal opportunity through education set out to ridicule these theories and their transformations in the work of others by labelling them 'reproduction theories' in an attempt to deny them a role in theorising social change[4]. But in none of these studies was there opposition to educational reform. Quite the contrary. But they were saying that unless the links between school and society were understood, isolated reforms would come to little. Class formation and gender formation must be understood as socio-cultural processes encompassing all aspects of life, with schooling but part of that process. Class, gender, ethnicity permeated the lives of the students before and during schooling, conditioning their strategies as creative social beings, preparing them for the world of work. Based in thorough research and all committed to the elimination of discriminatory practices, these studies basically agreed that:

> There is no way within capitalist society that children will not be born to unequal life experiences, faced with differing interpretations of the world to base their own on and in terms of which to develop their images of themselves. Class formations arise from the capitalist mode of production, not from education... (Branson & Miller, 1979 p. 163)

In theorising the link between education and work most studies concentrated on the formation and transformation of class structures. Few dealt with gender. Research which did include gender as a variable revealed an equally radical conditioning of thought and practice throughout the cultural experience of gender. The experience of gender, transformed in turn by class and ethnicity, radically conditioned cultural competence and orientations towards school and work, compounding the effects of overt sexual discrimination (see Branson & Miller, 1979; Wolpe, 1978). But whereas the link between class and the relations of production is direct, the link between gender and work is more problematic.

Gender and Work

That there is a gender-based division of labour in production, both within the public world of paid employment and between the public workplace and the private realm

---

4.   Prominent examples of such so-called 'reproduction theory' are Bernstein, 1975 & 77; Dale, Esland & MacDonald, 1976; Willis, 1977; Branson & Miller, 1979; and Apple, 1982.

of unpaid work, is not in doubt. Nor is there any doubt that in the public workplace women are marginalised by their femaleness, treated as interlopers from the private realm to be paid low wages - for the man is the breadwinner - and given little, or more probably no, security of employment. As such they occupy a vital place within the relations of production, variable capital to be hired and fired at will, filling gaps that the unionisation of male workers and their consequent achievement of increasing security of employment, had left in the labour market, continuing, by their femaleness, to downgrade the status, and thus the cost, of those service occupations associated with the nurturing role attributed to women - nursing, secretarial work and teaching, particularly of the very young (see Branson & Miller, 1977). The experience of these roles generates aspects of female sub-cultural behaviour and consciousness which permeate schooling. But is gender-based discrimination a *product* of capitalism?

Feminist theorising about gender and work during the 1970s had focused on gender divisions within the public world of work and on the relationship between housework and capitalism. As mentioned at the beginning of the chapter, the relative failure of programmes oriented towards the eradication of overt discriminatory practices revealed the need to theorise more intently on the covert processes of gender formation, the bulk of the iceberg of discrimination beneath the threshold of consciousness. Initially this took the form of essentially Marxist feminist attempts to understand the cultural and ideological construction of gender as a consequence of the demands of the capitalist mode of production. True to the conventional Marxist view that the form and even the content of the superstructure of ideology, culture and the juridico-political is determined by the base, the mode of production, the construction of gender was seen to occur as an integral part of the generation of the relations of production characteristic of capitalist production. The ideology of gender; the gender-based division of labour in the family; the male and female sub-cultural expressions of class cultures; gender distinctions in education, the church, politics, the law; all were seen as expressions of, responses to, the demands of the mode of production[5]. In this view, for enduring change to occur, the mode of production must change. Changes to the superstructure were assumed merely cosmetic.

Turning from the relations of production in the public realm to the relationship between housework and capitalism, problems associated with the articulation of domestic production and capitalist production generated a particularly profitable debate[6]. The need to theorise domestic production as relatively autonomous from

---

5. For coverage of the literature on housework and capitalism see Malos, 1980.
6. See for example articles in Eisenstein, 1979, Kuhn and Wolpe, 1978.

capitalist production and involving contrasting relations of production, seriously questioned the site for the construction of gender. Relatively autonomous but integral to capitalist production, the domestic realm became the focus of attention for feminist theorising. Examination of the ideological and cultural processes at work within the family led some feminist theorists to conclude that the family was in fact the sphere of ideological practice wherein gender was primarily constructed. Responding to the Althusserian view that 'superstructural' elements of the social formation are not only 'relatively autonomous' but through their relative autonomy contribute creatively to the overall structuring of the social formation, feminists moved beyond economic determinism to a more complex view of creative dialectical interaction between its various elements. The gender divisions of society did not derive from capitalist production, rather '.... the gender divisions of social production in capitalism cannot be understood without reference to the organisation of the household and the ideology of familialism' (Barrett, 1980 p.186 also Barrett & McIntosh, 1982). The demand by the capitalist labour market for unpaid housework and cheap, manipulable labour, feeds off and transforms the ideology of gender established elsewhere. The need is for variable capital, not for women. Women fill the bill because they are defined as marginal to the workplace by the ideology of gender.

But the concentration on the family as the source of gender construction was also too narrow. Feminists asked how the process occurred. They looked to the construction of meaning itself, a search which has led beyond the family to explore the roots of our cosmologies in childhood, religion, science and education. The ideological divisions between family, education and work, between the public and the private, break down as feminism explores the unity of sexist ideological and cultural practice across the whole socio-cultural spectrum. This is not to say that all feminists have abandoned the view of capitalist relations of production as the source of gender construction (e.g. Game & Pringle, 1983) or that all have abandoned the traditional political avenues of action for change, but the break by a significant range of feminist theorists with traditional revolutionary strategies, concentrated as they have been in the public realm of politics and the labour market, hemmed in by male-defined and controlled economico-political structures, has involved a new and intensively creative confrontation with gender, a deconstruction of 'the very historical identity on which feminist politics has traditionally been based' (Barrett, 1987 p.29).

This rethinking of the nature and purpose of feminist criticism involves a rethinking of the ultimate social, political and economic forms towards which feminists are orienting themselves. Is the aim 'equality' through socialism? Or is the possibility something entirely different? Most feminist politics has, like most socialist politics, assumed a form of socialism as its goal, the taken-for-granted 'other' in relation to their current lived experience. Controversies have simply raged over how this goal might be achieved, about priorities in the programmes for the revolutionary transformation of society, and about the relative importance of intellectuals and the labour movement in achieving revolution. Socialism has been seen as a natural historical supercession of capitalism, emerging from the raging of the contradictions inherent in the mode of production through revolutionary action in the public workplace.

Without necessarily rejecting the importance of the mode of production in the shaping of cultural practice, the revitalisation of the creative role of ideology and culture has injected new life into debates about the nature of gender construction, about the nature of gender itself, and about the role the 'female' might play in the development of a non-capitalist, non-exploitative society. The 'other' is being rethought, not taken for granted. This theorising has far-reaching consequences for the interpretation of the relationship of gender to education and work. It throws into doubt all our preconceptions about valued knowledge and valued work.

Gender, Education and Work

In turning to the links between gender, education and work we need to consider the current feminist preoccupation with 'difference'. These debates radically question, among many other aspects of socio-cultural practice, accepted views of curriculum development and the potential transformation of the workplace[7]. The basic question is, should feminists seek equality or difference?

In the search for an understanding of the foundations of gender, recent feminist theorists have concentrated on the contrast between the cultural qualities 'male' and 'female'. They have concentrated on the dominance of the organisation of thought and practice by maleness, investigated through the development of critical theory, through the exploration of techniques for the deconstruction of meaning in literature and of the development of the psyche. Literary theory and psychoanalytic theory constantly interweave in this search for an understanding of 'gender difference'. As with all feminist theory its prime objective remains thoroughly political: 'it seeks to expose, not to perpetuate, patriarchal practices' (Moi, 1985 p.xiv), through the detailed examination of the verbal and symbolic forms of signification and communication.

[7.] For discussion of so-called post-structuralist feminist theorising on 'difference' see Moi 1985 and Duchen 1986. For the best examples of such writing see Moi 1986, Duchen 1987, Irigaray 1985, Gallop 1982, Cixous & Clement 1986, Mitchell 1984, Rose 1986, and Spivak 1987.

The search goes deep below the threshold of consciousness to our deepest assumptions about nature and our place in it. Our neatly structured, logical, unitary view of nature, the polity, the economy, the law, of knowledge itself, emerges as distinctly 'male', oriented towards the construction and constant reproduction of transformations of a 'male' world in which the 'female' is devalued. The very foundations of Western science in the mechanistic theories of Newton and Galileo are themselves distinctly 'male' in their imposition of a unitary, logocentric cosmology. The 'female' that emerges from the critical analysis of literature and the psyche is, in contrast to the 'male', emotional and subjective rather than rational and objective; 'chaotic', in flux, rather than unitary, ordered; communal and other-directed rather than individuated and self-centred. The images of the contrasts are constantly likened to contrasting genitalia, both for their psychological and symbolic importance:

> As Luce Irigaray and Jacques Derrida have argued, patriarchal thought models its criteria for wart counts as 'positive' values on the central assumption of the Phallus and the Logos as transcendent signifiers of Western culture. ...anything conceived of as analogous to the so-called 'positive' values of the Phallus counts as good, true or beautiful; anything that is not shaped in the pattern of the Phallus is defined as chaotic, fragmented, negative or non-existent. The Phallus is often conceived of as a whole, unitary and simple form, as opposed to the terrifying chaos of the female genitals (Ibid p.66-7).

Whatever the source of these contrasting modes of thought and practice, their theorising has radical consequences for feminist views on every aspect of thought and action in Western society. So the very mode in which subject matter is approached, let alone the actual content of the curricula, is in doubt, as is the nature of the economic process towards which students are directed. The challenge for many feminists now becomes the ridding of society and culture of their phallogo-centric bias. The dominance of the maths and sciences, the logocentric subjects of ordered calculation, over the greater subjectivity and creativity of literature, the arts and humanities; the stress on individual retention of knowledge for competitive assessment rather than the sharing of knowledge for communal enlightenment. These are but the most obvious examples of the phallogocentric bias of education.

The recognition of 'difference' is of course the recognition of the massive contradiction that girls experience within the school and workplace. The embodiment of femaleness, they compete at school and work in a male mode. As they apply themselves to their subjects, particularly the sciences, they live a cultural lie, a lie experienced in the mode of organisation of all their subjects. In the workplace they must, if they move beyond the 'female' nurturing occupations, be 'male', further living the lie. Is that what women are aiming for? Is this equality, to be 'male'? If not, what is the alternative? Having theorised, revealed, the degree to which gender differences permeate our lives what should we aim for and how? Some writers have theorised a female curriculum and beyond that a female workplace - meaning defined in female terms, not meaning occupied solely, predominantly or even strategically by women. Whether this would necessarily involve the marginalisation of the 'male' depends on whether the 'female' and 'male' as we know them are incompatible. Given that we have, in capitalist society, a situation where the 'male' aspect has become dominant in all spheres of social life, thus segregated from the 'female' and consequently dehumanised, the orientation must be towards the reintegration of the female into all aspects of our lives, for without doing so we continue to live under the shadow of Blake's brutal 'spectre', now the threat of nuclear war, born of 'male' competition and insensitivity. Blake's 'dark satanic mills' are now the brooding stockpiles of nuclear missiles, equally phallic, equally inhuman and unitary in their purpose, bred of the same mechanistic anti-spiritual orientation towards a selfish future. The 'male' would of necessity, with the revalorisation of the 'female', not be marginalised since, while the 'male' aspect dominates, excludes, oppresses its opposite, the 'female' succours, includes, values its opposite. To valorise the 'female' is therefore to look towards a harmony which a 'male' dominated society can never achieve:

> ... cruel Works of many Wheels I view, wheel without wheel, with cogs tyrannic, Moving by compulsion each other, not as those in Eden, which, Wheel within wheel, in freedom revolve, in harmony and peace. William Blake, *Jerusalem* (Blake, 1934 p.338).

The sensitivities of women must be rediscovered, acknowledged, used, respected.

This analysis of a potential future is of course intensely idealistic, but ideals must be the basis for action. It is hard to conceive of men not being selfishly and single-mindedly 'male'. But the position taken here is that to be 'female' is to be culturally formed and defined. It is not a natural consequence of being a woman. It is tempting to posit that women are more inclined to be 'female' than men, and men more inclined to be 'male' but even if this is the case the inclination exists at a level beyond culture and is therefore so general as to be culturally meaningless. At most it would warn of the need to ensure that neither men nor women are marginalised from any aspect of social life. Some feminist theorists do claim a form of biological determinism in the development of the female consciousness[8], some psychoanalytic

---

[8]. For the most sophisticated of the essentialist positions see Irigaray, 1985 and Cixous & Clement, 1986. See also Toril Moi's discussion of their work in Moi, 1985.

others stressing the importance of the experience of childbirth, but in this chapter the stress has been on the cultural moulding of dispositions. Girls live the lie, manifest the contradictions at school and at work because they have been enculturated as 'female', where being 'female' involves an orientation towards thought and practice in opposition to the valued 'male' qualities that mould the public world.

Orienting ourselves towards programmes for change, and the curriculum in particular, what is patently obvious is that capitalism and its accompanying theology, scientific rationalism, are thoroughly 'male'. Referring to three of the more direct feminist confrontations with school curriculum, confrontations concerned precisely with theorising 'difference' though not all from the same point of view, Lyn Yates writes:

> What Grumet, Gilligan and Martin take up, though in different ways, is that if we put women to the fore we need to address a very different style of reasoning and a different content of the curriculum. The different style of reasoning they point to is one developed not around clear-cut cause-effect relations and abstract logic, but one which is alert to the human, interpersonal, emotional, contingent qualities of a situation (Yates, 1987a p.332)[9].

Our public behaviour, our performance at school and work, are dominated by and judged in terms of 'reason', 'rationality', a unitary, logocentric perspective based in a mechanistic, law-governed view of nature and humanity. Its orientation is *control* through technological mastery. But science has not always been relentlessly 'male'. It was only in the seventeenth century when, with the foundation of the Royal Societies, science was harnessed to serve incipient capitalism that it became so (see Uberoi, 1978). The reintegration of the 'female' into science involves the rediscovery of the spiritual side of nature, of the sensitivities that have been devalued as 'female' and identified with women. As Lyn Yates' researches showed:

> ... a case has now been well-established that traditional school knowledge and practice has distorted, omitted, trivialised the contribution of women ... (1987a p.359).

This omission, trivialisation of the 'female' has impoverished the curriculum for girls in particular but for boys as well, devaluing, inhibiting, belittling the development of their 'female' aspect.

Among feminists at least there is little argument with the claim that current educational practice is distorted, one-sided, and that 'good education' requires a

---

9. See for example Grumet, 1981; Gilligan, 1982; and Martin, 1984.

reorientation of the form and content of the curriculum. But the two-way link with the labour market is much more problematic and probably for that very reason is largely ignored both by the educational theorists and by those theorising the transformation of the workplace. The greatest danger in theorising the link is to assume a sexual division of labour. Some theorists still see women primarily as housewives and mothers but with housework and motherhood imbued with respect and recognised as integral to social production and reproduction. Such a position is sociologically naive failing to consider the overall relations of production. Also, to orient girls primarily towards motherhood and household management is to restrict not only their creative contribution to work in general but that of men as well. Child care and domestic work need not be gender specific. It is precisely through their creative contribution to the workplace in general, including teachers at all levels, to the quality of work and the relations within work, that women, as the embodiment of the 'female' in our culture have a vital role to play in its transformation.

The only way that the reintegration of the 'female' aspect into work and education can occur is by the full and equal integration of those who symbolically represent that 'female' aspect and whose consciousness is not blinkered by 'maleness', namely women. But *on their own terms*, encouraged to be female, to redefine priorities in knowledge, in the organisation of work and the distribution and investment of profits. They must be looked to for that vital aspect of humanity that the public world lacks and that remains subordinate in the domestic realm. Those few who have become used to being 'one of the boys' or who are by habit subordinate must rediscover and revel in their vital link with the 'female', encouraging men to discover their own 'female' side. There is no reason why these modes of thought and practice should be labelled 'female' rather than 'male'. That they are is historically and culturally specific: an historical development that dates from the sixteenth century in particular, part of the development of a fully-fledged capitalist mode of production.

Feminism's concern with the liberation of women is, through its revelation of the implications of the discriminatory evaluation of gender through difference, a call for the liberation of people in general from the domination of brutish, one-sided 'maleness'. The fact that recent feminist theory has revealed this process of gender differentiation to be basic to the development of the psyche and to the written, spoken and symbolic transmission of meaning, to the evaluation of space and time as elements vital to the strategies of communication (cf Bourdieu, 1977a), reveals the vital strategic importance, in the battle for change, of education; in the home, the school and the workplace. A concerted programme for the valorisation of the 'female' aspect in all thought and practice must include the transformation of the curriculum, of its relationship to tertiary entrance and work, and of the relations of production in work.

This is not to theorise with one's head in the clouds. The signs of change, not necessarily feminist in inspiration but none-the-less in the right direction, are there already, in the home, the schools and the workplace. The foundations are coming along even if the building has a long way to go. Moves to discourage intensive specialisation in the final years of schooling in Australia, to decrease the stress on competitive examinations as a mechanism for tertiary selection, reveal a softening and increased flexibility in the approach to schooling which must be encouraged and linked directly to the special role that women can play in the process. The relaxing of entrance requirements to science-based professional faculties such as for example the placing of humanities students on an equal footing with science students for entrance to medicine and veterinary science at the University of Sydney, also lays a firm base for the reintegration of the 'female' aspect not only into the heavily logocentric areas of scientific knowledge and practice but into the highly valued and strategically important areas of the workforce. Not only women but less phallogocentric men thus enter the most valued professions.

But these trends are only small moves in the right direction, indicative of the sort of changes required. Male opposition is strong and effective, seen recently for example in the nurses' fight for professional status, a fight for much more than higher wages. It is a battle for the redefinition of the relations of production away from the traditional recourse to gender. Their rejection of the 'Florence Nightingale' image is the rejection of the view of the 'female' as marginal to the public world and therefore as not in need of 'male' remuneration. Until the 'female' and thus women are valued in the public and private spheres of action, shock tactics such as those of the nurses were inevitable, the blame laying squarely with the politicians and doctors who cannot face the challenge of a threat to their vested interest in 'male' domination.

What is required above all is *a constant critical practice* among students, teachers, politicians, workers and employers which is informed by the feminist theorising of 'difference'. The idea of an alternative achieves nothing without action. Awareness of the one-sided, dehumanised nature of a unitary, logocentric 'male' position must be promoted to encourage the transformation of priorities in teaching, research and the organisation of production. For students, the *experience* of a transformed practice is at least as important as the learning of a transformed curriculum. The treatment of women teachers and girls as well as of the less overtly 'male' boys is as important as the promotion of alternative 'female' modes of reasoning which are not based on a mechanistic, unitary view of nature as governed by known laws and in need of technological control. Final year assessments must not downgrade 'female' skills and thus the potential success of girls in particular by, for example, requiring only a bare pass in English and thus not allowing those more 'female' students who do well in literary subjects to benefit from their particular skills. The hierarchical domination of the sciences and maths must be destroyed and their content critically revised.

What is particularly important with regard to the link between government policy and education, is that formal education must not be designed and funded 'to serve the needs of the economy'. This current familiar political rhetoric - particularly apparent in recent policy statements by the Australian Federal Minister for Education - not only gives priority to capitalist economic activity but assumes that the morality of the labour market and of investment strategies is a desirable morality for the society as a whole. In terms of the feminist theories of difference such an approach intensifies the 'male' qualities of our society running directly counter to necessary strategies for the liberation of women and society. We should remember that:

> It is only our Western societies that quite recently turned man into an economic animal. ... *Homo oeconomicus* is not behind us, but before, like the moral man, the man of duty, the scientific man and the reasonable man. For a long time man was something quite different; ...[only recently did he become] a machine - a calculating machine. (Mauss, 1967 p.74).

The increasingly fervent alliance between politics and the economy involves the rejection of any vestiges of 'female' values. While the same governments voice a concern for equal opportunity for women, encouraging girls to enter occupations dominated by men, even to the point of legislating for 'affirmative action', they are in fact only promoting the presence of women not the integration of the 'female'. Women must have a place as 'females' not simply as pseudo men, as 'male' women. Women must have the right to *redefine* curricula, school practices, labour relations. Currently they are allowed into a 'male' defined world.

Political policy is born of the contradictions inherent in society. These contradictions are the source of change. These are the contradictions that give rise to affirmative action, to changes in assessment procedures, to programmes for the integration of the disabled into mainstream education, to the transformation of entry requirements for tertiary education. In many cases governments may be doing the right thing for the wrong reason but they are providing the opportunity for further change, for the emergence of deeper contradictions which can then be the basis for further change. It is the role of educators to reveal these contradictions, to raise them above the threshold of consciousness. They must expose, for example, the duplicity of politicians who claim to represent all constituents equally; the destructive, dehumanising nature of so much of the popular media, so often sheltering in a self-congratulatory recourse to ideologies of creative 'freedom', usually one-sidedly 'male', certainly phallocentric; the exploitative ruthlessness of capitalist production shrouded in ideological recourse to 'freedom' to invest, 'individual' competition for profit, and 'equality' before the law; or the fundamentally disharmonious nature of much family life, apparent harmony based on 'male' dominance and the duality of the 'public' and 'private' domains (see Barrett & McIntosh, 1982); in general to reveal the unwillingness of those in positions of power and privilege to understand, let alone realise, the ideals they self-righteously mouth; and above all to reveal the interconnections between these various spheres of socio-cultural experience and strategic action.

But if educators are to play such a constructively subversive role they must first and foremost look inward to discover the contradictions inherent in educational thought and practice, to deconstruct the categories of their own practice to reveal the currently destructive but potentially creative power of difference. It is feminism's task to reveal and act on those contradictions based in gender. The way through to the transformation of our 'male' dominated society will only be found through the praxis of a feminist critical practice. In concluding this review of the interrelationships between gender, education and work two issues need to be highlighted.

First, subversive education involves not only 'knowledge' but the *experience* of a transformed and reflexive practice. Schools must practice what they preach. Second, a feminist education no matter how fervent will not generate social change towards a non-exploitative or even less-exploitative practice unless it involves the breaking down of the artificial barriers between family and school and school and work. The institutional isolation of schooling contains its potential subversive influence; creates a false sense of achievement among teachers who think only in terms of 'school results'. Education is much more than formal schooling. It is a lifelong experience. A feminist-inspired curriculum and teaching practice must link up with a feminist-inspired practice at home and at 'work'.

9

Technical and Vocational Schooling: Education or Work?

by Gary McCulloch

The development of technical and vocational schooling has been an important means of encouraging 'education for work', that is, orienting the organisation and curriculum of schools towards industrial and vocational needs. However, there has often been some tension in such policy initiatives between addressing the alleged requirements of 'work' and meeting accepted or received 'educational' criteria. This tension may be expressed in terms of control, as groups representing educational and industrial interests compete for involvement and influence. It is also likely to precipitate debate over the kind of curriculum appropriate for both types of concern. Such tensions and problems have been clearly evident in policies relating to technical schooling in the English context, and help to account for the general lack of impact of such schemes. We may assess these difficulties, and the challenges that they pose for the 'city technology colleges' now being promoted by the British Government, first through an historical perspective on technical and vocational schooling in twentieth-century England, and then through detailed scrutiny of a current project - the Technical and Vocational Education Initiative (TVEI). In general terms, the secondary technical schools of the 1940s to 1960s provide us with an example of an 'education-based' initiative in this vein; the TVEI on the other hand may be characterised as 'work-based'.

Secondary and Technical Education

Much criticism has been voiced over the failure of English education to prepare pupils more actively for the 'world of work'. Education for work has been chiefly associated with preparation for industrial jobs and skills which would improve Britain's economic and industrial performance. But the academic traditions of English secondary education in particular, it is said, have tended to neglect or downgrade such preparation. The Duke of Edinburgh, a prominent advocate of reform, suggested in 1967 that the pattern of education had been developed over a period when a particular type of end-product had been required (e.g. the Colonial administrator or the family business man) and when there had been little or no demand for the technologist. He asked how relevant was this out-dated structure to those who wish to become technologists; the system of training craftsmen and technicians required rethinking. The Prince also gave an example of where British educational processes were leading in industry: the British motor car fell down in world markets because it lacked rational design - it was the product of the academic approach.

Such views became especially influential in the 1980s, when it became common to attribute Britain's long-term relative economic decline and contemporary industrial problems to the character of its education system. Thus David Young, chairman of the Manpower Services Commission (MSC), argued that "the whole educational system is slanted towards academic and abstract standards and not towards pragmatic practical skills which are so often necessary in the world of work" (1984a p.456). Historians increasingly emphasised the social attitudes reflected in and reproduced by education in explaining Britain's low industrial productivity. According to Correlli Barnett, for instance, "the general ethos and thrust of British education are, if anything, hostile to industry and careers in industry" (1979 p.120; see also Barnett, 1986).

The strength of the grammar school tradition in twentieth-century England gave much weight to this general view. State grammar schools established under the Education Act of 1902 generally sought to imitate the liberal ideals of nineteenth-century English public schools. They also placed a strong emphasis on academic achievement. Only a small minority of the age-range reached the grammar school, and these in turn usually went on to higher education and professional, commercial or clerical careers. If this was education for work, it was so in only a selective and limited sense. After the 1944 Education Act, which introduced secondary education for all, the grammar school remained the chief route to the professions. In the 1950s, as the sociologist Olive Banks pointed out, the grammar schools, "enjoying in any case the reflected glory of their former esteem", continued to provide "the chief avenue, within the state system of education, to occupations of the highest social and economic standing" (Banks, 1955 p.7). They were still effectively "the goose which lays the golden eggs" (Whitfield, 1957 p.18). From the 1960s, the grammar schools were superseded by comprehensive schools designed for pupils of all abilities and aptitudes. Despite this, as Stephen Ball has remarked, "with a few notable exceptions, the expectations of parents, the demands of the examination system and the increasingly critical attitude of successive governments have tended to reinforce an emphasis on internal selection and differentiation among pupils"

(Ball, 1984 pp.2-3; see also Hargreaves, 1982). Grammar school values, traditions and curricula survived in the new setting of the comprehensives. Thus it seems no exaggeration to argue that the grammar school tradition has dominated English secondary education throughout the present century.

Any substantial reform of the curriculum and orientation of the grammar school, including a reorientation towards industrial and commercial work as opposed to middle-class, black-coated professions, therefore tended to be regarded as a betrayal of its liberal and academic values. As the secretary of the Norwood committee on curriculum and examinations in secondary schools pointed out in 1941, "I don't see how industry can be done in the Grammar school, or full-time commerce without such changes in organisation and staff as would destroy its 'grammar' nature". The alternative was to develop another kind of secondary education in the shape of technical schools, designed to prepare pupils for skilled trades and industry. But the problem here was that such preparation appeared decidedly inferior to the prospects offered by the grammar schools. Clive Griggs has recently documented how the interest of the Trades Union Congress shifted in the early twentieth-century towards providing authentic, as opposed to second-best, secondary education for the children of the workers: "Technical knowledge might raise a worker to the rank of foreman but it was secondary education in the mould set by Robert Morant and A.J. Balfour [in 1902] which was more likely to provide the social mobility needed to join the ranks of the white collared workers" (1983 p.117). Thus a basic tension emerged between a need, widely perceived, to prepare and train future workers in various skilled fields, and equally strong views on the proper values, curricula and orientation of secondary education. Technical education, in short, looked more like 'work' than 'education'.

In such circumstances it was bound to be difficult to reconcile 'secondary' with 'technical' education. The Bryce Report on secondary education had argued in 1895 that technical education should be regarded as a species of the genus secondary, but this view appeared unsustainable after 1902. It was not until 1944 that a substantial attempt was made to develop 'secondary technical schools' equal in stature to the grammar schools. This was based on the view upheld by the Norwood report of 1943 that there were in reality three different types of pupils, who could best be catered for through different kinds of secondary school: grammar, technical and modern. Charles Tennyson, chairman of the education committee of the Federation of British Industries, predicted with considerable accuracy "that boys [sic] taking a technical education would be likely to go on to the general commercial side of industry, while those at grammar schools would tend to enter a profession". In practice, the grammar schools almost completely overshadowed the newer technical schools. By 1955 there were still only 300 secondary technical schools, with 4.4

per cent of the total number of state secondary school pupils enrolled.

The most common response to this situation was for secondary technical schools to try to become respectable in educational terms, by emphasising their compatibility with liberal and academic ideals even at the expense of their ostensible relationship with industry and work. It was suggested that the true conception of a secondary technical school was "that of a selective school which is in no way inferior to the grammar school in quality of staff and buildings, age of recruitment, freedom to attract children of the highest intelligence, intellectual demands, standards of work, including capacity to prepare for GCE [General Certificate of Education] and advanced level courses, and the breadth of its vision and humanity". The Association of Heads of Secondary Technical Schools took pains to stress that "the secondary technical school provides a type of education which is satisfying to its pupils because of the purposeful nature of the courses followed and the harmonious blending of the academic, the practical, the moral and the aesthetic". Thus there was often some dilution of the work-oriented rationale of the technical schools in an effort to imitate the rhetoric and values of the grammar schools.

Such efforts could at times be painfully obvious, and led to some conflict among the schools themselves. Thus for example when the Head of a certain technical school 'paused outside a school workshop, saying: "Not plumbing - non-ferrous metal work. We teach them why - not how"', another Head complained indignantly that 'We suffer too much today, and particularly in the secondary technical schools, from individuals who, unaware of the significance of their work, spend much of their time apologising for the fact that their school is not a grammar school and trying to put an academic veneer on what is in itself a thoroughly cultural effort giving an experience of values which no 'academic' education can equal". The secondary technical schools were generally somewhat incoherent and unclear about their precise role, and this hampered their attempts to gain wider attention and respect (see McCulloch, 1984, 1985 and 1986 for full references to quotes here and elsewhere in this chapter). The most important and best publicised effort to publicise a distinctive 'secondary technical' philosophy, however, asserted their educational as opposed to their work-related value. This was the Crowther Report on the education of boys and girls from fifteen to eighteen years of age, published in 1959. Geoffrey Crowther himself, chairman of the committee which produced the report for the Ministry of Education, was anxious to enhance the educational aspect of such schools; as he emphasised for the benefit of his committee members in 1957, the key need was that "the whole of this area should be gradually transformed from being primarily designed to meet industry's needs (with some education thrown in) to being primarily designed to continue the education of a large slice of the nation's boys and girls (without destroying the usefulness to industry of the present system)". This was forcefully expressed in Chapter 35 of the final Report as 'The Alternative Road'. Not all pupils, it suggested, were attracted or motivated by "the academic tradition which inspires and is embodied in our grammar schools and universities". Some should therefore be encouraged to benefit from an alternative, more "practical" route; but this route should be marked not by "narrow vocational interest", but rather by a "broad scientific curiosity". The emphasis was therefore upon respectability in educational terms, which meant eschewing directly vocational curricula, instead of focusing upon active preparation or specialisation for the various spheres of work (McCulloch, 1984).

In terms of curriculum and control, 'educational' interests and criteria generally dominated policy in relation to the secondary technical schools. They were state schools, organised by their local education authority (LEA), responsible to the minister of education. They failed to establish themselves either as a reputable alternative form of education or as an effective training-ground for the world of work; and during the 1960s the experiment was abandoned.

The TVEI

The Technical and Vocational Education Initiative was established at the end of 1982 specifically to resolve the problems that the secondary technical schools had faced, in the interests of industry and enterprise. It proved to be a contentious policy initiative because it challenged educational control, criteria and traditions; indeed, industrial and employment interests were much more strongly represented in the new project.

'Education for work' was the key theme in the self-styled Great Debate launched by James Callaghan as prime minister in October 1976. A consultative paper published by the Department of Education and Science the following year acknowledged the widely held view that "the educational system was out of touch with the fundamental need for Britain to survive economically in a highly competitive world through the efficiency of its industry and commerce". Especially after the election of a Conservative government under Mrs Margaret Thatcher in 1979, this came to represent an important area requiring urgent reform. At the level of secondary education, the problem appeared to be as great as ever despite the eclipse of the grammar schools and the widespread adoption of comprehensives. The secondary technical schools had also succumbed to the advance of the comprehensives in the 1960s. According to David Young, "in the drive towards comprehensives the technical and vocational end of education somehow got lost" (1984b p.426). It was he indeed who came to spearhead a new initiative intended to succeed where the secondary technical schools had failed.

In November 1982, the prime minister announced the launch of a pilot scheme for fourteen to eighteen year-olds in selected schools that would be known as the TVEI. This was to prove a highly controversial development. Dispute arose because the TVEI appeared to threaten established 'educational' criteria and values in a way that the secondary technical schools had never done. Indeed, whereas the earlier initiative had been firmly controlled by the education service, the TVEI was from its inception a creation of employment interests. It was to be administered by the Manpower Services Commission, a body established in 1973 and responsible to the Department of Employment. The Department of Education and Science and the LEAs had little influence on its initial character (Dale, 1985; McCulloch, 1986; Gleeson, 1987). Thus Young, as chairman of the MSC, was able to give the initiative a strongly work-based rationale. "Next summer", he noted, "nearly half a million school-leavers will be coming on to the labour market, and every year that passes brings still more young people unprepared for the world of work on to the job market". But the TVEI could change all this: "By the time they leave, our youngsters will be highly employable".

Over the next years the TVEI was consolidated and expanded as a national project. In 1983 the TVEI steering group established broad criteria, and selected fourteen LEAs to run pilot projects. In 1984 and 1985 further projects were launched, and in July 1986 it was announced that the TVEI would be extended into a national scheme, part of the curriculum of all schools, from the autumn term of 1987. According to this policy statement, entitled *Working Together - Education and Training*, "Children go to school so that they can develop their talents, become responsible citizens and be prepared for work - for others and on their own account. The schools - and, for some, the colleges and universities - have the task of laying the foundations for effective learning and training throughout life". Within this context "the main purpose of the initiative has been to test methods of organising and managing the education of 14-18 year-olds across the ability range to improve the provision of technical and vocational education in a way which will widen and enrich the curriculum and prepare young people for adult and working life". This conformed with MSC's aims for the TVEI, that it would encourage more young people to seek and achieve "the qualifications/skills which will be of direct value to them at work". Young himself was elevated in spectacular fashion in September 1984, becoming Lord Young of Graffham and Head of the prime minister's Enterprise Unit. He was soon to become secretary of state for employment, and continued to pursue his belief that although "the purpose of school is not just to prepare you for work it should be a help and not a hindrance" (1984a p.453). Meanwhile the new chairman of the MSC, Bryan Nicholson, was optimistic that the influence of the TVEI would soon pervade the education system as a whole.

The sponsors of the TVEI were soon using more reassuring language to ensure wider acceptability and the consolidation of the policy. Young himself could suggest, for example, that although the TVEI would give young people 'employable skills', this was not what it was 'essentially concerned'to do: "TVEI is about educating people, about broadening the curriculum to give them new subjects to which to relate" (1984a p.457). It would have been mollifying also to see, as one critic noted, that "TVEI has proved to be very varied - so varied that there is no such thing as a TVEI stereotype" (Maclure, 1985). Even so, the MSC's control of the venture still seemed to ensure an essentially work-oriented and employment-based development. For this reason it aroused much hostility and resentment from educational groups and interests, despite the fact that it represented a major national investment in curriculum development. It was quickly labelled 'Norm's Academy', after the then secretary of state for employment, Norman Tebbit. Young, it appeared, was "the polished bogeyman of the education world", because he "personified the attempted takeover of the classroom by the training world", (TES, 1984). Such opposition was well expressed by Maurice Holt, a principal lecturer in curriculum studies, who has complained of an "industry-led view of the purpose of schooling" in which "'working life' is to determine both the knowledge and the 'personal skills' addressed by the school curriculum" (1987 p.61). According to Holt, "given its direct connection, through the MSC, with a government committed to radical right-wing dogma, one would have to be remarkably purblind not to see TVEI as a very serious, if not fatal, threat to a tradition of liberal education that has survived two world wars and the narrowness of the grammar-school curriculum, but may not yet survive the market-economy technocrats of the 1980s" (Holt, 1987 pp.81-82). For such critics, the TVEI was symptomatic of a 'new vocationalism' that disregarded the needs of education in favour of those of work and the economy (see Bates, 1985; Dale, 1985). Those concerned to defend the comprehensive schools and the idea of the common curriculum against what they see as a politically-motivated attack, were especially critical of the TVEI's ambitions. The general secretary of the Trades Union Congress insisted that the initiative should "ensure that vocational preparation does not mean early specialisation and narrowing of study options". The Labour Party, in the words of its shadow minister Giles Radice, also sought to foster "a more generous, less narrowly 'vocational' vision of education than the Tories". Such doubts and opposition made the TVEI, however well resourced and managed, politically vulnerable in the longer term.

Thus, if the secondary technical schools had tended to emphasise their 'educational' basis, the TVEI generally stressed its work-oriented character. The secondary technical schools' attempt to achieve educational respectability failed to convince; the TVEI's more radical, employment-based approach threatened to confirm the suspicions of educators regarding the unsound, potentially alien tendencies of technical and vocational schooling.

Towards the City Technology College

In the wake of the TVEI exercise, the new secretary of state for education, Kenneth Baker, announced to the Conservative Party annual conference in 1986 plans to develop 'city technology colleges' (CTCs) for pupils from eleven to eighteen years of age, in collaboration with local industries. These, it appeared, would be akin to the earlier secondary technical schools in that they would be separate institutions with the status of secondary schools, but they would be administered by local industrial and business interests independent of the education service. The now familiar tension between 'education' and 'work' seems likely to affect the new enterprise. Critics were quick to note that the new proposals "look like a throw-back to the technical schools of the 1950s", and "certainly toll the knell for many a shrinking inner city comprehensive maintaining a sixth form". But one 'grain of comfort' for such observers was that the DES rather than the MSC are running the scheme. Its success may well depend on the extent to which it is able to establish and reconcile both educational and work-based criteria and objectives. The control and the curricula of the CTCs will be subject to intense scrutiny. If they are to be effective in promoting education for work, they will surely need to steer a path between the educational Scylla of the secondary technical schools and the vocational Charybdis of the TVEI.

10 Leisure, Work and Education

by Harold Entwistle

Leisure and Employment

One assumption which has grown out of post-industrial technological innovation is that it will greatly expand the spare time available to most workers. Indeed, it is often assumed that the shift towards automated, labour saving technologies has put us on the threshold of a Golden Age of Leisure. If diminishing opportunities for employment seem to be an inevitable consequence of the kind of technological innovation characteristic of the post-industrial society, it seems only rational to assume that work could be spread more thinly amongst those in the labour market, making for a radical reduction in the working day or the working week; or, perhaps, there is the possibility of longer vacations, even 'sabbatical' leaves for industrial workers.

However, it is only by thinking about work and leisure in an economic and political vacuum that it is possible to conclude that opportunities for leisure will increase as a consequence of automation. If we ignore political and economic constraints it does appear axiomatic that if the application of new industrial technologies should spell redundancy for large numbers of workers, this ought also to lead to reorganisation of the work force so that everyone benefits from the dramatically increased productivity which is implicit in the new industrial techniques. Unfortunately for this analysis, 'Western' societies are rooted in free enterprise, capitalist economies in which (as a matter of fact - this point is not made polemically) production is for the sake of profit and not primarily for the satisfaction of human needs. No doubt, satisfying human needs and wants is often also profitable (in making a profit the baker, the shoe and clothing manufacturer, the builder, the show business entrepreneur are all meeting human needs and aspirations), but if satisfying a particular need is not profitable, it remains unfulfilled in a free enterprise capitalist society. People are in business to make profits; they are not, on the whole, philanthropists. This is, essentially, why we develop mixed economies: the rationale for developing the public sector is that there are human needs (in the areas of education, health, etc.) which would not be addressed in any economy which is primarily fuelled by the profit motive. Indeed, a major justification of socialism hinges on the notion that the quality of life depends upon the public financing of goods and services, the universal provision of which private industry would not find profitable. Even scientific research is decreasingly devoted to projects concerned with the elimination of poverty and disease or raising the standard of life: the main purpose of research and innovation is to counteract the tendency of the rate of profit to fall and to create new opportunities for profitable investment.

The reason for insisting that in capitalist economies the profit motive ultimately overrides human need, is that the worker's need for more spare time (or, when threatened with redundancy, his or her need for a job) is not a 'service' which industry can provide consistently with the pursuit of profit. The fundamental weakness of the view that with the intensification of automation, vastly increased 'leisure' is an imminent probability, is that it can bear little relationship to the facts of life in capitalist economies. Under capitalism, labour-saving innovations are made to reduce costs and increase profitability, not benevolently to create leisure for workers. As the managing director of Standard Motors once put it: 'We are not installing £4 millions worth of equipment in order to employ the same number of men. We can't carry people for fun'. Given this kind of economic imperative, technologically induced 'leisure' becomes merely a euphemism for unemployment. For however productive an economy may be, potentially, from a technological point of view, so far as technological innovation requires a significant reduction in the work force it operates to reduce effective demand for goods and services. Unless compensating opportunities for work are created in other private or public enterprises, the only way we have of financing mass 'leisure' is through the dole, welfare benefits or pensions. For workers, technologically induced redundancy is not an invitation to leisure so much as an imperative towards their finding other jobs elsewhere in industry or in the public sector of the economy. Hence (this constitutes a further reason for assessing the work-leisure relationship in terms of particular economic and political systems) structural redundancy in a capitalist society also creates the problem of maintaining a satisfactory level of economic activity through its effect on demand for goods and services. In a market economy, people have to be in receipt of income in order to keep industry in business. Yet the rhetoric of futurism often seems predicated upon the assumption that an increased capacity to supply goods and services automatically generates its own effective demand.

As well as in qualitative terms of how many jobs are available and how much leisure time workers can expect to have in an automated economy, in qualitative terms also, the future of leisure is inseparable from the quality of work. One common assumption about the relationship between work and leisure is that leisure can compensate for alienation at work. Indeed education for leisure is apt to be proposed on behalf of those whose work appears to be routine and mindless. To the extent that such people might experience a reduction of the time spent at work, it is thought desirable to ensure that their spare time is filled profitably and creatively. The assumption is that the average man lacks the personal cultural resources towards that end. Advocacy of education for leisure tends to focus upon the need for initiation into a variety of pursuits, usually of a 'play' or 'recreational' nature. No doubt there is often a genuine concern that the quality of a person's life should be enriched in this way. But one critic of what have been called 'professional leisurists' sees the emphasis upon developing 'leisure industries' and 'leisure training' as a modern version of the nineteenth century's concern for 'gentling the masses': leisure is to be the new opium of the people. As Parkin puts it, in a modern society subtle ways are found of 'ensuring social discipline and conformity by entrusting this task to the welfare professions in their capacity of moral entrepreneurs' (Parkin, 1979 p. 18). One apologist for 'professional leisurists' has argued: 'Since the average citizen is unable to invent new uses for his leisure, a professional elite shares a heavy responsibility for discovering criteria for ways of employing leisure and creating enthusiasm for common ends within the moral ends of the community' (Quoted by Parker 1971 pp. 128-129). As Parker observes, this point of view is not only elitist: the notion of 'moral ends of the community' also implies 'that only certain kinds of leisure are to be promoted and that they are intended as a means of social control' (Parker, *loc. cit.*). there is also an implication of change for the sake of change in the criticism that the average person is incapable of inventing '*new* uses for his or her leisure'. This presumes, without explanation, that *old* uses for leisure are somehow inadequate.

It may be, of course, that the way in which many people in our society occupy their spare time leaves much to be desired from the perspective of what constitutes an educated life. A conclusion of this kind necessarily involves value judgements about the kinds of activities which are considered worthwhile components of the good life. And although these judgements which are made about other people's lives are apt to be dismissed as elitist or paternalistic, they are inescapable for social reformers and, especially, for educationists. In one form or another, the judgement that most people make less than the best use of their spare time is commonplace amongst scholars and intellectuals. Sociologists and historians from Engels down to the present day (often actively involved in the working class movement) have pointed to the deleterious effect of industrialism upon popular culture, and to the tendency of the working class to search for irrational, escapist solutions to the problems of life. However, in correlating the prevalence of mechanical, escapist, soul destroying spare time preoccupations with the existence of a particular kind of industrial and economic organisation, these sympathetic critics of the quality of much activity spent outside the workplace are also pointing to the unreality of the compensatory conception of education for leisure; the assumption that you can redeem people from the dehumanising effects of their work by teaching them how to make constructive and profitable use of their spare time. For there is an air of unreality about a notion of education for leisure which assumes that you can educate a person whose work is trivial and repetitive away from the pursuit of trivial, mechanical, spare time activities and towards those which are intellectually and aesthetically demanding. A number of modern industrial sociologists have concluded that the relationship between work and leisure has to be one of correspondence. As W.E. Moore has put it: 'leisure is a problem where work is a problem and probably proportionately. The "constructive" use of leisure is likely to depend in considerable measure on the constructive definition of jobs'. Life-styles, that is, are a package of essentially sympathetic activities, at work, at play, domestically, politically and culturally.

This conclusion opens the way towards a conception of leisure richer than one which conceives it merely as a vacuum which remains to be filled when the economic imperative to earn a living has been accommodated, and which poses the problem of education for leisure as one of helping people 'to fill their leisure hours' consequent upon a reduction of working hours or even 'the enforced leisure of unemployment'. It is more fruitful to conceive of leisure as itself a way of life, a manner of conducting all life's various activities. It is mistaken to conceive of work, play and recreation, home life, political activity and social service as discontinuous. Work, especially, cannot be circumscribed from the rest of life. Whether or not work provides intrinsic satisfactions it tends to determine one's style of living. Work frequently determines the character of our personal relationships, our friendships and, hence, the quality and pattern of recreational activity. It may be the mainspring of our activity as citizens, determining whether and how we perform social service, as well as our political allegiances. To change one's work is often also to alter one's entire pattern of life.

This conclusion that work is integral to life and, especially, to leisure is shared by diverse intellectual, religious, political and popular traditions within Western civilisation. Variously, work is regarded as an opportunity for worship and for sharing with God the Worker the task of creating and renewing the universe; as the essentially human activity which distinguishes Him from the beasts; as the *raison d' être* of social organisation; as the mainspring of human culture, especially of the arts (Entwistle 1970, Ch. 2). The educational implications of this assumption that work is the central life activity, since a civilisation is the creation of human work, are most rigorously pursued in the principle of polytechnical education, the theory and practice of education in Marxist states. Dewey's educational theory and the Project Method which he inspired are also rooted in the assumption he shared with Marx that what brings people together in a community is the organisation of different economic tasks to minister to human welfare. The celebration of work by different cultural traditions is paralleled by the common and widespread fear of unemployment. This is not simply a fear of economic deprivation which could be overcome by generous welfare handouts. As Lord Beveridge put it in his classic report, *Full Employment in a Free Society*: 'idleness is not the same as want, but a separate evil, which men do not escape by having an income. They must also have the chance of rendering useful service and feeling that they are doing so'. Nor is it only a matter of enabling a person to contribute towards the common good. Especially in the kind of society where a good deal of political power is exercised through the major economic institutions of both capital and labour, those cut off from these institutions are also politically impotent. Some politicians and media pundits, as well as some educationists, have concluded that people will have to accept the fact of prolonged, even lifelong, unemployment and there is even talk in 'official' circles of education for unemployment. One is at a loss to understand what this last could possibly mean, but it is inconceivable that educationists should even contemplate this notion. What the bland insistence that people can be persuaded to accept unemployment as inevitable leaves out of account is its political implications. According to what principles do we select those who are to be denied employment, not only as a source of political power, but also as the only means to an economic existence beyond mere levels of subsistence? The prevailing political and moral climate remains one where social insurance payments have to be kept so low that they are not a disincentive to work. Those fortunate enough to remain in employment will need considerable persuasion to agree to the diversion of revenues from taxation towards welfare benefits capable of sustaining even a moderately affluent standard of living for the unemployed.

The conclusion that leisure is linked closely to work and, indeed, that leisure is most profitably conceived as a way of life compounded of a variety of sympathetic life activities is underlined by the notion of a leisured class. Historically the leisured class was not a social group without the obligation to work, dedicated to idleness and the mere pursuit of pleasure. The leisured class pursued what Veblen called 'honourable employments', as landowners managing their own estates, for example, thus providing employment for others, as well as government and the administration of justice at various levels in the State (Entwistle 1978, Ch. 6). The leisured class was also the ruling class. Its work was in government and in the management of a rural economy, functions that have economic significance. But although in one sense leisured class employments were obligatory (its continued privileges depending on the provision of good government and work for others), the essence of its leisure consisted in the freedom with which it could pursue its distinctive work. Freedom or flexibility about how and when work can be done is the essence of leisure.

For Marx too freedom was a necessary condition of the worker's delivery from alienation, and it is interesting that his brief description of the ideal working life in a Communist society should evoke the lifestyle of the leisured class:

> In Communist society, where nobody has one exclusive sphere of activity but each can become accomplished in any branch he wishes, production as a whole is regulated by society, thus making it possible for me to do one thing today and another tomorrow, to hunt in the morning, fish in the afternoon, rear cattle in the evening, criticise after dinner, in accordance with my inclination, without ever becoming hunter, fisherman, shepherd or critic.

Idyllic and redolent of upper class life as this is, it has been taken as a point of departure for modern reflection upon the ways and means of improving the quality of working life and, hence, of the quality of leisure. Dahrendorf has asked, why not 'collect people's taxes in the morning and repair their cars in the afternoon, assemble television sets in the morning and go to polytechnic in the afternoon?' (Dahrendorf 1975 p. 76). This notion of redeeming workers from the alienating effects of industrial specialisation by sharing society's work so that everyone enjoys creative tasks and suffers the unpleasant chores would require an entirely novel mode of economic and industrial organisation and, so far as this kind of flexibility could be a possible outcome of technological innovation, it posits a need for political education as a necessary component of vocational education. This is to say that workers and citizens need to learn the dynamics of post-industrial economies and the structural (economic and political) changes which they must influence if they are to share the benefits of technological innovations.

Hence, vocational education must be conceived more widely than in its pejorative identification with technical training for manual occupations. Even in that context, as in historical examples of apprenticeship, there was a moral dimension to the training of craftsmen. As well as the 'mystery' of his craft, the apprentice was expected to acquire a cultural orientation in which acceptance of moral and social responsibility towards the client, the community and the fraternity of one's craft was of major importance. Also, to the craftsman the notion of 'a job well done' had aesthetic overtones: especially, the aesthetic dimension was implicit in the creation of art forms associated with these economic communities, particularly drama and music. And prior to the intensification of industrial discipline which resulted from collecting craftsmen into factories, the work patterns of industrial artisans shared some of those characteristics of 'leisure in work' (especially in relation to timing) that we have suggested are the prerogatives of a leisured class.

Thus, to have a vocation in its traditional sense is to do a job in a cultural context requiring an appreciation of the close connection between technical skill, personal taste, citizenship, morality and, perhaps, religion. In this sense, vocational education requires technical and professional training, but also political, aesthetic and moral education. It is this necessary reference to other cultural dimensions, as well as to the individual's capacity for acquiring 'technical' skills, which can ensure that vocational education becomes a liberating experience. A liberal education is one which frees the learner from whatever constraints might hinder his or her development as a person. And if our conclusion that future problems of work and leisure are likely to be as much a matter of political organisation and of the choices we make about what constitutes 'the good life' (including the obligation to make that available to as many as possible of our fellow men and women) as they are of the commercial and industrial management of technological innovation, then political and moral education are inescapable components of vocational education and education for leisure.

No doubt all this points, conservatively, to something like the traditional, humanistic, liberal curriculum, suitably modernised to encompass new forms of knowledge and properly concretised to speak to a variety of student interests, talents, aspirations and needs. But as is often the case in periods of normative confusion, a return to educational first principles may be the most appropriate way of finding our way out of current social dilemmas and of establishing signposts towards ways of harnessing technological innovation for the humanisation of work and leisure.

Social and Technological Change

Diversity or Commonality in Post-School Education

by Douglas Weir

11

This paper concentrates on the educational needs of those beyond the minimum school leaving age but outside the higher education sector. The group under review in Britain therefore comprises young people in the post-compulsory years of school, those in further education, those in the Youth Training Scheme, those in employment with associated education and training, and those unemployed but with access to education through the so-called '21 hours rule' and other devices.

That group is the target population for the new curricular prescription called vocational preparation, a group for whom a large fund of new resources has been created, partly in order to disguise the true extent of unemployment (nearer five million than three million) and partly to demonstrate the accuracy of facile equations developed by the government such as: more vocationally relevant education = more skilled manpower = more take-up of labour by industry = more competitive production = more wealth = reduction in unemployment and/or its effects.

In determining what should be the major elements of vocational preparation there is such a variety of alternative prescriptions that it is not yet possible to see how vocational preparation contributes to coping with social and technological change. For example:

(a) Is vocational preparation part of the curriculum for all, or is it for those below the group who can obtain higher education places?

(b) Is vocational preparation primarily training, with an emphasis on job skills, or primarily education with an emphasis on personal effectiveness?

(c) Does vocational preparation concentrate on the direct applications of information technology such as keyboarding, programming, systems analysis, or on the indirect applications such as cooperation, flexibility, problem-solving, greater participation in the community?

(d) Should vocational preparation take the view that since social and technological changes affect or will affect all of us then every young person should be prepared now; or should it take the view that these changes will have a different effect, both in time and place, and that therefore we should be prepared for change only when there are particular effects relevant to us as individuals?

While the choices are not as stark as the questions suggest, it is vital to take a view now on the needs of young people, and determine the priority tasks.

On the matter of 'who is the curriculum for?', we have seen for too long a division in curricular structure where value judgements have been made to the effect that there is a category called academically able young people who require to be stretched in preparation for higher education. They do not require vocational education since they will not 'work' and they do not require social education since their own ability, extra-curricular provision, and support from the home will take care of that need. The converse value judgement is to the effect that there are less-able young people who cannot achieve sufficient cognitive mastery for university, who do not partake of extra-curricular provision and who lack home support. For them, a social curriculum is required. And since they will be workers or unemployed in preparation for work, a vocational curriculum is also required.

These value judgements have resulted in the low status of social and vocational studies in schools and colleges, in the low status ascribed to professionals such as engineers, and the oft-quoted path to leadership in industry and commerce which is open to accountants and lawyers more often than to engineers and scientists. These phenomena and others are directly associated, by some writers, with the relative economic standings of Britain and the Federal Republic of Germany.

If social and technological change will require us to reverse the status position of the academic and vocational curricula, or at least to bring them into balance, then the priority would seem to be vocational preparation for all. That in turn would require a different balance to teacher education, both in content and methods, and a re-examination of the entry requirements to higher education since, without these two changes, it would be unreasonable to expect parents to invest in vocational preparation.

On the matter of whether vocational preparation is primarily concerned with the manual and associated intellectual skills which have dominated the further education curriculum, or the social and emotional skills which have dominated community education, there is clear evidence of conflict at present.

Taking a short-term view suggests that young people who leave school at the age of 16 are primarily motivated by the desire to enter full-time employment or training which leads to some specific range of occupations. That view demands a curriculum in post-school education which is at best job-specific or at worst, occupation-family specific, and which appeals to young people because it allows practice in skills which they see existing in the present labour market.

The trouble with the short-term is that it leads to a backlash from the young people involved and to a backwash extending to younger people who might be considering the same curriculum. These effects occur because at the end of the specific, job-oriented course it is realised that the jobs which have been aimed for are not available to most of the learners and, further, by concentrating on a narrow range of jobs, the learning or training has effectively closed off other entry points to the labour market.

A further element which enters into the short-term view is the political pressure from government to be seen to be doing something about jobs. In their view that means distorting the curriculum towards jobs (which in effect do not exist) and towards the visible, i.e. practical, aspects of employable skills.

The longer-term view, on the other hand, tries to distinguish between young person wants and young person needs. It is willing to take the risk of having an initial lack of motivation in young people by facing them with a curriculum which does not promise a face-value correspondence between the learning and present jobs.

The longer-term view derives from speculation about the future shape of society and the economy. That speculation leads to a number of conclusions such as:

- full-time employment will continue to fluctuate at between 80% and 90% of those available for work
- information technology will, at worst, aggravate the unemployment trends and, at best, provide more opportunities for people to take a larger part in their society, both in its decision-making and in its social services aspect
- those who are employed will find the content of their jobs changing regularly
- employment patterns will be characterised by frequent job-changing

Out of all of these, a picture is created of the need to create a curriculum which enhances those skills of decision-making, flexibility, and problem-solving which some new society requires rather than a curriculum which enhances the narrow range of practical and personal skills associated with conventional job-holding.

The alternative curriculum which one view of vocational preparation permits is not incompatible with the desires of government. Like all good vocational preparation it will be experience-based and practical, it will be open to all young people and it should, in the long run, create more jobs. The present system of vocational education and training creates shortages and surpluses of labour by trying to match training capacity to manpower needs (an impossible task), or by training for stock. The alternative system would break free of that morass by training for adaptability and transfer so that, as new manpower needs emerged, there were always people available with the disposition and capability to be trained for these new needs.

That line of argument then throws light on how we should approach the challenge of information technology. Any training approach to social and technological change is always embarrassed when the demands of the labour market change faster than the training system can cope, either in producing personnel or in utilising equipment. That potential embarrassment is all the greater in a situation such as information technology where we have gone from first-generation to fourth-generation hardware in the twinkling of an eye.

The task of vocational preparation therefore is to identify the underlying skills in using information technology and to separate these from the skills which are peculiar to this year's equipment or applications. It is important to identify the dangers in over-specialising in information technology. Some of the dangers have already come to pass in schools and colleges where computers and associated hardware are seen in one of two ways - a means of training computer specialists or a means of increasing the cognitive mastery in subject areas such as mathematics, physics, geography, etc. Each of these applications ignores two further and more important applications - information technology as a means of facilitating social skills such as discussion and problem-solving, and as a means of helping young people grasp the relationship between technological change and social change in the workplace.

In the case of information technology as an aid to the development of social skills, care must be taken to link this with a continuing concern for the maintenance of good relationships within family groups and social groups. An extreme version of information technology would give priority to each of us sitting in isolation facing a screen and interacting with it, rather than using the person-machine interaction as a method of developing social skills for quick transfer to the interpersonal interaction of social and family life. In the case of information technology as a force for change in the workplace, its successful implementation does not require that all workers necessarily understand the technical working of their data source or machine tool, but it does require that workers are prepared for the changes in the way they work, the way they relate to fellow workers, their need to control the machines rather than *vice versa*.

While therefore it is heartening to see vocational preparation schemes such as YTS include topics like 'computer literacy' in the common core studies, it is discouraging to see teachers, lecturers and supervisors translate this into 'here is how the computer works'. Of much greater importance is to use the experience of working with information technology and its applications to help people reflect on and adapt to its implications and opportunities for themselves as people.

The discussion so far leads to the key question of how far vocational preparation should assume a uniform spread of social and technological change across a society. If we do make this assumption then clearly significant investment is required in national programmes designed to heighten awareness and speed up the development of expertise amongst all citizens. That seems to be what is intended by government bodies with an interest in promoting change. Their case seems to be founded on a premise about the impact across the country of pervasive media like television and its spin-offs, or an international economy, based on inter-dependent national economies.

Reality is somewhat different. Despite television and other unifying factors, some parts of countries are stubbornly different from other parts of countries. Despite 'a computer in every school' many young people will not be introduced to that tool of information technology. Despite 'the car built by robots' many jobs are barely affected by technological change.

If we have learned one thing from further education since the war, it is that 'training for stock' is a waste of time when the time between training and employment is long and when the training concentrates on specialist occupational skills rather than broader vocational skills. While retraining followed by a six months gap before the chance comes to use the new skills is tolerable, training one 17-year-old in specialist skills which he or she cannot use for four or five years, if ever, is not acceptable. The same lesson must, therefore, be learned from the current rush to impart information technology skills to everyone.

The solution rests on a careful diagnosis of the impact of change, possibly categorising it as follows:

(a) Most people will be faced with 'change X'
(b) Many people will be faced with 'change X'
(c) Few people will be faced with 'change X'

and then proceeding to work out the knock-on effects of particular changes so that we can establish how a change which directly affects a few people, nevertheless has a consequential impact on the lives of most others.

Such a diagnosis would produce a vocational preparation curriculum with a small core of change elements which everyone needs to be exposed to and two major branches representing direct impact and indirect impact respectively, with connections made between the two. For example, my children may be into a particular technology but require to be reminded of the effect that that overwhelming interest could have on our survival as a family, while my concern for the maintenance of the family should be flexible enough to accommodate the introduction to our home of any particular technology.

That at last brings us to the resolution of the distinction between diversity and commonality in post-school education. If we continue to practise diversity of provision to the extent we have during this century, and even since the introduction of comprehensive schooling, we will exacerbate the social, political, racial and geographic tensions which exist in societies. If, on the other hand, we see technological change as a means of raising the common competence and common stock of knowledge and understanding, we may reduce these tensions.

In curricular terms that implies an enlarged common core of knowledge, attitudes and skills across all education and training, within which the small common core of new technology skills resides, and a core to ensure that even when programmes of study diverge into specialisms, each specialism not only takes account of local needs but above all retains a measure of common 'social' or 'technological' content with other specialisms.

The uses of information technology and other aspects of technological change must be steered away from a tool for governments to use in mass propagandising, and for capitalists to use in creating an international mass of identikit consumers, towards a tool which, when placed in the hands of individuals, enables them to enhance their personal identity within a liberal social consensus.

New technology and vocational preparation have been misunderstood and misapplied so far. They have to be subjected to close scrutiny and seen as a means of producing a curricular change where commonality based on social need dominates diversity based on technological need.

Youth Unemployment: A Review of the Literature

12

by Adrian Furnham

Since the early 1970s, when the problem became most acute, there have been a number of important studies in youth unemployment (Baxter, 1975; Fowler, Littlewood and Madigan 1976; Roberts, Duggan and Noble, 1982; Main and Raffe, 1983). Many of these have looked at the same factors - health, self-esteem, causal explanations - that have been investigated in the adult population, but some have been quite specific to young people.

The underlying causes of increased youth unemployment are of course manifold. They include demographic factors (change in the birth rate and an extension of the school career), micro and macro economic changes (change in technology, different productivity agreements) and educational and training factors (the relevance and appropriateness of education). Changes in youth unemployment are naturally associated with changes in adult unemployment but move with a greater amplitude. It has been calculated that if the unemployment rate for males rises by 1 per cent, the unemployment rate for young males under 20 years (excluding school leavers) rises by 1.7 per cent (Makeham 1980). Compared with other groups, young people change jobs more often or start without jobs, hence, as the recession deepens and recruitment is cut, young people are among the most vulnerable.

Psychological adjustment

A number of studies have looked at the emotional, social and psychological adjustment of unemployed school leavers. Using a questionnaire developed from the ideas of the neo-psychoanalytic thinker, Erikson, Gurney (1980a) looked at over 400 unemployed Australian school leavers. It was hypothesized that having a job helps school leavers to clarify their perception of their identity, and not being able to get work leads to a confused perception of self or no development due to a moratorium. The hypothesis was confirmed for females but not males. Furthermore, the unemployed males showed a significant shift towards the mistrust pole of the first dimension of *trust-mistrust*, and the employed of both sexes shifted significantly on the *industry-inferiority* subscale. He concludes "... it seems reasonable to conclude that unemployment has the effect of inhibiting development in school leavers, rather than inflicting trauma as is sometimes popularly supposed" (p. 212). Gurney (1980b) also found that over a 4-month period after leaving school, self-esteem increased only for those young people who obtained work.

More recently, Donovan and Oddy (1982) investigated the social and emotional development of a small, but carefully matched, group of employed and unemployed school leavers. They found that school leavers who were unemployed were more depressed and anxious, had lower self-esteem and poorer subjective well-being, were less well socially adjusted and showed a higher incidence of minor psychiatric morbidity than school leavers who had acquired jobs. They also found a significant interaction between employment status and gender on the locus of control scale - unemployed males tend to be more external than employed males, whereas these differences were minimal for females. They write: "Certainly the apathy and hopelessness frequently associated with unemployment could be linked to an increased tendency to attribute events to uncontrollable forces" (p. 24).

Similarly, Feather (1982) found both male and female, young, unemployed people had higher depression scores, lower self-esteem and Protestant Work Ethic, and reported that good and bad outcomes to everyday events were less important to them compared with employed male subjects. He notes:

> These results therefore indicate that both lower self-esteem and less effort to find a job were associated with increasing time out of work. They also show that the active pursuit of employment tended to be more frequent among those with higher self-esteem, stronger Protestant Ethic values and higher levels of concern about positive and negative events (lower apathy). But frequency of job search was lower among those unemployed who reported more depressive symptoms. These findings may imply a sort of reciprocal determinism in which the state of continued unemployment has effects on the person, and the person, so modified by his or her experience, begins to behave in ways that alter the probability of finding a job (p. 320).

Stafford (1982) examined the impact of the Youth Opportunities Programme (devised to offer 16-18 year-olds opportunities for training and work experience to increase employment prospects) on young people's employment prospects and psychological well-being. She found a significant improvement in employment prospects after participation in the scheme, which also acts as a buffer against any detrimental effects of unemployment. However, the beneficial effects of the programme do not last and the detrimental effects of unemployment return for those ex-trainees who remain unemployed.

Other studies have noted the medical and psychological health costs of being unemployed. In Britain, Banks, Clegg, Jackson, Kemp, Stafford and Wall (1980) gave 647 recent school leavers the General Health Questionnaire (GHQ) - a self-administered screening test for detecting minor psychiatric disorders. There was a large significant difference between those unemployed (3.78) and those employed (1.27), but there were no significant sex differences. Further analysis showed that although the unemployed scored higher on the GHQ, this relationship was moderated by their motivation to work, such that the unemployed with a high motivation to work scored higher than those with lower work motivation. Similarly, in an American study, Greenberger, Steiner and Vaux (1981) compared the health and behavioural consequences of 16-18 year-old schoolchildren who had part-time jobs to those who had never worked. Although they recognized the potentially positive influence on adolescents, their work focused on the costs of job stress. Their study focused on self-reported frequency of psychological and physical health symptoms, school absence, and the use of cigarettes, alcohol, marijuana, and other things. The results indicated that the working youths (especially boys) reported fewer somatic symptoms than the non-working youths, and that even boys who worked under stressful job conditions report fewer somatic and psychological symptoms than boys who hold less stressful jobs. However, the results did show that exposure to job stress is related to alcohol and marijuana use for both boys and girls. The authors proposed four explanations for their finding that work is associated with fewer symptoms in boys but more in girls: differential selection (hardier boys are likely to take more stressful jobs); differential attrition (hardier boys are likely to remain at stressful jobs while those less sturdy are likely to leave); differential reporting about health (boys who work under stress are less likely to report health problems than are girls); and sex differences in socialization (boys are led to expect more stress than girls).

Other studies have been concerned with the effect of youth unemployment on rapid labour turnover and delinquency. For instance, Baxter (1975) studied chronic job changers in the early 1970s. Job changers tended to be less intelligent, more neurotic, from poorer homes, and less socially and occupationally skilled than their counterparts who did not change jobs so rapidly. However, Raffe (1983), in a study of employment instability in young people, found that although instability was generated more by occupational than personal factors (unstable jobs not unstable workers), their chances of finding new employment depended on personal factors more than on their earlier occupational experiences. Similarly, Raelin (1981) found that early career unemployment is not a critical factor in retarding personal economic growth (relative to educational background and first job experience), but does have negative job attitudinal consequences. Young males who are early entrants in the labour force and who spend the bulk of their work in part-time employment do as well economically, and better occupationally, in their later work experience than do full-time employed youth.

Millham, Bullock and Hosie (1978), in a study of over a 1000 boys in approved schools, found that employment experiences were a crucial factor in promoting economic and social well-being. Though the authors were careful not to draw causal links between unemployment and delinquency, they did find that regular work did build up offending boys' confidence, changed their job aspirations, enhanced their self-perceptions and remotivated their interest in numeracy and literacy.

The problem with nearly all the studies on youth unemployment and psychological adjustment is that one cannot infer cause - only correlation. That is, it is quite possible that poor psychological adjustment leads to a young person being unemployed, rather than the other way around. The only study that attempted a longitudinal analysis of the problem, however, yielded ambiguous results. Warr, Jackson and Banks (1982) interviewed two cohorts of recent school leavers over a 2-year period and found that measures of psychological stress and self-esteem were found to be correlated with the duration of unemployment for young men. In one cohort of women, the young people appeared to be better adjusted the longer they were unemployed, apparently because of their reduced commitment to the labour market along with a stronger personal involvement in family matters. The authors offer two compatible explanations for their puzzling findings - the association between well-being and length of unemployment may differ between age groups (older people with more commitments may experience greater distress) and, secondly, that longer periods of unemployment than those studied in this study (over a year) lead to distress.

Similarly, Banks and Jackson (1982) interviewed two age cohorts of young people up to 2 $^1/_2$ years after leaving school to investigate the association between unemployment and risk of minor psychiatric morbidity. They found a positive relationship between unemployment and morbidity after controlling for sex, ethnic group and educational qualifications. Further longitudinal analyses showed that the experience of unemployment was more likely to create increased psychological symptoms, rather than the reverse. More recently, Jackson, Stafford, Banks and Warr (1983) studied longitudinally two cohorts of young people in the first 3 years of their working lives. They found, as predicted, that psychological distress is higher for the unemployed than for the employed, and that changes in employment status lead to changes in distress score. Furthermore, this relationship is moderated by the person's commitment to work - the more committed suffer more from the experience of unemployment.

Attribution and expectation about employment and unemployment

Although there have been some studies of adult explanations of unemployment (Furnham, 1982a, 1983), considerably less work has gone into establishing young people's beliefs about, and actual attempts at, getting a job. Feather and Davenport (1981) tested their expectancy valence theory on young people: a person's actions are seen to be related to the expectations that a person holds *and* to the subjective values of the outcomes that might occur following the action. They found, as predicted, that higher motivated, more depressed, unemployed youths blamed stable external factors for unemployment and rated the attractiveness of work more highly than less depressed youths. Although incompatible with learned helplessness theory, the results supported their theory which assumes that positive motivation to seek employment is identical to the multiplicative combination of expectancy of success in getting a job *and* the perceived net attractiveness of unemployment. They note:

> One might assume that work will have stronger positive valence for individuals with strong Protestant ethic values than for those people for whom these values are weaker. If this assumption is valid, then it follows that people with a strong Protestant ethic value will be more persistent in their efforts to get a job and that they will suffer more negative effects if they fail to obtain employment (p. 337).

Gurney (1981) in fact examined the attributions for the causes of unemployment in both employed and unemployed groups of school leavers. In a first study he attempted to discover, among a population of Australian school leavers, whether the unemployed differed in their attributions of employment from those who succeeded in getting work and, secondly, whether any differences were antecedent to, or consequent upon, unemployment. Subjects were asked to ascribe the ability to get work either to internal or external factors to the job seekers, and to fill out a simple eight-item scale devised by the author. He found that unemployed males attributed both getting *and* not getting work significantly more to external factors as has been found previously, but there were no differences in the female groups. Gurney suggested that the lack of differences among the female groups may be due to their lesser defensiveness and need to blame external factors for being unemployed. In a second longitudinal study, students were given a 12-item attribution-for-getting-jobs questionnaire prior to leaving school and again approximately 4 months later.

He suggested that:

> The unemployed may believe themselves powerless to change the circumstances of their lives (external locus) but the fact that they are without work, whereas others are not, and that they remain so may lead them eventually to see themselves as responsible for their condition (internal attribution) with consequent self-blame and self-derogation (p. 89).

The results showed that prior to leaving school the groups did not differ, yet later it was not the unemployed who changed their attributions, but the employed who shifted significantly toward a more internal set of causal ascriptions. Overall, Gurney (1981) seemed unable to account for his "counter-intuitive and unexpected" findings, suggesting perhaps that subjects of this age have their self-esteem based on numerous other things such as parental evaluation and peer group's approval, rather than exclusively on work which is more often the case with adults.

In a rather different study, Dayton (1981) looked at the way in which young people looked for a job. He set out to determine what job-seeking approaches were being used by young people and what factors they found positive and useful (aids) and what negative and worthless (barriers) in a job search. Using a population of 250 young Americans, Dayton found they regarded their own positive personal attributes (personality, flexibility, academic ability) as the most important aids in their job, and external factors (labour unions, welfare and unemployment insurance, government training programmes) as least important. Employment success and satisfaction was correlated with careful analysis of which job suited them best, the assemblance of a placement file, letters of recommendation and a c.v., combined with persistence in the job search.

Research within the framework of attribution theory would, however, lead one to make a number of predictions about school childrens' expectations and beliefs about getting a job (Furnham, 1982a, 1982b, 1983). For instance, people more prone to unemployment, and the unemployed themselves, tend to make more external attributions for the causes of unemployment, in contrast to those in jobs and unlikely to become unemployed. Furthermore, studies have shown that external attributions are to some extent protective of self-esteem in the context of achievement. Hence, Furnham (1984) predicted that females more than males and working-class subjects more than middle-class subjects - for whom unemployment is statistically more probable - will be prone to make more external attributions about getting a job. Further, it was suggested that these attributions will also be reflected in the number and type of job-search strategies adopted by young people and the barriers and aids that they consider operate in job-hunting success. In this study, Furnham set out to examine sex and class differences in 240 British school leavers' attributions about unemployment, the most and least job-search strategies, and which school course they believed most and least useful in getting a job. The results of the four different parts of this study suggest that, overall, attributions about getting a job are frequently internal (i.e. to personal attributes or abilities) rather than environmental or societal factors. Confidence, perseverance and qualifications were all considered to be primary factors responsible for success in finding employment, yet this is moderated by the belief that jobs are not currently available (a fact which is attributed to the government). Yet failure to get a job was rarely attributed to the personal short-comings of the job-seeker himself. Thus, these results tend to support the well established, attributional finding that success is attributed to internal factors and failure to external factors.

Where there were significant sex differences, it was found that females were more external in their attributions than males. This conflicts with Gurney (1981), who found that unemployed males were more external in their attributions about employment than employed males, but that there were no differences between employed females. However, the extensive locus of control literature has shown that where sex differences exist in generalized locus of control beliefs, females are more external than males. Similarly, class differences tended to show that working-class subjects tend to place more emphasis on structural or external factors (Furnham, 1982a). Again this is to be expected and in accordance with previous literature on the topic (Furnham and Gunter, 1984).

The results on the aids and barriers confirms the findings of Dayton (1981), who found that the subjects saw their own personal attributes as the greatest aids and external factors as the biggest hindrances. Similarly, regarding strategies, class and sex differences showed that the middle class tended to rate all job-hunting strategies as more useful than the working class, and girls showed less faith in following up specific job choices than boys. The subjects all stressed the importance of summer and after-school work for experience, but tended to rely on personal contacts rather than direct approaches to employers. It would be interesting to compare these beliefs with those of employers, who may have quite different beliefs concerning which factors make an applicant more employable. The belief in the usefulness of A-level courses revealed that both males and females believed science courses (and English) were the most useful in getting a job, although females tended to opt for arts courses and males for science at A-level. Females also believed that arts courses were more useful than science courses, so providing a rationalization for the choice. However, a study such as this was unable to determine whether females chose arts subjects and then felt it necessary to justify their choice, or whether they actually believed them to be most useful per se and hence selected them accordingly. It is of course also possible that when candidates select a particular course they do so for many reasons, only one of which is its usefulness for getting a job. Further, the believed importance of science courses may reflect recent government emphasis and funding towards the "hard" sciences, rather than the arts or social sciences. These results also indicate that attributions are to some extent a function of the expectation of work.

Education about unemployment

Because it has become so widespread, various researchers have argued for some sort of education about the problems and prospects of unemployment. Some (Stirling, 1982) have gone so far as to suggest that we need to prepare school leavers for unemployment, arguing that because as many as one-third of school leavers in Britain (in 1982-83) may experience unemployment they need to know what to anticipate and how to cope. Furthermore, high levels of youth unemployment have produced a questioning of, and disenchantment with, the whole education system (Hargreaves, 1981).

Darcy (1978) argued that young people need to be educated in all aspects of job-sharing and to be encouraged to have a new definition of work, to include not only paid employment but a variety of other activities. To this end he believes a careers education programme should involve such topics as the mechanics of collecting benefits, the acquisition of job-seeking skills, the experience of unemployment, leisure and community roles, and the politics of the right to work. Watts (1978) also considered the implications of school-leaver unemployment for careers education in schools. He argues that careers educators have not seriously dealt with the problem of unemployment because they do not feel competent to tackle it effectively; they are aware of its highly political and emotional overtones; it might affect deleteriously the work ethic within and outside the school; and because the teachers feel instinctively hostile to the concept of preparation for unemployment. A number of possible curricular objectives are listed, including equipping children with employability, survival and leisure skills. Four alternative aims are described, depending on whether one is focussing on: change in society (to help students see unemployment as a phenomenon resolved by social and political measures); change in the individual (to maximize students' chances of finding meaningful employment); status quo in the society (to reinforce students' motivation to seek work); and status in the individual (to make students aware of the possibility of unemployment and how best to cope with it). Many of the educational responses and strategies are dependent on whether one believes unemployment to be voluntary (aversion of the will to work), cyclical (cycles of recession and expansion) or structural (a major change in the relationship between capital and labour). These solutions may include a deeper inculcation of the work ethic, job creation schemes, etc. Careers education is seen as the education of central life interests and personal growth and development, rather than the matching of people to (non-existent) jobs.

As a practical measure, Lavercombe and Fleming (1981) attempted to identify (by using attitude measures) those schoolchildren at risk of longer periods of unemployment and hence in particular need of support, information and skills. Although they found that their measures did not predict which pupils would take longest to find jobs, they believed all pupils should be prepared for unemployment. Their results suggested that employers have little confidence in what teachers report concerning expected examination results, attendance records or attitudes to school authority or work, when selecting among young applicants.

Fleming and Lavercombe (1982), in a study of 29 professionals working with young people, found that the professionals varied considerably in their topics and approaches. The sort of topics discussed by the professionals in schools were: whether work itself is the major basis of self-respect and how the unemployed can compensate; how to spend one's leisure/free time; the mechanics of claiming supplementary benefits; and possibilities of continuing education and the politics of unemployment. In talking with unemployed school leavers after school, the professionals believed their primary role was giving support while being as honest as possible. They also believed that their activities helped combat boredom and anxiety, helped the young get a job, and helped personal development. The professional who believed that there was a chance of a youth's return to work emphasized job-seeking and -keeping skills, while those who were more pessimistic about the future of work concentrated on developing survival skills suitable for the unemployed. This seemed a basic division among the professionals, some of whom believed their job was primarily to help young people get a job, and others who believed it was to help young people cope and amuse themselves because they never had a job. Not surprisingly, many of the professionals seemed depressed and exhausted by a job that confronted so starkly the discrepancy between young people's aspirations and the lack of jobs available.

More recently, Coffield (1984) has considered the future for the whole of education in a world without jobs. He suggests that young people are learning to live with unemployment as a result of moving in and out of jobs and government schemes. Furthermore, he notes how the education system and particular schools should be willing to adapt their curriculum for new circumstances. He proposed a new organisation formed by schools, universities and colleges of education that would translate research findings into industrial terms and vice versa; give educational institutions rapid and reliable feedback on the general and specific skills needed by young workers at the beginning of their careers; and use latest research findings to update educational curricula.

Thus:

> in return for a steady stream of articulate, literate and numerate young workers
> and managers with the appropriate skills, local industry would pay to keep both
> the University and local schools in the vanguard of progress (p. 41).

Although somewhat optimistic, this visionary but practical approach appears to be necessary to help prepare young people for the future.

Job choice and work experience in the young

High rates of unemployment naturally affect school leavers' perceptions, expectations and experiences of employment. Although it has often been suggested that modern youth are reluctant to accept menial and non-menial employment, have lost the willingness to work, and are no longer believers in the Protestant Work Ethic, studies have shown this not to be the case (Borus 1982). One example of young people's eagerness to work is the number of part-time jobs that they have. There has been a general assumption that working teaches young people "responsibility", fosters "social cooperation" and helps in the attainment of new and important job skills, though there is not a great deal of hard evidence in support of this (Rugguro and Steinberg, 1981).

As Stafford and Jackson (1981) have pointed out, the literature on the transition from school to work has been derived from two approaches - the psychological, which stresses individual choice in work, and the sociological, which sees entry to work as a process of allocation.

A case study of 24 young people's work aspirations and job-seeking in an area of high unemployment showed that it is through the job-search process that young people learn about the accessibility of jobs when these influence their aspirations. Because families and friends are so important in the job-search process, young people from unemployed or unsupportive families are most at risk. This suggests the importance of the family in the choice of job, the ability to get a job, and the coping strategies used while unemployed.

However, search-for-work strategies are in part a consequence of opportunities and experience. Education, age and race might act in favour or against young people getting work. In a study of immigrant school leavers' search for work, Fowler et al. (1976) found a larger proportion of native Britons had access to, and enters, the "primary labour-market" through jobs with formal training, relatively good pay and promotion prospects than did immigrants who were relegated to the secondary market. They found that explanations in terms of unrealistic aspirations or inadequate job-hunting strategies are satisfactory in only a minority of cases, while discrimination seemed the most obvious explanation.

Values

School leavers develop aspirations about the types of jobs that they would like. These aspirations - or work values - can and do affect their job satisfaction and personal adjustment. Where there is a large discrepancy in such things as skill utilization, influence and job variety there is likely to be a high incidence of job dissatisfaction. Various studies have shown that the unemployed feel progressively less able to use their abilities and influence their environment in order to obtain desired outcomes.

Dowling and O'Brien (1981) predicted that school leavers who had experienced a significant period of unemployment would lower their desired levels of skill-utilization, influence and variety in employment. They administered a questionnaire to 652 Australian school leavers and then again a year later when some were employed, some unemployed and some in further education. They found that the employed showed a significant increase in their desire for skill utilization but no change in desired influence and variety, while the students showed an increase in all these work values. Contrary to their prediction, there was no significant change in the work values of those unemployed. These results are explained in terms of methodological errors or insufficient attention to individual differences. Rump (1983) has argued that in the study of unemployed and employed young people one needs to:

> distinguish those whose unemployment has been tempered by earlier employment from those who have never been in work; those studying by reason of preference from those studying only by reason of failure to obtain employment and those in employment who have been so for most of their post-school experience from those currently working who have nevertheless been unemployed for a long period prior to obtaining work (p. 90).

Dowling and O'Brien (1983) reanalysed their data in line with Rump's suggestions, but found no significant differences. Studies on adults have, however, shown a change in values as a consequence of unemployment.

Job interview training

One consequence of mass youth unemployment has been a focusing of attention on the job interview and the skills required in it. Many people became aware of the fact that because of skill deficits on the part of both interviewers and interviewees, potentially able candidates were getting rejected because of their poor performance in the job interview.

Subsequently, there has been a great deal of careful detailed work on the verbal and non-verbal skills required to be successful in a job interview setting (Hollandsworth, Glazeski and Dressel, 1977; Tessler and Sushelsky 1978; Hollandsworth, Kazelskis, Stevens and Dressel, 1979). Hood, Lindsay and Brooks (1982) allocated school leavers to either an interview training or discussion control group. The interview-training group received a combination of modelling, coaching, role play, feedback and discussion to train both verbal and non-verbal skills. Later, the school leavers were assessed using video-taped and role-played interviews which were made at the beginning and the end of each training phase. The trained group showed significant improvements on global, as well as specific, ratings: question asking and answering, fidgeting, smiling, eye contact, gesture, posture and interest compared to the control group. The researchers all demonstrated the generalization and maintenance of these treatment effects over time. In conclusion they noted:

> Studies that have been concerned with interview training for various populations of adolescents indicated that such training may have a worthwhile contribution to make in preparing them for seeking employment. In view of the current employment situation, performance in the interview is more critical than ever before and interview training may fulfil a preventive function in interrupting the process of failure in interview, lack of work experience, and further failure in interview, before it becomes entrenched and leads to other psychological problems (p. 592).

Heimberg, Cunningham, Stanley and Blacenberg (1982) conducted a similar study in America which aimed to investigate the effect of social skills training in preparing unemployed youth for the job interview. Firstly they conducted a series of detailed interviews with unemployed youths, their employment counsellors and potential employers to obtain information about the appropriate "target" behaviours in a job interview. Subjects were then given a trial run in order to determine how much training they needed. The performance of the training group was compared to two groups of controlled subjects - one *role* played the interviewee in an actual job interview. Although this study did have some limitations (only quasi-randomization of subjects to conditions), it was established that subjects receiving social skills training surpassed control subjects on a number of verbal paralinguistic and other measures employed in the role play assessment *and* overall performance as rated by an independent set of observers. Furthermore, role-play ratings at the post-testing session were found to moderately predict ratings by employers in the actual interview.

Although this interview training for young people is probably more an outgrowth of social skills training validation than a response to youth unemployment, it clearly will be of considerable use to prospective job applicants.

Conclusions

Research on youth unemployment is scattered across a wide number of disciplines: economics, education, psychology (clinical, educational, occupational, social) and sociology. Nevertheless it can be divided roughly into two areas: those studies concerned with the cause and consequences of youth unemployment, and those studies concerned with preparing or training young people for unemployment and employment respectively.

As in nearly every area of social science research, the results are equivocal; nevertheless, various themes emerge. For instance, studies on the psychological consequences of unemployment tend to point in the same direction - namely that unemployment causes stress, a lowering of self-esteem and a change in expectations. Similarly the work on attributions and expectations has revealed some consistent findings. Taken together, the literature implies a vicious circle for the unemployed school leaver. If, for any reason, the young person is unable to find a job, he or she might loose self-esteem, become physically ill and might change expectations of getting a job. Lowered job expectations will no doubt affect job-search strategies which in turn lower the probability of getting a job, so confirming the belief. Hence a self-fulfilling prophecy or reciprocal determinism (Feather, 1982) may account for the despair of many school leavers.

The literature on education and training is clearer and more optimistic. Older educational topics and values are being challenged, though there remains some disagreement about the precise direction in which we should move. On the other hand, there is close agreement and a moderate degree of success in the training of young people for job interviews.

Although research in this area is comparatively recent, difficult and expensive, this is no excuse for poor studies. One reason for the equivocal, ambiguous and unconfirmed findings is clearly methodological. Certainly individual differences need to be taken more into account. There are three categories of individual differences which need to be controlled for in experimentation in this area. Firstly, there are *psychological* differences in *personality, self concept, beliefs* (e.g. work ethic), etc. of young people before and after any unemployment, or employment, experiences. Secondly, there are *demographic* differences in *age, sex, national group, religion, schooling* etc. which condition any young person's world view, expectations, etc. Thirdly, there are work experience differences in that some young people have had *full-* or *part*-time work experience, *voluntary* work experience, and *no work* experience. Each and all of these variables have been examined in one or other of the above studies. The problem has been that in concentrating on one variable others have been ignored or, worse still, confounded. The reactions of young people to unemployment seem sufficiently different to those of adults, and are clearly of utmost importance in their adjustment to the adult world, to merit good research.

State Policy And Employment

B

by Ian Shirley

To the ancient Greeks work was a curse, a brutalizing of the mind conditioning "man" and making him unfit for a truthful and virtuous life - it was a necessary material evil which any visionary elite should avoid. Similarly, the Hebrews thought of work as a painful necessity, the product of original sin - it was the means by which human beings might atone for their sins and cooperate in the redemption of the world. Luther went further - he identified work as the base and key of life, the underlying assumption being that perfection in one's work was the best way to serve God.

Whilst these and other perceptions of work have altered over time, the most dramatic change occurred with the advent of capitalism and with what Keane and Owens (1986) refer to as "The Employment Society". By employment society is meant a certain 'mode of production' in which work is conceived as a commodity to be bought and sold in the market place along with other commodities. Work in this sense is synonymous with a particular type of employment, namely that which conditions individuals to sell their capacities to employers in return for some form of remuneration. Although the mediation of capital and labour interests is highly specific to each country, the capitalist State has played an increasingly significant role in the formulation of employment policies and in responding to the escalation of unemployment in the wake of the world recession.

This chapter sets out to examine the role of State employment policies during the 1970's and 80's as the global economy went into recession. The focus is not on the nature of this recession, but rather on the alternative policies adopted by nation States in response to the international crisis.

Capitalism and the State

In order to examine the degree and nature of State involvement in our social and political lives, it is necessary to trace what Habermas (1975) refers to as the two historical tendencies which have radically altered contemporary forms of advanced capitalism. These tendencies are - the escalating power of the State and the transformation of science and technology. Habermas addresses both issues by tracing the origins of capitalism from its philosophic base through to the systematic use of science as an ideological instrument of the State and in this process he identifies four social formations.

The first of these formations is defined as primitive in that familial and tribal structures played a crucial role in bringing order to the social and political lives of the citizenry. Change was related to factors such as age and ecology, with dependency between tribes subject to economic exchange, war and conquest. World views and norms were integrated with rituals and taboos and the satisfaction of basic needs such as food and shelter appeared to be the major motivating factor in the production of goods.

With the advent of traditional societies there was a shift from familial forms of organization in the production and distribution of social wealth, to private ownership of the means of production. The kinship system surrendered its central functions of power and control to the State. In the course of this transfer, the family lost all of its economic functions and some of its socializing functions. With private ownership of the means of production, a power relationship was established which allowed the privileged class to appropriate the socially produced wealth and along with appropriation came class repression and the exploitation of labour. These conditions led eventually to the transformation of the political system and to what Habermas refers to as liberal capitalism.

During the early stages of liberal capitalism, the State played a somewhat limited role, mainly concerning itself with providing the conditions under which the market economy might expand and flourish. Although State and private sectors appeared to be independent of one another, the State received its power from the economy and in turn, the polity used its knowledge to extend the interests of capital. These interests advanced the notion of 'fair exchange' between capital and labour as the epitome of individual freedom and competition.

By the early 20th century the system was in crisis. A series of depressions culminating in the Great Depression of the early 1930's brought the crisis to a head and the State re-engaged the economy. Instead of acting as a complimentary organization to free-ranging market forces, the State became directly involved in economic policy. It began to establish long term and non-competitive contracts with the market sector in areas such as defence. It set up a system of incentives and subsidies for capital. It guaranteed the financial sector against collapse. It nationalized certain elements of economic life and it actually replaced the market in non-profitable sectors, thus creating and improving conditions for the realization of capital.

During the development of what might be referred to as monopoly capitalism, old class conflicts were absorbed into the structure of the Welfare State. Arbitration and mediation systems were developed and pension plans emerged. The apparatus of welfare in the form of social security payments, health and education services, unemployment benefits, state housing and compensatory payments of one sort or another were designed to deal with the worst excesses of market forces.

At the same time, increasing State involvement in both production and distribution highlighted the conflict of interests between socialized production and private appropriation. As the State was now actively engaged in the reproductive process, it had to find a way in which it might balance the contradictory interests of accumulation and legitimation. This was achieved with varying degrees of success by advancing the State as an independent arbiter representing the public interest and the common good and thus politics was portrayed as being largely irrelevant in the light of such 'benign' administrations. Questions which were regarded as political matters in previous times were now defined as technical issues requiring objective, scientific analysis and resolution.

This process of legitimation clearly required a particular form of science which treated knowledge as a politically neutral commodity devoid of value imputations. In essence, it corresponded with the 'mainstream' tradition in that it accepted existing economic and social relations and in line with the natural sciences it sought to organize the world into discrete categories for the purposes of accurate description. By adopting this form of science, State practitioners were able to define social phenomena such as unemployment in narrow technical terms, thus excluding the possibility of political action.

In contrast to this mainstream position, 'critical' theorists maintain that it is epistemologically impossible to distinguish between fact and value in analysing and describing human development. Whereas mainstream theorists distinguish between belief and technique in the tradition of the natural sciences, the critical tradition argues that all language is socially constructed. This means that the very categories by which we describe and interpret human behaviour arise out of specific social and political situations and even where we use a technical language we are fabricating categories which are rooted in values and beliefs. As we examine the different ways in which national states respond to the economic crisis of the 1970's and 80's, the significance of these value and belief systems will become apparent.

State Responses to the Global Recession

The economic achievements of the global economy during the 1950's and 60's created what Armstrong *et al.* (1984) have called the golden age of capitalism. The post-war economic boom made it possible for western states to develop a concern with distribution as well as production and with social wellbeing as well as material progress. Many believed that it was feasible to build welfare States unmarred by conflicts such as gender, class and race and in America Daniel Bell (1973) confidently predicted an end to ideological and political differences.

A broad consensus certainly appeared to be established right across the political spectrum and although this consensus varied from country to country, the major political parties generally accepted the notion of a mixed economy - that is a capitalist system of production and distribution with the State accepting responsibility for economic policy and the enhancement of social welfare. Trade unions secured employment as a component of the social wage and workers responded to these assurances by accepting capitalist ownership and control. Employers' associations tolerated workers' rights and provisions in return for a profitable economic environment and governments of all political persuasions planned for economic growth and for a future of apparent affluence. Political consensus was based on widespread public confidence and this in turn helped maintain accumulation. Accumulation generated jobs, regular increases in living standards and resources for welfare as well as profits - these factors in turn reproduced the consensus.

By the end of the 1970's, the consensus was fractured. Production slowed and unemployment soared. These conditions represented what Armstrong *et al.* (1984) have called an overaccumulation crisis in relation to the labour supply - a crisis marked by excess productive capacity and a decline in the rate of profit.

> The basic idea of overaccumulation is that capitalism sometimes generates a higher rate of accumulation than can be sustained and thus the rate of accumulation has eventually to fall. Towards the end of the post-war boom, an imbalance between accumulation and the labour supply led to increasingly severe labour shortages. The excess demand for labour generated a faster scrapping of old equipment. Real wages were pulled up and older machines rendered unprofitable, allowing a faster transfer of workers to the new machines. This could in principle have occurred smoothly: as profitability slid down, accumulation could have declined gently to a sustainable rate. But the capitalist system has no mechanism guaranteeing a smooth transition in such circumstances. In the late 60's the initial effect of overaccumulation was a period of feverish growth, with rapidly rising wages and prices and an enthusiasm for get-rich-quick schemes. These temporarily masked, but could not suppress, the deterioration in profitability. Capitalist confidence was undermined, investment collapsed and a spectacular crash occurred. Overaccumulation gave rise, not to a mild decline in the growth rate, but to a classic capitalist crisis. (Armstrong *et al*, 1984, p. 235).

Whilst the fundamental problematic is defined as the declining rate of profitability, it is important to note that the era of consensus did not substantially undermine the essential relationships underpinning capitalist economies. Despite the gains of the labour movement as reflected in welfare provisions and in moves towards industrial democracy, workers were still obliged to sell their labour power to employers and whilst the actions of these employers could be limited, they were not able to be controlled. The essential decisions over investment were taken by the owners of capital on the basis of private profitability. When this process of appropriation was interrupted during the 1970's, it produced steering problems for the advanced industrial societies and endangered social integration. Not only was the consensus shattered, but class differences were unmasked and in this process, the fundamental conflict over power was exposed.

As far as this chapter is concerned, the most interesting aspect of the breakdown of consensus centres on the way in which nation states responded to the international crisis. It is here that Goran Therborn's (1986) work is important because his primary objective was to explain why the economic crisis of the 1970's and 80's as encountered by different institutions and policies resulted in radically different rates of unemployment. By assembling national profiles for each country so that policies could be historically and culturally tuned to the particular context from which they were drawn, Therborn noted that "the gulf between high and low unemployment countries (was) widening" (Therborn, 1986, p.67). Whereas countries such as Belgium, the Netherlands, Britain, Canada and Denmark plunged into mass unemployment, Austria, Sweden, Norway, Japan and Switzerland were able to maintain unemployment rates of between 0 - 5% of the labour force.

By focussing on policy process as well as outcome, Therborn was able to expose a number of popular myths. These included the prevailing concern over public versus private sector development and export orientation versus domestic demand - as arguments they appeared to be fueled more by ideological heat than by scientific knowledge and analysis. Indeed, both opponents and proponents of the welfare state were criticized for selecting profit rates, levels of social expenditure and taxation or the size of public sector employment as key explanatory factors in comparative levels of unemployment. Whereas the Welfare State of Sweden, with generous social commitments and a relatively developed public control of the economy, had been extremely successful in maintaining full employment, Belgium, Denmark and the Netherlands which also have extensive social policies, were most unsuccessful. Of those countries which can be described as market states, Japan and Switzerland were successful, whereas Australia, Canada, Britain and the United States, were spectacularly unsuccessful.

It was also apparent at a general level that differences in the level of economic growth accounted for minor differences in the level of unemployment. The same was true of the numbers of people seeking work and as far as wage restraint was concerned this did not in itself lead to full employment or international competitiveness. Further myths were exposed when key tenets of right wing liberalism were examined. There was no significant relationship to be found between inflation and unemployment - in fact this relationship was close to zero - whilst factors such as labour costs, social expenditure and unemployment compensation were also relatively insignificant.

Therborn offers two main lines of explanation for the differential success rates of the sixteen nations. The first line of explanation centres on the economic and political history of these nations and suggests that during the cyclical troughs of the economic crisis, certain nations displayed a capacity and resolve to resist redundancies by institutionalizing a State commitment to full employment. These countries were Austria, Japan, Norway, Sweden and Switzerland - "the only low unemployment countries in the contemporary crisis"? (Therborn, 1986, p.23).

By contrast, nation states such as Belgium, The Netherlands and Britain followed restrictive monetary policies in an attempt to bring down inflation. Whereas the late Keynesian notion of an inflation/unemployment trade-off became widespread just before the onset of the crisis in the early seventies, the monetarist advisers to Thatcher and Reagan unconditionally accepted the notion of trade-off as a short term solution to their country's economic ills and gave priority to combating inflation. They implied that a rise in unemployment was necessary for economic success and these strategies were accompanied by ideological statements which have since become the hallmark of the New Right. Statements such as "cut down the public sector" and "strengthen the market" ensured legitimation for economic strategies which in turn provided the shortest and fastest route to mass unemployment.

The second line of explanation advanced by Therborn, focussed on policy constraints and pressures. By tracing macro economic and labour market policies over time, he was able to consider the pressures generated by factors such as the labour supply as well as constraints such as an imbalance in international trade. This line of argument negated the OECD (1977) emphasis on wages and prices and demonstrated that the five successful countries all developed a range of State intervention policies which were designed to promote full employment. In the Swedish case, these interventions took the form of active labour market policies based on special public works and public vocational training programmes. In Norway the State provided substantial public subsidies for private employment, a tradition that was established even before the development of North Sea oil.

In Japan, the emphasis centred on expanding public investment and on a publicly co-ordinated private labour market policy organized by the big industrial and business concerns. Behind the sustained growth and exports of Japan throughout the period of the recent economic crisis lay a comprehensive restructuring of Japanese industry; first from textiles then from ship building and steel into car making, electrical engineering, electronics and services. This restructuring programme took place without first making people redundant.

In Switzerland, policy makers concentrated on controlling the supply of immigrant labour and this was complimented in the Austrian case by a public investment programme and investment incentives. The State, in each of the successful five, had more power vis-a-vis international and national markets than was evident elsewhere and they avoided the stop-go policies and inconsistencies which characterised countries with high unemployment. The five successful countries all generated a remarkable national unity around a set of concrete policy priorities and this unity convinced the various parties involved in tripartite negotiations, that there would be consistency in the level and form of State intervention.

While the five roads to success were all different, several dominant factors in the fight against unemployment can be isolated. These factors can be summarized as follows:

- A commitment to full employment both as a political priority and as the dominant ethic of economic policy. The countries which were successful translated this policy objective into action and as such it was embodied in the policy making structures of both public and private enterprise.
- State intervention geared to productive investment, both public and private, was favoured over boosting consumer demand.
- Active labour market policy measures including public works, vocational training and special employment in public services. These measures were designed to adjust supply and demand factors in the labour market within a broader policy framework of full employment.
- The creation of part-time jobs with full social rights and in co-operation with the trade union movement was favoured over a general reduction in working time.
- A tax structure which reflected a trend away from pay-roll taxes and social contributions toward taxes on capital assets and consumption.
- A labour movement committed to technological change and job flexibility under conditions of full employment and to wage moderation under conditions of rising real wages.
- A conscious decision by all parties not to use high unemployment as a means

of securing other policy objectives.

Although the political persuasion of government had nothing to do with the success or otherwise of employment strategies, the five successful countries were all outside the common market and their economies were not deeply penetrated by foreign capital.

By summarizing those factors which promote employment and unemployment, it is possible to identify two alternative development paths which appear to be at the forefront of State policies in the 1980's. The first option as advocated by the New Right argues that market forces, the free exchange between capital and labour and competition between capitalists, is the only "natural" way to satisfy basic human needs. As a consequence, social phenomena such as unemployment are best resolved by leaving market forces to find their own solution.

The alternative option which can be classified as Left Revisionism is based on economic sovereignty, a secure domestic market and an institutional commitment to full employment. In policy terms, this means an emphasis on productive investment and a consistency of purpose both in terms of state intervention as well as in the fiscal and monetary policies being pursued. Whereas the New Right strategy induces mass loyalty, but avoids participation, the Revisionists seek a just, participatory and sustainable development path. In the Swedish context, this means "the whole people at work" because full employment is considered a necessary prerequisite for development.

The New Right and the Revisionist Left

In order to appreciate both the strengths and limitations of these development options, it is necessary to examine the theoretical frameworks and assumptions on which these strategies are based. As Dobb (1973) suggests, this means starting with those socio-economic conditions which shape the class relations of society. One of the more perceptive interpretations of class relations in the modern era is advanced by Jessop (1987) who describes the central feature of welfare capitalism as a mode of economic growth based upon a combination of mass production and mass consumption. This mode of growth was distinctive because it represented the first formation under capitalism which produced a productive alliance between capital and labour. The alliance was important in providing a strong material foundation for Keynesian economic policies committed to full employment and to the expansion of the welfare state. These expansionist policies ensured working people a share of the action on the basis of rising profitability, rising productivity and rising patterns of consumption.

By the 1970's the alliance between capital and labour could no longer be sustained. In order to counter the declining rate of profitability, international capital successfully demanded for itself trans-national mobility and the State played a significant role in this restructuring programme. Global "states" such as the International Monetary Fund and the World Bank created the conditions necessary for the restructuring of capital and within the western world, national States such as the United Kingdom, America, Australia and New Zealand aligned themselves with the philosophy of the New Right giving it a certain legitimacy.

In policy terms, the strategy of the New Right is based on flexible production with short runs of varied products oriented toward particular markets. Flexible production is based on highly differentiated patterns of consumption and it is associated with what Jessop refers to as portfolio lifestyles for the affluent. It is also associated with the inevitability of surplus populations. Whereas mass production and mass consumption are identified with the growing importance of the semi-skilled worker and with a leveling of income standards, differentiation is centred on a skill flexible core and a 'marginal less skilled, more part-time, sometimes in work, sometimes out of work, periphery'. (Jessop 1987). A central feature of this strategy is the subordination of all individuals to the logic of a free market in commodities. Traditional income and employment security is traded for a cheap, young and mobile workforce, a low wage regime and a highly speculative development path. Whereas the goals of this programme are defined in terms of efficiency, consumer choice and user pays, its means centre on a restrictive monetary policy, deregulation of the economy, the privatisation of the public sector and the dismantling of social services.

The theology of the New Right is an amalgam of three strands of thought. The first is the doctrine of economic individualism which assumes without question that markets are beneficial and governments harmful, and that individual freedom and government action exist in inverse ratio to each other. The second strand emanates out of extreme libertarianism, which bases its case for laissez faire capitalism on moral grounds and the third strand comes from Austrian economics and its disciples Schumpter and Hayek. The ideas are not new and the practices date back to anti-union pressure groups established before the Second World War.

The doctrine of economic individualism is based on the belief that the history of western civilisation is the history of free individuals engaged in intellectual thought. It is strongly rooted in the tradition of welfare economics, (Hunt, 1980) which maintains that all human behaviour is conditioned by the hedonistic aspirations of each individual wanting to maximize his/her productive capacities. It ignores the fact that individual desires are themselves the products of a particular social process and, in essence, it is an apologia for existing economic arrangements.

Even when advocates of economic individualism claim that they are motivated by progressive and humane intentions, they inevitably view individuals as one-dimensional beings committed to a basic moral position that exults infinite greed. It is a tradition which produces an ahistorical view of isolated, alienated competitors, thus ignoring their cultural history, the institutions they have established and the reality of power differentials.

Despite the flawed assumptions on which the New Right theology is based it has successfully changed the agenda for economic and social policy debates in the 1980's and this is where the monetarist theories of Milton Friedman have been significant. As Gamble (1986) observes, monetarism in the 1960's was merely one position in a technical debate on how best to stabilize the economy. It grew in favour along with the liberalisation of world trade and the internationalization of production. In a period of floating exchange rates and world recession, governments either had to adopt monetarist policies or contemplate stringent controls on trade and capital in order to insulate the domestic economy against international fluctuations. The rise in the influence of monetarism has to be understood against this background with the theoretical rationale based on one of the oldest ideas in economics, the quantity theory of money. It is this theory as defined by Barker (1982) which has important ramifications for employment. According to monetarists:

money is a unique asset which is held, in the long run, on a predictable and stable ratio to aggregate monetary expenditure. The government gives money its status and controls its supply so that proper control will determine aggregate expenditure. Since in the long run the economy will return to a natural full employment level from any temporary disturbance, monetary control will effectively determine the price level. The lag in this process is variable, with its most likely value between 1 and 2 years. In reducing the rate of inflation by this mechanism, some costs of adjustment are manifested as unemployment. But these costs will be reduced the more rapidly trade unions and workers adjust their expectations and accept lower wage increases (Barker, 1982 p.320).

Whereas the theoretical problems of monetarism centre upon the substitutability of money, the failure of markets to clear through price changes and the way expectations are formed, the political significance of this doctrine is the way in which it rejects Keynesian modes of intervention as being overly ambitious. In the monetarist world the only policy governments need to have is a policy for controlling the money supply - if the State delivers sound money then the economy will be stabilised. The level of employment and the rate of growth both depend on the conditions prevailing in particular markets. These conditions cannot be altered by State intervention, and thus monetarism subscribes to the doctrine of the natural rate of unemployment.

Although New Right adherents parade as 'libertarians', few adopt a classical liberal position when it comes to lifestyles, gender or race relations, defence, or law and order. On these and many other issues they are fundamentally conservative. Thus the "individuals" of the New Right are not really individuals at all, but households represented by male wage-earning patriarchs. Consequently, the individualism of the New Right is not a theology of universal opportunity for all irrespective of race or creed - it is the doctrine of privatism, patriotism and economic "man".

The alternative development option identified in this chapter as the Revisionist Left is based on counteracting what Armstrong refers to as the "inherent characteristic of capitalism to decide employment and investment on the criterion of private profitability". In order to counteract this deficiency, revisionists seek to transform the basis on which the economy operates and this requires either the nationalization of major sections of industry or the imposition of controls on the private sector to achieve the same results.

Two theoretical strands have been significant in the development of the Revisionist Left. The first of these strands is consistent with what has been referred to as the modified market tradition (Wilkes & Shirley, 1984), and with what came to be known throughout the era of consensus as welfare capitalism. Keynes, a central theorist in this tradition, advanced a practical message in his "general theory" asserting that capitalism left to its own devices was economically unstable in that it alternated between periods of protracted stagnation and unemployment and bursts of booming economic activity and inflation. By rejecting the automatic reconciliation of conflicting interests as conveyed by Says Law of Markets, Keynes advocated rational State intervention in order to increase the money supply and counter deficiency in aggregate demand. As to the level and form of State intervention, then, there are variants within the Keynesian tradition. These variants range from a limited role for the State where government simply influences private investment indirectly by managing aggregate demand to a wider governmental role where State expenditure supplants private investment as the driving force behind economic activity.

Although planning and capitalism are perceived as being compatible, Keynes and those who subscribe to the modified market tradition are primarily concerned with the preservation of the market system as the source of individual initiative and the bastion of personal liberty. They have clear connections with orthodox liberal thought in that they accept existing relationships of dominance and subordination. At the same time, they do not approve of these conditions and thus the political commitment of these revisionists to freedom and individualism is modified by an old-fashioned humanism and by a certain sensitivity to human suffering. This concern does not lead the modified marketeers to argue for a transformation of power relations in society, but it does lead them to alter the market towards a more benevolent path.

The second strand of thought within the Revisionist Left emanates out of the socialist tradition which attacks the free market system as inequitable, undemocratic, unjust and inefficient. The socialist critique focuses on the capitalist system of organizing production and draws attention to the division which exists between those who own or possess the means of production (capital and raw materials) and those who possess labour power (their ability to work). The fact that capitalists control the productive process means that they are able to retain any surplus profits for private appropriation and thus revisionists seek State action in order to ameliorate these inequities and promote economic and social well being.

Socialist theory as advanced by Paul Baron (1957) advocates freedom as an extension of rights and powers in direct contrast to the libertarian tradition which emphasises freedom from restraint. To advance freedom and reduce disparities between rich and poor, socialism promotes both economic and social growth. The cumulative impact of this growth as evidenced by the level of productivity and knowledge possessed by human beings in the modern era leads socialists to believe that it is possible to transcend capitalism and replace it with a socialist society committed to the sovereignty of individual beings. Therein, the individual might be formed, influenced and educated within a system of rationally planned production "oriented towards solidarity, cooperation and freedom" (Baron, 1957: xvii).

Although planned intervention is an essential component of socialist thought, there are divisions within socialism when it comes to theories of the state. Whilst socialist critiques of capitalism all focus on class relations as the driving force of the welfare state, the Marxist/socialist tradition maintains that only socialism itself, the public ownership of property, can alter the basic inconsistencies and contradictions which plague advanced capitalism. By contrast, Revisionists argue that the welfare State has been successful in modifying market forces and they maintain that existing State structures are capable of being transformed. It is this latter position which is consistent with the development option being pursued by the Revisionist Left.

Development models in action

When the two development options examined in this chapter are translated into programmes of action, then the implications for both work and education become self-evident. The New Right perspective is consistent with the policies advanced by the Thatcher Administration in the United Kingdom which has based its economic and social agenda on five central elements:

1. Restrictive monetary policy based on the economic theories of Milton Friedman and Ferdinand Hayek. A tight monetary policy is designed to cause a recession in order to restore the profitability of production and investment. Its success depends on the extent to which wage increases are reduced more than price increases.

2. Dismantling of social services based on a residual notion of welfare which views the State as agency of last resort. Welfare reductions enable governments to hold down expenditure and they serve to discipline a workforce which is subject to high unemployment.

3. Tax reductions based on supply side economics which asserts that reductions in personal income tax will result in people becoming more productive. As described by J.K. Galbraith, supply side economics is a theory which suggests that the way to improve incentives is to make the affluent more affluent, in the belief that these "benefits" will eventually trickle down to those who are economically and socially disadvantaged.

4. Privatisation based on opening up profitable areas of state activity to private capital through the sale of public assets and the contracting out of work previously undertaken by State employees. It also involves the introduction of commercial criteria into any residual public sector which remains.

5. Deregulation or the opening of the economy to international forces and a rolling back of major State responsibilities accepted by western governments during the post-war consensus - namely that of protecting workers from excessive pollution and other factors which might be detrimental to their health and well being.

Since 1979 the impact of these policy enactments within the United Kingdom has been dramatic. The productive capacity of the British economy was substantially reduced and official unemployment doubled to register 12% of the labour force by May 1981. Unemployment varied considerably from one region of the country to another with areas in the north of England registering unemployment rates of up to 30% of the labour force. Manufacturing output fell by 15% in 12 months from December 1979 and by 1982, company liquidations were running at 12,000 a year which was two and half times the 1979 rate. Along with these economic indicators, Taylor (1987) draws attention to the social disorder which accompanied Thatcher's economic strategy. Crime statistics for the period 1979 - 85 rose by 40%; in a country which throughout the entire post-war period to 1979 had experienced a total of three discreet sets of urban disturbances, the past seven years produced a dozen major riots. Thus the application of restrictive monetarism has not only provided "the quickest and surest road to mass unemployment" (Therborn, 1986 p. 25), it has also produced a legacy of social costs which have yet to be assessed.

The alternative development option which has been termed the Revisionist Left is consistent with the characteristics identified by Therborn in his assessment of countries which successfully maintained full employment in the face of a global recession. Although the "successful" countries are not easily compared, several dominant themes have clearly contributed to their employment records.

1. Employment Policy
    Austria, Japan, Norway, Sweden and Switzerland all displayed an institutional commitment to the development of an employment policy. This commitment involved the use of counter cyclical mechanisms and policies, adjustments to labour market policy and a conscious decision not to use high unemployment as a means of securing other policy objectives.

2. Order and Stability
    The drive for employment security has always been a central feature in policies advanced by union movements, but the successful countries also exhibited a strong conservative concern with order and stability. This concern was assessed as being "of equal importance to capital accumulation" (Therborn, 1986, P. 24).

3. State Interventionism
    The successful countries all pursued expansive Keynesian type policies complemented by a consistent monetary policy. These fiscal and monetary policies were supplemented by a range of interventionist strategies designed to maintain full employment. Education and training programmes represented one of the central strategies employed, but these retraining programmes were merely one component of an overall development option committed to full employment. The pursuit of this development option also demanded a high degree of economic and political sovereignty.

The Revisionist Left position is best illustrated by Sweden which has pursued an active labour market policy throughout the duration of the economic recession.

The geographical maldistribution of work in Sweden was tackled by regional development policies and by assistance with employee mobility. Policies aimed at improving the skills and mobility of the labour force and direct subsidies to private corporations especially in ship building and steel were designed to prevent redundancies. These interventions were supplemented by a range of special measures designed to assist the least privileged competitors in the labour market. Training subsidies in sheltered employment facilitated the restructuring programme and provided new job opportunities in depressed regions.

The outcome of these interventionist policies, as assessed in 1986, reveal a registered unemployment rate of 3% with an additional 3 - 4% of the labour force employed in subsidized work. The inflation rate was recorded as 3% and at the same time Sweden continued to support a highly developed welfare system which provided superannuation, free health and education services and extensive provisions in child care and employment leave. The full employment policy continues to be jointly advanced by labour and capital interests under the auspices of the National Labour Market Board and this alliance has clearly been an important stabilising factor during the period of restructuring.

Implications for Work and Education

In comparing these development options within the context of "employment societies" two fundamental differences emerge. The first of these distinctions relates to the significance of work and the second is concerned with the purpose and form of education.

The concept of work is conditioned by what Johan Galtung refers to as the "30 year life". The period from birth to death can be placed on a continuum with life defined as the period in which we engage in "productive" work. The concept of production as measured by economists refers to that period of our lives in which we earn money in the market place and in this sense the concept of life is contracting. In the early years of existence education and training programmes are extended in order to prepare students for work and at the other end of the continuum people are pensioned off into redundancy. Life represents that contracting section of existence in which we earn an income and establish ourselves as individuals in the market place. In other words what is done on the job is production and work - what is done away from the job is consumption and leisure. Thus:

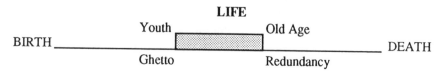

This type of thinking is exemplified in economic constructs like Gross National Product or G.N.P. which in economic terms represents production, income derived from production and expenditure of income. Yet it simply measures goods and services produced for market exchange or in return for taxes and the rate and efficiency at which land, capital and labour are employed to those ends. It excludes what might be described as the "informal economy" and that means child rearing and education, house keeping and even home maintenance and renovations where these services are not hired out. It also excludes other productive processes which are not intended for market exchange such as the provision of food, clothing, shelter and heat for one's own use or for exchange within familial or communal settings.

The implications for sectors of our society such as women should be obvious. Whereas the "beneficiaries" of development exercise considerable power within the so-called productive sphere of the market, women are largely confined to the private and non-productive arena of the home. By definition, women are unproductive members of society and this relative sense of powerlessness can be extended to members of the working class and indigenous populations. These groups are generally excluded from "life".

If this critical interpretation of employment societies as advanced by Galtung is related to the development options considered in this chapter, then there are apparent advantages in the policies enunciated by the Revisionist Left. Although revisionists accept the existing relations between capital and labour as the basis upon which production is organized, they argue that the market system is inherently unequal and thus State action is required in order to ameliorate these inequities. In development terms, this means ensuring some form of economic sovereignty, the maintenance of a secure domestic market and an institutional commitment to full employment. Revisionists acknowledge the social implications of an employment society as well as the economic and social consequences of unemployment and although they have yet to address the power relations which condition the "30 year life", they have advanced a range of strategies designed to improve the interests of labour. These strategies include the concept of a social wage, access to employment opportunities for women by favouring the introduction of part-time work and the fostering of industrial democracy so that workers are able to participate in decisions which directly affect production.

By contrast members of the New Right remain committed to economic individualism which assumes that all human behaviour is motivated by the hedonistic aspirations of acquisitive individuals seeking to maximize their own productive capacities. In policy terms this means trading income and employment security for a mobile workforce, a low wage regime and a highly speculative development path. Although Friedman (1980), one of the leading theorists of the

New Right, maintains that the only side effects of this economic agenda will be "modest reductions in output and employment" the reality is that restrictive monetarism has created a "fast track" to mass unemployment. Instead of order, stability and economic growth, this development option has created insecurity, disorder and relative deprivation. At the same time, its true social costs are yet to be assessed. Whereas the philosophy of the New Right endorses individual freedom and competition, it inevitably enhances the power of capital and the position of economic "man".

As far as education for work is concerned, then again some important distinctions emerge. The New Right views education as an investment product designed for individual consumers who are encouraged to purchase their product in the market place. A price is extracted in some form or other by those producing education and this price is to be paid by either the consumers or their agents (Treasury, 1986). Education is accordingly reduced to an individual construct in the belief that human behaviour emanates from a moral position which exults infinite greed. This moral position inevitably means that the desires and aspirations of individuals (weighted by market power) constitutes the basis on which social values are assessed. Thus concepts such as user pays and voucher education emphasize individual choice and personal rather than social responsibility.

The Revisionist Left is also influenced by the liberal tradition and by notions such as individual freedom and liberty, but this political philosophy is tempered by humanitarian concerns and by a commitment to some form of social responsibility. Although the social and cultural impediments to equality through education have never been adequately resolved, revisionists have long viewed the educational process as an important component of the social wage with the capacity to alter life opportunities. It is this relationship between education and other components of life that is subject to alternative interpretations. These interpretations are not only conditioned by work, but also by the way in which knowledge is perceived.

As Habermas observes, education was once an integral component of living, but the process of modernisation has distorted its purpose and meaning. In the progression and advancement of capitalism, the production and distribution of social wealth was transferred from the family and the tribe to private ownership. Education was separated out as with other aspects of social and political life and in this process of separation, the kinship system surrendered its power and control. The loss of power was not only related to control over the productive process, but also the ability to define knowledge and how it should be used. Whereas the New Right views knowledge as a politically neutral commodity devoid of value imputations, revisionists maintain that it is impossible to distinguish between fact and value in analysing and describing human development.

In adopting a position which is consistent with the mainstream tradition, the

New Right accepts existing economic and social relations as given and in line with the natural sciences it seeks to organize the world into discreet categories for the purposes of description and understanding. Aspects of our economic and social lives, which were previously regarded as political matters, are redefined in narrow technical terms thus excluding the possibility of political action. This economistic view of the world reduces education to a commodity which can be purchased by individuals for their own enhancement and well being. The outcome is a form of development which is individualized and privatized thus reducing the human prospect to a mere caricature of reality.

The alternative development option as advanced by the Revisionist Left views economics, society, culture and education as aspects of one in the same reality, arguing that to isolate these components of human development would be arbitrary. The logic of this holistic approach is articulated by critical theorists who maintain that the categories by which we describe and interpret human behaviour arise out of specific social and political situations and even where we use a technical language we are fabricating categories which are rooted in values and beliefs. What ideas are produced, by whom and for whose benefit have always been the fundamental problematics in any critical examination of science and human development. Whilst the revisionists have embarked on this journey they still have some way to go because it eventually means addressing the connection between work, income and power. This is not just a question of 'perspective', but rather confronting those cultural practices which emanate out of the economic and social relations of domination.

Part Four

School Policy and Curriculum

14 Introduction: Studies in Work Across the Curriculum

by David Corson

School Policy and Curriculum

In Part Four, we deal with the limited sense of 'policies' in which the term refers to plans made for the operation of a school and its curriculum. Policies of this kind are widely discussed and consented to before their adoption; they are available in written form so that they can be referred to and regularly used as guidelines for action; and they usually address matters that are of obvious curriculum importance. In the first section of this Introduction I examine the process of school-based policy development, suggesting that all secondary schools need to have a policy for 'studies in work across the curriculum'; in the second section I recommend the characteristics of 'craftmanship' as benchmarks for use by school curriculum planners who are interested in educating about 'work' as part of a worthwhile form of life; and in the third section I extend the idea of 'studies in work across the curriculum' to include practical strategies in reaching suitable curriculum aims.

School-Based Policy Development

The amount of theoretical work that has been done in the area of constructing policies at the school level in education is slight. Although there is a wealth of information relevant to large scale policies that have their impact across educational systems, very little work has been done to improve our knowledge about policy making and planning at the level of the single institution in education. Part of the problem, of course, is that we cannot have a lot of knowledge about policy construction at the school level since each institution is so very different in its needs and arrangements.

There is one commonly used definition of policy that is not very helpful to us:

the view that policy-making in educational organisations is whatever administrators in the field of education choose to do or not to do. Caldwell and Spinks (1986) see policy in a much less abstract and more useful way: a policy is a set of guidelines that provides a framework for action in achieving some purpose on a substantive issue. This suggests reasonably that not all issues need a policy but only those of substance and importance.

Most curriculum issues in education come into the category of being substantial and important. We need policies in modern schools for assisting a wide range of children with special curriculum needs, for allocating scarce resources needed by teachers in developing their curriculum programme, for rostering facilities, for integrating the help of parents and the community into the school, and so on. One policy that reaches across all of these and other areas is a policy that sees language as the central instrument in learning and a chief methodology across the curriculum (Corson, 1988). Another policy that seems essential in the modern senior secondary school is a policy for 'studies in work across the curriculum'.

A school policy that is well defined and publicly available has the advantage of lending form and structure to the school's operation. If it is acted upon, it brings rationality to that operation since it asks that decisions and actions be based on objective and generally acknowledged criteria. A school policy is a device for guarding against practices that may be insensitive to the needs and interests of children: practices that often may not be deliberate professional malpractice but derive rather from a lack of reflection or from following personal whim, caprice or habits of patronage.

A school that is amoral in its organisational practices is a powerful force for doing harm; it may be massively 'miseducative' by giving children clear but unstated examples of human behaviour that are contrary to the explicit messages about human behaviour and personal ethics that the school itself seeks to disseminate through its formal curriculum. As a small example, many schools in the Western world in recent decades have moved quickly and compellingly to develop policies on smoking, by their staff members, in and around the school environment. The point of these policies is to eliminate the double standard that was witnessed by earlier generations of children who saw some staff smoking freely in and around schools while other staff were warning children about the health consequences of smoking and trying to discourage smoking by students themselves.

In schools, then, well written policies help us in managing complex ethical matters. We can readily appreciate why schools and school systems present situations for decision making that are value laden and complex. The school is far more complex, I believe, in the ethical relationships it harbours than any other institution that humankind has developed (Corson, 1985b). Problems of value complexity are inevitable in a system established on the premise that in order to prepare young people to be 'free' and responsible in a free society we should take away their freedom by having them attend compulsory institutions for 11 or 12 years (Lawton, 1981).

Problems of organisational and ethical complexity often arise in schools because of our need to accommodate two seemingly opposed inclinations that teachers hold as professionals: on the one hand we are rightly anxious to treat children fairly and as individuals in schools; on the other hand we are aware that schools are places run on essentially utilitarian lines, where the greatest good of the greatest number is usually and reasonably the guiding ethical principle that has some relation to pragmatic reality (Corson, Cowling and Wenn, 1986). Goal confusion can result, frustrating our efforts as administrators to accommodate to either of these inclinations with ethical consistency.

We can meet this ethical challenge. At the same time, knowing as we do that schools are belief systems reflecting each participant's different goals and values, we can deal with the effects of the organisational and ideological constraints that this situation creates. One way to confront these challenges in schools is to adopt a collaboratively produced set of policy documents, responsive as far as possible to the perceptions of the organisation that each individual has; indeed this may represent the only hope of a satisfactory plan of action. The alternative for principals and teachers who are concerned to educate for work may be to see their task as no more than a series of situations requiring decisions governed by short term exigencies to be met by whatever expedient measures are to hand: 'piecemeal' decisions, in the bad sense of the word. I prefer the policy approach.

Cooperative and collaborative group structures, of the kind needed to construct policies that attract general assent, are influential in improving attitudes and the reception of new ideas. In Greenfield's work (1978) we find reasoned support for the view that schools collaboratively managed and with agreed policies are better places for all concerned, since they tend to escape the trap of having their procedures and styles of operation modelled on the dominant points of view only. In the eyes of the public they are also more 'legitimate' places, a point that relates to the theorising of Habermas (1985) which is at the forefront of social philosophy. His conclusion is that a new form of 'institutionalised discourse' is needed in social institutions in Western democracies if they are to recapture their legitimacy, their sense of direction and the motivation of their participants and adherents. Habermas writes of 'an ideal speech situation' in which there are no external constraints preventing participants from assessing evidence and argument, and in which each participant has an equal and open chance of entering into discussion. Reinterpreting this idea of Habermas' into the everyday context of managing schools, we find support in it for the methods of policy discussion and construction that are recommended these days in many quarters: for example the system of 'self-reflective meetings' recommended by Carr and Kemmis (1983) or the stages of 'school development' suggested by Prebble and Stewart (1981).

The starting point may be in having a policy about policy-making itself that sets up, as far as is possible, an 'ideal speech situation' for determining how decisions are planned or implemented in the school. This 'policy about policy' could include sections on how priorities for discussion and policy making are arrived at; the process of selecting policy working groups; matters of resources and accountability; procedures for reporting back; steps in final decision making; the location of responsibility for and methods of implementing decisions; and the steps in the evaluation and reform of policies. If this policy is itself collaboratively produced, and regularly revised, then there is a good prospect of staff supporting later policies created in line with its prescriptions: such as a policy for 'studies in work across the curriculum'. Policy making is a precise process that can work at the school level if the steps in the process itself are well formulated.

To say more at this stage might not be helpful since every school has its own set of contexts and circumstances that bear upon the kind of policy for studies in work across the curriculum that it might design. Here are some examples of these factors:

1. the way that work is practised in the local community and the kinds of work available will influence the kind of curriculum strategies that might be appropriate; this does not mean, though, that the school should accept any blame for community unemployment rates; nor should it attempt to provide solutions for local unemployment (see Ivan Snook in Chapter 17);
2. the degree to which the local community is involved with the school will determine how much community integration a policy can have in its early days (although the policy's long-term aim should be the maximum degree of community involvement in any studies in work across the curriculum);
3. the kinds of 'youth cultures' inhabiting the school may be major considerations for planning (see Jim Walker in Chapter 15);
4. any resources for vocational guidance and careers counselling within the school will need to be integrated into the policy to ensure that, while addressing the needs of all students, the particular needs of individuals are not overlooked (see William Taylor in Chapter 16);
5. the nature and scope of transition-to-work programmes operating in the local community will influence school level policy decisions and there may be opportunities to relate these more closely to the school's formal programme (see Wanda Korndörffer in Chapter 18).

I am suggesting that the development of policies for 'studies in work across the curriculum' of individual schools is a reasonable and proper course for education in English-speaking countries to be taking in response to contemporary needs. The development of a school policy in this area depends on a number of factors. All of these are located within the school's ambit of control: the commitment of the teaching staff to the needs of 'education for work'; a willingness to undertake some research into the 'education for work' needs of a particular school community; the openness to consult with parents and the wider society in deciding possibilities; and the leadership of the school executive and the enthusiasm of the whole school community in making the policy work.

Work as Craft

It is a simple truism to say that recreational work is part of a worthwhile form of life: recreation is an end in itself. Occupational work can also be pursued for its own ends. In Chapter 1 this form of work is referred to as 'unconstrained occupational work' or 'meaningful work'; the presence of skill or judgment is a necessary part of this kind of work. This work is similar to recreational work in having value for its own sake. On the other hand constrained 'labour' is less likely to be part of a worthwhile form of life since it is directed elsewhere; it is performed under circumstances that are not voluntary; and its worth is measured by scales of value outside itself. Schooling that prepares students for entry into work of this kind does not have education as its goal. This is a species of training, not education. Education allows its students to see work more as recreational work is viewed: an activity of life that is worthwhile for its own sake.

The curriculum aim I am suggesting here is that occupational work could come to be viewed by more students as a desirable alternative to leisure, since its point would approach so near the point of recreational work, which is the activity of leisure. Leisure 'work' could become a distinct aim in education, as Dewey implied it could (Dewey, 1940; Sherman, 1974). For him the actual training for work should be the least important part of a vocational curriculum. In the contemporary world there are practical reasons to support Dewey's case: the rapid obsolescence of training and even of occupations themselves suggests that we need a broader not a narrower preparation for work. For Dewey 'education for work' should develop intelligence, initiative, ingenuity and executive capacity in order to allow workers to be "their own masters" (1915, p. 42).

All of this suggests promoting a shift in values about 'work': perhaps for many students these proposals would create, for the very first time, a value for work that is implicit in it. By developing workers who love their work for its own sake this curriculum direction might produce graduates who view their work as craftsmen view theirs. I have adopted six features of 'craftmanship' from a list provided by C. Wright Mills (1973, pp. 10-13), a list that he extends to 'intellectual craftmanship' elsewhere (1970). Nor is there a ready substitute word for 'craftsmanship' that is gender neutral; readers will know, then, that the word in this context denotes men and women involved in activities of craftmanship.

The following descriptions could be used as benchmarks in designing 'studies in work across the curriculum' to ensure that programmes are within a framework reinforcing the value that students see in their work and the significance of that work for themselves and for their society:

1. there is no ulterior motive in work other than the product being made and the process of its creation;
2. the details of daily work are meaningful because they are not detached in the minds of workers from the product of the work;
3. workers are free to control their own working action;
4. craftsmen are thus able to learn from their work and to use and develop their capacities and skills in its prosecution;
5. there is no split of work and play or work and culture;
6. the work activity of craftsmen determines and infuses their entire mode of living.

In recommending these features of 'craftmanship' as benchmarks for curriculum planners, I am taking a very strong stand against the widely cited 'Theory X' account of management: the view that the average human being has an inherent dislike of work and will avoid it wherever possible (McGregor, 1960). This account of mine is broadly consistent with a humanistic conception of work and a management 'Theory Y' view of workers: the expenditure of effort in work is as natural as play or rest; human beings will exercise self-direction in work if they are committed to it; and the capacity for imagination, ingenuity, creativity, and responsibility is widely distributed among people, yet only partially utilized in modern industrial work situations.

Work viewed as craftmanship is quite different from work viewed as constrained labour. There are rewards implicit in work when workers recognise that they are the producers of products or services that enrich or sustain life; when their own purposes and meanings are involved; when qualities such as exercise of judgment, sense of style, and the practice of a sense of craft are demanded. From work of this kind, as Arthur Wirth points out, comes a satisfaction of the human search for potency, as workers measure themselves against their work, sensing their powers and finding human dignity and worth in the process (1977, pp. 56-66). He instances the situation in Sweden where the automobile companies were forced to accept that they could not hold their educated youth in the constrained settings of traditional plants. The result was the redesign of workplaces to lessen the constraints and to satisfy workers' desires for achievement, recognition and interest: to offer them meaningful work. For Dewey work of this kind plays a critical role in self-fulfilment and in continuing education: it becomes a vocation or a calling:

> A calling is of necessity also an organizing principle for information and ideas; for knowledge and intellectual growth. It provides an axis which runs through an immense diversity of detail; it causes different experiences, facts, items of information to fall into order one with another (Dewey, 1916b p. 362).

In this quote from Dewey we can see the links clearly revealed between craftmanship, work and the meaning of education that was highlighted in Chapter 4: to be educated involves the possession of a body of knowledge along with a conceptual scheme to raise that knowledge above the level of a collection of disjointed facts; this means some understanding of principles for the organising of facts, the reasons behind things. Studies in work across the curriculum, that explore the links between 'work' and 'craft', are compatible with this view of education. Student attitudes to the curriculum, to schoolwork, and to work in general could be transformed by a well-conceived and integrated course of study of this kind.

Studies in Work Across the Curriculum

In this section I centre discussion on the education of children in middle to late adolescence: students nearing or passing the minimum school leaving age in most English-speaking countries. Although my approach to the topic suggests some broad form of curriculum integration, I am not advocating the abolition of subject boundaries or a totally integrated curriculum: the loss of the subject specialisation of teachers at this level is probably greater than the gains to be made from a fully integrated curriculum (see Lawton, 1983; Pring, 1976; Reynolds and Skilbeck, 1976). Nor am I urging major changes in what schools do or in the knowledge they convey; rather I am simply suggesting that senior schools might *conceive of their task* in a slightly different way. What I am advocating is that 'studies in work across the curriculum' should become a broad organising idea for the senior secondary school, a major theme to be pursued as a curriculum goal that will link what Bernstein calls 'the uncommonsense knowledge of the school' and 'the commonsense knowledge, the everyday community knowledge' of pupils, their families and peer groups (1975). Recent experiences in education suggest that we need to tread cautiously in pursuing an integration of this kind. Bernstein argues that four criteria need to be met if schools are to have a culture in which both staff and pupils retain a sense purpose. In summary these four conditions are as follows:

1. there must be consensus about the integrating idea and it must be very explicit;
2. the nature of the linkage between the integrating idea and the knowledge to be coordinated must also be coherently spelled out;
3. a committee system of staff may have to be set up to create a sensitive feedback system;
4. without clear criteria of evaluation, neither teacher nor taught has any means to consider the significance of what is learned, nor any means to judge the pedagogy.

Considered in the light of experience in a variety of versions of 'open plan' education at different Tasmanian primary and secondary schools (Corson, Merrington and Wenn, 1986) Bernstein's warnings are powerful and impressively accurate. Where his conditions are met, staff and pupils do have a clear sense of time, place and purpose. Elsewhere, where one or more of the conditions are missing, teaching, learning and evaluation all suffer from vagueness about what is to be done in the school and how.

Denis Lawton (1983) suggests a possible committee structure to facilitate school-based curriculum planning. He mentions three levels of decision-making: a director of studies committee; departmental committees; and a committee of the whole teaching staff. I believe, though, that we can go much further in developing 'studies in work across the curriculum'. In this instance we can address several problem areas at once in our school planning: the 'education for work' needs of the students; the need for a school-level policy in 'education for work'; the need to promote work experience for all; and the need to make the school itself more organic to the community in which it is set. The current move in many places to develop effective Schools Councils for all schools (Wenn, 1986) relates to Bernstein's four conditions, especially his third point. These bodies for curriculum planning and for school management generally are far more involved in the education process than are the 'boards of governors' that have been common in some places. The task of a School Council is to assist the school executive wherever possible with educational policy-making and planning. If we expand Bernstein's committee concept in point 3 to include in curriculum discussion teachers, students and the parental community in an active relationship, then his other three points become an essential frame of reference within which the School Council might operate. In the senior secondary school a democratic organisation of this kind could find fulfilment of its curriculum purpose in the task of coordinating studies in work across the curriculum. Further details are outside the scope of discussion here. Guidance of a practical kind for councils or school curriculum policy groups may be found in the curriculum matrix planning advocated by Lawton (1983). My concern here is with the kinds of questions that curriculum planners in this or any area should ask in designing their proposals.

A.V. Kelly (1986) bypasses the rationalist questions that are often asked about school subjects: what subjects have a right to a place on the curriculum; or, what subject content should we be aiming to transmit to pupils? He also bypasses the politician's and economist's questions: what economic value or use has the teaching of this subject; or, what is its vocational potential? Instead he asks very different questions: what forms of development can subject x [or theme x, or work experience x] promote; and how can we justify its inclusion in the curriculum in these educational terms? For Kelly it is not the kinds of knowledge that matter; he places priority instead on the kinds of engagement with knowledge that are promoted by engaging in given curricular activities

Kelly borrows from Raymond Williams (1958) the idea that education's task is to anticipate cultural change, a form of development that links directly with development at the personal level. I think we can conclude that initiating into a worthwhile form of life will certainly require a preparation for cultural change and the development of the personal strengths that are needed at least to understand, if not to contribute to, cultural improvement. Educating in order to promote these two kinds of development was a major thrust of Dewey's philosophy so it is not surprising that it enters pointedly into discussion here. We do well to think first about 'competencies', then, or 'potentials for development', in planning a curriculum for studies in work.

The following checklist of competencies is one that is already in use in schools for overlaying on curriculum proposals. Clearly these competencies relate directly to 'education for work'; this means that they are also central to education in general since the former, as I have argued, is a part of the latter. The competencies fall into two groups. First there is a set of competencies associated with learning to converse, read, write and calculate. Second there is a set of competencies that depends considerably on the prior acquisition of the first set. This list is borrowed freely from a curriculum document (Schools Board, 1986 pp. 22-23). It may be helpful for readers to know that the list was compiled by principals, senior staff and tertiary affiliates (including the author) from all the senior secondary colleges of Tasmania. It therefore represents an amalgamation of views from across the curriculum of upper secondary education; it encapsulates the kinds of developmental aims that schooling at this level is widely thought to pursue.

Prior Competencies

acquiring information

This includes listening accurately and critically to oral presentations; using data from computer information systems; identifying the main ideas from print and graphic material as well as from film, television and radio presentations; reading different kinds of fiction and non-fiction; observing and recording practical experiences.

conveying information

This includes talking and writing for particular purposes; using a range of media to tell a story or present factual information; using models to explain ideas; demonstrating the difference between major ideas and less important ones; and doing all these for a range of audiences.

applying logical processes

This includes inferring from observations, analysing and interpreting information, calculating number relationships and values, solving practical and theoretical problems, forming hypotheses, anticipating and predicting consequences, identifying assumptions and evaluating requirements.

undertaking practical tasks as an individual

This involves choosing, planning and organising a range of tasks, including those that require a range of physical dexterity and seeing them through to completion without supervision.

undertaking practical tasks as a member of a group

This includes activities similar to those above with emphasis on cooperation, negotiation and leadership.

making judgments and decisions

This includes identifying alternatives, evaluating evidence and ideas, selecting appropriate courses of action.

working creatively

This includes the ability to use ideas and materials inventively - recombining ideas to meet new situations and contexts, extrapolating beyond what has been given explicitly. These creative activities should not be restricted to art, drama and music.

Dependent Competencies

act autonomously

by displaying initiative, self-confidence and control, resilience and entrepreneurial skill across a range of human activities.

act responsibly

by considering how actions will affect others as well as oneself, being tolerant or firm when appropriate, and valuing democratic processes.

show care and concern for other people

by being sensitive to the thoughts and feelings of others, respecting different opinions and ways of doing things, being friendly and helpful, being able to express love and affection.

consider questions of beliefs and values

by examining how ideas and actions reflect beliefs, giving careful consideration to personal, individual and group values in all aspects of experience.

These competencies have clear relevance across the full range of human activities. Graduates from a form of schooling that managed to equip all its students with all of these competencies would be welcome as beginners in any work or non-work environment. Reading over them I am reminded of the kind of education that was practised for the leisured classes of earlier centuries whose aim was to make the student 'agreeable company' or 'socially acceptable'. The list would also overlap considerably with a list compiled by a Marcus Aurelius or an Aquinas or a Socrates. If these competencies do seem historically conservative then perhaps there is a message in that fact: our views about what is needed in a desirable member of civilised society are reasonably stable and enduring ones (like our views about what constitutes 'classical music'); there is a certain 'canon' of socially necessary human competencies that are only subject to slight variation across time, not wholesale change or even much supplementing.

Schooling today, though, is not much directed to educating the leisured classes. These competencies are still essential ones but the context of their application in education has changed and is changing. If we accept that 'initiation into work as part of a worthwhile form of life' is a task for education, then studies in work across the curriculum will give attention to the meaning and place of work in that worthwhile form of life; it will, I suggest, promote a view of work as craft. Suggested below are practical strategies, in no special order, that might be effective in reaching these aims:

1. Studies in work across the curriculum could emphasise work skills rather than job skills; the list of competencies above gives a practical guide here. The task of finding and mastering what is common to work, rather than what is specific to 'a job', will inevitably help the discovery of the meaning and place of work in a worthwhile form of life. A good starting point might be an explicit investigation by teachers and students of the competencies listed above: how do they relate to the work setting?

2. Programmes could be student-centred and individualist. For example, the 'No Kidding' project in the Post Sixteen Centre at the University of London Institute of Education seeks to involve groups of young people actively in the development of curriculum materials; it produces a series of photographic exhibitions and related texts based on students' work; it runs a cultural event on the theme of 'Livelihoods' and develops video programmes on the same theme. There is a need to give individual student capacities and interests more weight at this level as the curriculum begins to reflect career aspirations and cultural factors. Jim Walker in Chapter15 gives a clear lead; he recommends that negotiation between teachers and students be the basis of curriculum

planning in this area.

3. Programmes could explore the context of work by case study with groups engaged in activities that might provide partial answers to the following questions : where does work fit in the scheme of things? what place does remuneration play? can work be separated from the constraints of time, venue, duration and intensity that affect it? is it always enjoyable? A purpose for including this last question is to avoid setting students up for possible disillusionment and defeat that might come when the realities of work turn out to be rather different from the idealized view of work that is often passed on in schools and among peer groups. Work experience programmes could also do much to head off false impressions about the world of work. In Chapter 16 William Taylor discusses student expectations about work: after a period of exposure to work many young people find even the most menial forms of work to be preferable to the indignity of being treated as children in schools.

4. Programmes could include counselling, group discussion sessions, role play activities and simulation games examining the non-remunerative rewards to be gained from work: for example, the opportunities for social intercourse and its related benefits; reflective pleasures; the sense of mastery and achievement; the sense of service; the feeling of responsibility etc. All these things are close to the dynamic interests that occupy adolescent talk and meld their relationships; not to have them in the curriculum is to outlaw from schools a chief ingredient of adolescent lifestyle.

5. The place of work experience receives special attention from Wanda Korndörffer in Chapter18. What we know about work experience and transition education is so far largely negative: we are beginning to know what not to do. In Chapter 7 I recommended the incorporation of work experience for all in secondary schools, an undertaking that requires deliberate policy change at the system level. The Ontario Ministry of Education gives a lead with an explicit policy providing guidelines for work experience (1984). To achieve the curriculum aim that is introduced in this present chapter, work experience could highlight interaction with workers who are themselves craftsmen and who offer an example of craftmanship in practice. This means a more careful matching in future of students with workers and work settings; it means paying more attention to educational factors and to questions of competency development than is probably paid now. Specifically, recreational workers and unconstrained occupational workers have an important place as exemplars in any work experience programme; the nature of the work is of less importance educationally than the developmental experience given to students by engaging in it.

6.   Programmes in work experience might advance the position that the way in which work activities are carried out in communities provides an organising principle for approaching the particular community under study.

7.   Programmes in work experience need not begin and end in the school. Adolescent attitudes to school are often so restricting that very little of value about the real world (of work) can be dealt with in the school. The school organisation itself shapes the social relations of students and teachers. Relations with teachers are friendly and more equal at a school camp or social event; this suggests that the divorce between school and non-school can be bridged by teachers doing things in the company of students outside of schools, not just by sending them off and seeing them again when they return. The need is really to take the school into the world of work, not to bring that world inside the school.

8.   An organising idea within the theme of 'studies in work across the curriculum' might link studies of the language of the culture with work experience by deliberately expanding the communicative repertoire of students, both its lexical range and its functional and contextual applications. The point, value and significance of work becomes real to students when they are able to organise the vague ideas that they have about it and link them with language which becomes available to them for reflection and interaction. A wide range of oral language pedagogies and activities suited to adolescent interests and abilities are available, but they are rarely used in modern senior secondary schools (Corson, 1987).

A key organising principle in all these recommendations is that the studies should be *experience-based.*. What I am advocating is that we try to recapture, in our socialisation programmes in 'education for work', those traits of socialisation about work that still occur 'naturally' in agrarian societies. More than this, though, and consistent with the complexities of modern societies, experience-based studies of work across the curriculum will allow young people to view work from the different knowledge perspectives that a broad school curriculum offers. These studies will inevitably introduce the satellite social problems of work that provide constraints different from those of time, venue, duration and intensity: the aliena-tion of worker from worker; the maintenance of group motivation from within the group; difficulties in communication; inter-group conflicts; technological change; and the morality of engaging in certain kinds of work (see Colin Wringe in Chapter 3). From their experience of work and the processes of education that are based upon it, young people can be edged to the conclusion that our expectations of work differ according to the perspectives through which we view it.

Key Issues for School Policy and Curriculum

In Chapter 15 Jim Walker argues that youth cultures in the secondary school setting provide a foundation on which to build a curriculum in work. Adolescent problems relating to work and the world of work can be better understood by teachers who are familiar with the various youth cultures that exist in schools. This is not to say that problems are markedly different from youth culture to youth culture; Walker's claim is a lesser one: the perspective that individuals have on problems related to work will be coloured by their cultural allegiance and will be better understood by outsiders familiar with that cultural perspective. He identifies key educational questions in coming to understand youth cultures and in developing a coherent curriculum that responds to differences in cultural beliefs and practices. In part there is a need to address both the perceived and the real problems of students. He takes up the idea that studies in work across the curriculum may provide an avenue to successful policy development in education for work.

As examples of youth cultures, operating at the borders between school and work, Walker draws on two ethnographic studies: the one looking at boys in a youth culture styled 'the footballers'; and the other looking at girls in a youth culture styled 'the troublemakers'. He finds that the members of these youth cultures possess a wealth of knowledge and experience of real work situations, commonsense knowledge that contrasts markedly with the obscure knowledge of work located in teacher cultures. He recommends the creation of curriculum 'touchstones' between teachers and pupils, and between pupils and work. These touchstones, for Walker, are points where different cultural bodies of knowledge come together; they provide avenues of communication across pupil and teacher cultures that can be based on the sharing of problems, interests, experiences and standards of behaviour. The central method Walker recommends is negotiation: making deals with students about solving mutual problems and acting upon them. He offers five steps towards curriculum development of this kind.

In Chapter 16 William Taylor looks at developmental needs that individual students have in making the transition from school to work. He outlines changes in the practice and the conception of vocational counselling that have occurred in recent decades; there has been an overdue move away from the ritualistic practices of earlier times that attempted to match square pegs to square holes. He traces the impact on schools of 'careers education', translated to Britain from the United States in the early 1970s (see Robert Sherman in Chapter 6), and the development of the Schools Council Careers Education and Guidance Project. As in the United States there have been difficulties in matching the careers education ideology, as it operates in schools, with the realities of the world of work. Taylor concludes his first section with a plea that the genuine need for individual guidance and counselling of children in schools not be overlooked by educationists concerned with the wider issues of education for work.

Taylor's second section examines the criteria that people have for judging quality of working life and the ways that education can help satisfy these criteria. His conclusion, from a broad study of the sociological evidence, is that schools do best for their students if they equip them with the range of competencies that are considered desirable acquisitions by educators wherever they may be. He links these competencies with Bloom's concept of 'mastery learning' [an approach to syllabus design in the secondary school that has had a wide impact on the realignment of certification procedures by accrediting authorities in several Australian States]. Taylor concludes by making a number of recommendations for policy, research and practice in education.

In discussing Bloom's 'mastery learning' Taylor makes the point that a serious problem is arising in societies where generations of compulsory schooling have produced more skilled people than there are roles for them to perform. This is a situation closely related to that addressed by Ivan Snook in Chapter 17: there are many who blame schools for not equipping enough students with the skills needed for employment, who argue that schools should be blamed for unemployment and that teachers should be asked to take a role in eliminating it. Snook argues that schools are in no way responsible for unemployment. Drawing on statistical evidence he shows that in developed countries there is no serious mismatch between the jobs available and the skills that the unemployed lack. If schools have not caused unemployment, Snook asks, can they provide part of the solution to it? He sees difficulties here since the things that schools are able to offer their students may not greatly compensate for other 'prestige' factors in societies that act for or against job-seekers from different social or cultural positions. Jan Branson's chapter on 'gender' points to one of these factors; high status language is another (Corson, 1985). Training in skills may miss the point. An alternative curriculum in 'education for leisure' (see Chapter 10) is also unsatisfactory as a possible direction for schooling: "it reflects a cynical neglect of the social situation of the unemployed". Snook is not prepared to dismiss vocational education courses as lightly, however. They do give a lead to teachers about what to offer in schools because of factors in their broad appeal to students: vocational courses are active; they are relevant to student inclinations and hopes; and they integrate commonsense knowledge with school knowledge.

There are lessons for teachers planning any form of curriculum activity in what Ivan Snook has to say. In the context of 'education for work', though, his points can be noted and applied especially to programmes of work experience: he mentions the near irrelevance to real learning of direct instruction; he stresses the need for children to have a rich engagement in activities if they are to acquire traits thought desirable by people outside schools; and he advises teachers to find ways to excite and challenge the young, even while presenting them with a curriculum that must inevitably pay attention to conservative educational virtues.

In Chapter 18 Wanda Korndörffer uses field work studies to uncover the strengths and weaknesses of training for work programmes that are aimed specifically at young people among the 'at risk' group. She begins by examining the theoretical assumptions on which 'transition education' is based. It offers a response to a crisis of capitalism. The emphasis on equipping 'at risk' students with easily learned and barely relevant 'skills' in senior secondary schools and technical colleges thinly disguises the real intention of such programmes: the inculcation of social discipline. Korndörffer's interpretation of the social mechanisms preparing socially marginal children for alienating manual work takes us full circle, back to the distinctions made in Chapter 1 between meaningful work on the one hand, which is desirable, contributes to self-respect and is part of a worthwhile form of life, and constrained labour on the other. Transition education attempts to initiate most of its graduates into the latter.

In her second section Korndörffer examines transition education programmes in practice. The programmes she discusses are typical of programmes of this kind tried in various countries: they are neither outstanding nor poor examples of practice. While there is some encouragement in her findings for some of the activities of these courses (notably the kinds of engagement in real-life events that Ivan Snook asks teachers in schools to give more attention to) her general conclusions are not encouraging for courses of this kind. Transition-to-work and other stop-gap programmes do not adequately cater to the perceived needs of the clients or to the educational criteria that the programmes ignore. When training of this kind is conducted away from education it serves purposes that are other than the purposes of education: the needs of the state; the needs of employers; the needs of the instrumentalities that grow in power through mounting the programmes; and the narrow political aims of governments. A straightforward conclusion seems to arise from these latter chapters by Snook and Korndörffer: if training for work is necessary for young people, then it needs to be integrated into a school curriculum that has education as its goal.

Building on Youth Cultures in the Secondary Curriculum[1]

by Jim Walker

15

Introduction: A View of Work, Culture and the Curriculum

Work fits differently into different ways of life, or cultures. It is unlikely that a perspective on work can be understood adequately in isolation from the complex cultural whole of which it is a part. If this is so, then our approach to curriculum development needs to recognise that adequate understanding of students' perspectives on work, and suitable assistance to students in the problems they face in this part of their lives, requires some understanding of their cultures.

Different cultures not only contain different perspectives on work, but these perspectives are related to distinct problems concerning work and personal life, requiring different solutions. Indeed, it is fruitful to view a culture as a problem-solving repertoire which has developed out of the historical experience of the group in dealing with its environment, and which is adapted by individuals to their own particular circumstances (Walker 1987d). Individuals sharing the same culture not only vary in their personalities and abilities, but are assigned different social roles (for instance sex/gender roles), and so may differ in their work orientations and problems. Within one culture, males and females may have different perspectives on work, indeed distinct subcultures, but these need to be understood in relation to each other.

Differences between cultures are not complete or absolute. They frequently occur simultaneously with some overlapping of perspective and with shared problems in school and work, and they can change. Thus we need to view cultures dynamically: they are internally complex, they interact, and they may be open to reconstruction (Walker 1987d).

Cultural overlap derives from the material context shared by groups with different cultures. For instance, changes in the economy and in employment to which people respond differently are nevertheless the common origin of many of their diverse problems. Indeed they are widely shared basic problems which are mediated through complex social relationships which form the context to which particular cultures are responses. Similarly, the education system within which teacher and pupils must address the problems of their students is a common context within which to develop educational solutions.

The problems a person faces also vary according to the person's age. Given a dynamic, problem solving view of culture, this means that cultures are to a large extent age-specific. In the secondary school, for example, teachers encounter youth cultures, which combine ethnic, sex-gender, social class, recreational and other elements in response-repertoires more or less adapted to the problems perceived by young people. Here there are four key educational questions. First, how real are these perceived problems? For example, are migrant groups a real or an imagined threat to the employment prospects of already established groups? Second, are there other real problems facing students which are not perceived by them? For example, are students aiming at apprenticeships in traditional blue collar occupations aware of how they might be affected by changes in the labour market? Third, how effective are youth cultures as resources for handling the problems facing young people? For example, do the cultures of groups of working class girls provide an adequate set of responses to the problems of employment and family life they are likely to face? Fourth, how does one youth culture enhance or constrain the options available to young people in other cultures? For example, do some of the "macho masculine" youth cultures prevalent among boys in secondary schools adversely affect the chances of positive learning and development of other boys and girls whose cultures are dominated and subordinated by the "macho" cultures?

Any attempt to develop a curriculum orientation to "the world of work" will need to address these questions. Above all, if it is to succeed in a context of cultural diversity, it will need to take account of both similarities and differences between cultures, of shared and unshared problems, and find a way of developing a coherent curriculum which nevertheless does not obscure or ignore the complexities (Walker 1988c).

Teachers, of course, have their various cultural backgrounds too (Connell 1985). These become mixed in with their shared general professional culture (Hargreaves 1980) and the specific staffroom cultures of teachers of humanities, mathematics, the natural and social sciences, and so on (Ball & Lacey 1980). Moreover, just as pupil cultures are related to wider ethnic and class cultures, teacher cultures are related to wider cultures in the arts and sciences, the educational system, and government bureaucracies (Bernstein 1977). Like the youth cultures of students, teacher cultures have their perspectives on work, deriving from the problems and contexts of the work teachers understand and have to perform. Teachers need to be aware of how their perspectives on work relate to those of their students.

In this context, two major problems face teachers. First, there is the problem of effectively addressing students' cultural perspectives as these are played out in daily life and as, in the minds of students, they link present realities with future possibilities and personal aspirations. Solutions to this problem require the development of intercultural understanding, a precondition for tackling the second problem, which is to develop educational strategies which can maximise students' employment options and promote desirable change in students' perspectives on work. I suggest that the solution to this problem requires addressing both the perceived and the real problems of students. Furthermore, the curriculum needs to take into account all these problems in as coherent a way as possible. One aspect of a coherent curriculum relevant to the world of work might well be the study of work across the curriculum (Corson 1985a).

To illustrate this cultural approach to curriculum development, I shall draw on two ethnographic studies of the transition from school to paid employment, unemployment, and domestic work: studies of groups of girls (Moran 1988) and boys (Walker 1987a, 1987b, 1988a, 1988b, 1988c). Both studies employed an approach to the study of culture which emphasises problem-solving activity and the dynamic relations between different cultures.

Example 1: "The Footballers"

"The footballers" were a group of boys in an Australian polyethnic inner-urban single sex school in the early to mid 1980s. They represented a particular form of "Aussie" male youth culture, placing a premium on rugby football; they formed the backbone of the senior grade rugby union teams, and at every opportunity played "touch" football (rugby league with touching substituted for tackling) at school. They controlled the largest and best section of the school grounds, and when they moved around they expected others to make way. Rugby league, their preferred game, is bound up with traditional Australian working class culture in the area. Most footballers were of Anglo-Saxon-Celtic (ASC), or "Aussie" backgrounds.

"The footballers" were at the top of a youth culture hierarchy, setting the "agenda", as it were, for other boys. To be accepted by them, others had to develop the capacity to trade real or mock physical violence, jokes and insults, and overtly to reject non-Aussie values. Footballer culture placed a strong emphasis on mobility—preferably by car on evenings and weekends—moving from one pub or club to another as the fancy arose, striking aggressive postures to other males, and performing ostentatious displays or conducting propositioning raids on females— "hunting".

Short-term goals, especially "having a good time with your mates", took precedence. Assertive masculinity worked as a repertoire of solutions to short-term problems of personal identity, self-esteem and legitimation of one's actions in very concrete practical contexts involving eating, drinking, moving, relations with females and, as the post-school years went by, the pressures of working life.

Although footballer culture was far removed from the professional cultures of teachers and from most of the content of the formal curriculum, the footballer group was not alienated from school. Because the school recognised and celebrated their sporting prowess, the footballers had ample opportunity for short-term reward and status at school. Teachers used sport as a bridge to youth culture and largely succeeded in establishing reasonably good relationships with these boys, whose competitiveness transferred to the classroom and provided some motivation for perseverance with the culturally alien contents of much of the curriculum. The footballers, at least around the age of sixteen, tended to accept teachers' credentialist arguments for the necessity of gaining a School Certificate to enhance employment prospects.

Such competitive and credentialist motives, however, were educationally limited by the short term orientation of the traditional working class culture of the area, and so ASC footballers tended to aspire to little more than the kind of employment they saw around them, what had been achieved by their fathers, for example. In the long run, this limited their employment flexibility and their earning prospects in a changing labour market. The only exceptions to this were non-ASC members of the footballer group whose family backgrounds, reflecting immigrant ethnic culture, provided them with higher aspirations. These boys, by gaining entry into the culturally dominant footballer group, achieved higher youth social status, but were not restricted by the short-term perspective on work. Thus at the age of twenty one, ASC footballers remained in occupations similar to those of their parents, and continued to live in the area, while non-ASCs had moved out of the area to higher status occupations.

Footballer culture contrasted strongly with the culture of another group of boys, "the Greeks", whose family backgrounds stimulated them to stay longer at school, to seek the Higher School Certificate, and to go on to higher education or to establish their own businesses. By the age of twenty one, "the Greeks" were becoming very successful in their ambitions; and many of the footballers, who had looked down on them at school, were either envious of their achievements or expressed the wish that they had themselves worked harder and persisted longer at school.

Example 2: "The Troublemakers"

"The troublemakers" comprised two groups of girls in an Australian polyethnic inner-urban coeducational school in the early to mid 1980s. They were often described by teachers and other girls as "troublemakers", "dummies", "ratbags", "sluts" and "moles", They were generally antagonistic to other girls they regarded as "goodie-goodies". Their main interest was in attracting boys; indeed talking and worrying about boys was their major preoccupation. Girls without steady boy-friends spent a lot of time plotting how to meet "Mr Right"; while those with boyfriends constantly grappled with disappointments at the hands of males and agonised over sex. Other major concerns were closely related: dress, hairstyle, make-up, weight, and so on. The girls came from a variety of ethnic backgrounds, although the smaller group was entirely ASC.

Family ethnic differences had a pronounced influence on the girls' relationships with males. The non-ASC girls went out only with non-ASC boys, and would not associate with boys (ASC and non-ASC) whom they regarded as beneath them: boys who were not well presented; or likely to be in trouble with the law; less well-off; less likely to have cars or much money to spend. When their parents knew of their outings with boys, the non-ASC girls were usually chaperoned. For the Turkish and Lebanese girls in particular, steady, intimate relationships with boys were generally impossible. The families of all non-ASC girls expected them to be "good girls", which meant retaining their virginity and showing "ladylike" behaviour, such as not swearing, smoking or wearing sexually provocative clothes. Within limits, how-ever, these girls tried to look "sexy", finding it gave them a greater choice among males. All girls were prepared to place a much higher short-term premium on their relationships with males than were other girls in the school, and would downgrade their participation in schoolwork accordingly. Thus, in contrast to the footballers, some of whose preferred activities were integrated into "official" school life, to maintain the preferred activities of their culture these girls risked conflict with teachers, punishment, and failure to get their School Certificate to a much greater extent than other girls.

This was linked to their relationships with males at school. Although they were not interested in males of their own age as potential boyfriends, preferring older boys, they were friendly with an equivalent group of male "troublemakers" at school, and with other people from different forms who shared their interests. They had much less mobility and independence than males at their own school and than "the footballers".

Schoolwork, rules and teachers' directives were resented and often rejected when they prevented the girls from talking with each other. The girls spent their days at school finding places where they could talk and smoke. In the playground they were attracted to the fence where boys drove past in "hotted up" cars. Moreover, especially for girls from the most restrictive families (Turkish, Lebanese and

Portuguese), a major reason for truanting was to take up opportunities to meet boys. Their youth culture, oriented to attracting and talking about boys, was a major factor in the girls' rejection of school and, in turn, in their rejection by the school and other pupils who were more disposed to conformity. The sexual stigma implied by "slut" and "mole", therefore, combined with "troublemaker" in the girls' case. The culture's rejection of school in pursuit of males was met with a condemnation of the culture as a way of life inappropriate for female students in particular.

Their relations with boys, however, were fraught with ambiguity and tension. Especially in the non-ASC girls' case, their male counterparts maintained a double standard, distinguishing between girls whom they wanted to marry, who should be ladylike virgins, and girls they wanted to have "fun" with, who were "sexy" and less inhibited, more likely to be "troublemakers". The girls then felt placed in a position where they had to meet both standards. They would fail to attract or would lose a boyfriend if they did not fulfil the "sexy" standard; they would not be acceptable for marriage if they lost their virginity or their reputations as "good girls". Their problem was that their boyfriends wanted both.

Thus for non-ASC girls the female youth subculture was under the dominance and contradictory demands of male youth subculture which reflected the double standard of the wider ethnic cultures. Because relationships with males were so problematic, the friendship groups functioned as supports for their members' attempts to construct and maintain relationships with males. They would close ranks behind a member who was competing with another girl for a male's attention, and they constantly discussed each other's problems with boys, trying collectively to work out solutions.

Whereas none of "the footballers" or "the Greeks" foresaw problems in the relation between paid employment and their potential domestic situations, "the troublemakers" did. They regarded marriage, parenting and domestic work as their primary role in the future, but many expressed disillusionment about the role, hoping for some economic and personal independence based on full or part-time work, at least for a period. The tensions foreseen arose from two sources, the complications imposed by the relationship with their future husband, and the presumption that it would be the wife who undertook the bulk of the parental and domestic work.

Although they had sometimes conflicting beliefs about the relation between school achievement and job prospects, they were not convinced, given this scenario, that achievement at school mattered much *for them*. Their expectations of their future were closely tied in with their present preoccupations with males. This preoccupation was connected with the girls' failure at school, reinforced by what they perceived as teachers' rejection of the worth of their way of life. This reinforced their view that working hard at school was not a viable solution for them.

The careers teacher worked hard to make his classes interesting and "relevant", to provide an accurate and realistic picture of the options open to the girls when they left school. He encouraged the girls to participate in a simulated experience of "work life" through drama but, in his words, "The kids who need it most won't participate ... they are just not interested". From the girls' perspective, however, the problem was that it did not bite on their problems: "Oh, that's boring stuff, Mr — — he's all right, he tries to help us but ... it's boring an' all the goody goodies do that ... teachers think they know what's best for us ... I dunno."

Similarly, although the school curriculum did nothing overtly to reinforce the sexual division of labour, the teachers' apparent failure to articulate in any other than a negative and judgmental way with the girls' boy-oriented, "troublemaking" culture reinforced the cultural alienation and so helped to further entrench the girls' perspective on work. Teachers' responses failed to get at this. In general they were perceived by the girls as uncaring, even punitive, labelling the girls as socially and sexually deviant. The school failed to come to grips with the fact that the girls' perspective on work was deeply embedded in their youth culture and mediated through their relationships with boys, other girls, and teachers. It could not be dealt with in isolation in careers lessons; it needed to be confronted holistically across the curriculum and in the articulation between teachers' and pupils' cultures.

The general problem, then, was quite clear. The combination of a sex/gender urgency associated with a crucial stage of social and sexual development, with the basic desire for a secure identity, self-esteem, and acceptance in an achievable set of goals, given the culture in which they were growing up, made them perceive the wife/mother role as their only long-term option. They then saw the school as irrelevant to strategies for achieving this. Unable to relate positively to the girls' cultures as wholes, teachers were unable to devise strategies for helping the girls to consider realistically and work towards a wider range of options.

The point to emphasise here is that a culturally specific perspective on work is largely what underpins the "irrelevance" judgements made by students on school and teachers, even when teachers themselves hold a progressive approach to the question of gender and work, especially women and work.

Touchstone: Building a Coherent Curriculum

Although both "footballer" and "troublemaker" cultures had limitations which were recognised sooner or later by the young people, they also contained a wealth of knowledge and experience of real work situations, in paid employment and domestic work, and of the socio-cultural relations in which these situations were embedded. Much, indeed often most (especially in the girls' case), of this knowledge remained hidden from teachers. A curriculum which builds on youth cultures needs to recognise the genuine knowledge embedded in each cultural perspective, whether it is held by pupils or teachers. On the other hand, apart from credentialism, much of the knowledge of work located in teacher cultures remained obscure to or was rejected by the young people who were unable to relate it to their own perspectives.

The educational task, clearly, is to locate those points where different cultural bodies of knowledge converge, and start from there, building a coherent curriculum. We attempt to locate what we might call *touchstone*: the ways in which youth cultures articulate with each other and with teacher culture, through shared problems, interests, experiences and standards of appraisal (Walker 1988b Ch. 6, 1988c). This will involve a strong component of school-based curriculum development (Reynolds & Skilbeck, 1976; Skilbeck, 1984). Moreover, to incorporate, across the curriculum, an approach to "the world of work" which is both holistic and practical will mean emphasising not only points of coherence between teacher and student cultures, but touchstone between the "academic" subjects and the teacher subcultures in which they are embedded. The search for touchstone needs to extend to the informal experiences of pupils and their families in work of all kinds, whether sponsored by the school (e.g. work experience) or not (e.g. domestic work, part-time employment while at school). Learning about the needs and problems of students needs to be supplemented by building coherently on what is shared between work and schoolwork. That is to say, learning (by teachers and students) and curriculum development can proceed through the discovery and extension of the touchstone common to different perspectives. Appreciation of touchstone, of what is common, is a necessary condition for understanding the real significance of cultural differences, and for making informed and intelligent decisions about which ones should remain and which should change.

To discover the touchstone, teachers need to understand, concretely, just how students' repertoires function in practice, how they generate particular strategies for dealing with work and schoolwork (Woods 1980a). For example, "the troublemakers" strategies of "switching off", truanting, and talking things over with friends resulted from the girls' common preoccupation with males which was a key part of their perspective on work and schoolwork. Teachers need to understand how such problem-solving repertoires and the cultural perspectives reflected in them influence students' aspirations and their beliefs about the realistic options facing them, such as further education, specific employment options, or marriage and parenthood. Especially in the case of girls, there is a need to positively recognise and respect the problems for which the cultures are attempted solutions, rather than simply negatively to condemn behaviour which might be regarded as unacceptable. There was an obvious inequity of treatment as between the "macho" culture of "the footballers" and the "sexy" culture of "the troublemakers". Each culture was in large part the outworking of sex/gender problems, but whereas the most assertive boys were integrated into their school's "official" life, the most assertive girls were not. This no doubt reinforced gender inequities in the world of work.

The search for touchstone will also mean helping students to learn from each other's cultures as well as from teachers. For example, the ASC "footballers" eventually realised some of the advantages of the culture of "the Greeks", but this came too late. At school they tended to reject the other culture out of hand. In such cases teachers might well explore the details of each culture so as to develop curricular touchstone and expand the horizons of all students.

Intercultural learning among youth cultures is especially important when the problem-solving repertoires of other groups of young people function at their expense (Walker 1987b). The "macho" dominance of "footballer" and "Greek" cultures limited the learning options of other boys in the school, notably those regarded as "poofters". The changing of perspectives, and therefore of aspirations and beliefs about options, is more likely when intercultural understanding, harmony and cooperation is promoted among young people themselves, and they can learn to recognise actual and potential convergences between each other's problems and perspectives. (For examples see Walker 1988a, 1988b Ch. 4). Power differentials between groups of young people can be positively addressed through the kind of learning which leads to cultural change. Such learning starts with touchstone, and leads to shared experience and a more coherent curriculum.

No doubt this sounds all very well, but, it could be asked, is not more required than simply learning about each other? The answer depends on the kind of learning envisaged, the kind of interpersonal and inter-group processes involved. The stress on problem-solving means that both teachers and students need to be active participants in determining the course of learning, and of curriculum development itself. They will need to see how the learning process addresses their problems as they understand them. In the process of curriculum development stemming from the cultural approach I have been advocating, the central procedure is negotiation (Boomer 1982). Within a coherent curriculum, knowledge is built up out of touchstone by negotiation. In this process, a degree of cultural convergence is achieved, as students' and teachers' cultures are brought into closer and more productive engagement with each other. For there to be realistic and hardheaded— in a word, pragmatic—curriculum development, deals will need to be proposed and agreed to (Walker 1987c). It is more a matter of discussing what each party wants, or is prepared to accept; it involves examining what contribution each party can make towards solving the problems and underlying cultural perspectives of all parties. This understanding becomes the basis for a particular curricular coherence. Teachers endeavouring to develop or implement coherent curricula in a practically effective way could break this up into five steps:

1. Find out what the relevant people, i.e. pupils and teachers, regard as their problems, either explicitly through their own words or implicitly by their responses to situations and by their more settled practices.
2. Given their understanding of what their problems are, we next ask how they see their options for dealing with them. Can we find out what they think are the available solutions to their problems?
3. Analyse these accounts of the problems and solutions, to discover how coherent are the various cultural perspectives generating the analysis of problems and solutions. Are there contradictions in the views and practices of the people concerned? (Our assumption is that contradictory frameworks lead to less effective capacities for producing solutions.)
4. How do the perceived problems and solutions of one individual or group match up with the perceived problems and solutions of other individuals and groups? Is there any overlap? Any conflict? If so, how much of each, and how significant, practically speaking, are they?
5. Given our answers to the preceding questions, how realistic and how effective are the problem-solving perspectives being used by people involved in the overall problem-situation? What would have to be changed for the people involved to change their perspectives, in order to change the overall situation?

These steps should enable us to recognise the different styles, contexts and problem-perspectives implicit in the cultures, including the knowledge of both teachers and pupils.

Work Across the Curriculum

Within such a coherent curriculum, I believe, we should stress the importance of individual choice. To enhance it, the prime aim should be for the secondary school to provide, through a common curriculum, a broad understanding of the "world of work", in all its aspects, relating this to the specific backgrounds and future options of pupils through school-based developments and applications. Expansion of individuals' options, rather than specific vocational education, should be our orientation in gearing the curriculum to "the world of work". The basic problem facing many girls, for example, is their belief that their options are severely limited, and that therefore many of their particular problems cannot be solved, but simply have to be "lived with".

So far as possible, given present credentialist structures and likely future modifications of them, introduction of such a "work-orientation" should not be confined to a particular curriculum subject. It should be on a holistic basis, across the curriculum, at all levels of the school. Obviously certain studies are easier to adapt to this orientation than others; but overall coordination of studies is as important as adaptation of any particular subject.

There is therefore a parallel between the point about perspectives on "the world of work"—that they have to be understood as part of a whole culture and as mediated through many responses to school—and the present argument for a holistic treatment of work across the curriculum. The greater the coherence across the curriculum, provided this is anchored in teacher-student touchstone, the greater its appeal and relevance to students. Confinement of important concerns, needs and problems of young people (such as those relating to the world of work) to one school subject limits the appeal and relevance of the rest of the curriculum. The alternative, working cooperatively towards a coherent curriculum, not only maximises relevance and problem-solving capacity; it also opens up new possibilities for learning and development for both teachers and students.

[1.]   This chapter contains extracts from J.C. Walker, *School, Work and the Problems of Young People: A Cultural Approach to Curriculum Development* . Canberra: Curriculum Development Centre, 1987. Permission from the Curriculum Development Centre to reprint these extracts is gratefully acknowledged. The studies reported in this chapter were conducted with the permission of the New South Wales Department of Education. The cooperation of the Department, and the principals, teachers and students of the schools is also gratefully acknowledged.

16

School To Work

by William Taylor

There is in most countries a long-standing concern with improving the means whereby young people make the transition from school to work, and a history of reorganization and reform within the responsible agencies. Until quite recently, both as a practical process and as a subject for study, the education-work transition has been overwhelmingly in the hands of psychologists, and has been analysed principally at the individual level. Such theoretical elaborations as existed were rooted in the importance of relating an individual's knowledge, disposition, personal needs and possibilities of rendering service to the characteristics of particular forms of employment.

The history of such vocational guidance has been comprehensively reviewed by K. Miller *et al* (1973) who record a move during the 1960s away from the concept of vocational guidance, seen simply as the provision of satisfactory job opportunities, and towards "... on the one hand, the broader concept of helping the individual to decide upon the style of life that he wishes to lead, and on the other the more specific purpose of teaching decision making skills. The latter is seen as a necessary pre-requisite for coping with accelerating social change" (p. 266).

Other recent trends have included a greater stress on the *developmental* as opposed to the crisis-oriented nature of guidance; a more non-directive approach, calculated to enable individuals to identify and assess their own strengths rather than simply accept advice provided by the Careers Officer or teacher; recognition that the skills involved in providing vocational guidance and counselling are specific and important and require training; a wish to offer such guidance to *all* students, not just those following the less academic courses who had hitherto been the chief customers of the service; and a recognition (especially on the part of more radical critics) of the strain between a "client centred" and a "manpower centred" approach.

It would be a mistake to believe that these ideas are new. C. Millar (1961) quotes an article by Jones and Hand in the *1938 Year Book of the National Society for the Study of Education*, in which guidance is defined in terms that seem entirely contemporary:

> Guidance is coming to be regarded as the inseparable aspect of the educational process that is peculiarly concerned with helping individuals discover their needs, assess their potentialities, develop their life purposes, formulate plans of action in the service of these purposes and proceed to their realisation. The total teaching process involves both guidance and instruction as these terms have commonly been employed in the past, and as inseparable functions. Neither can be delegated in any discrete manner to separate functionaries ... ideally, there would be no such thing as a separate or self-contained guidance programme. Rather, guidance and instruction would be functioning as inseparable parts of a unitary educative process. The needs of students would constitute the stuff out of which a broadly defined scope would be formulated for the school curriculum ... (p.6-7).

Alongside these modifications to the philosophy and practice of vocational counselling, the effects of sociological research have begun to be felt in discussions of the education-work transition. The naivete of viewing this as a process of 'talent matching' of individuals and jobs has come in for criticism. March and March (1978) have challenged the theoretical rationality behind the "square pegs for square holes" philosophy:

> ... the world of work is viewed as consisting of a pool of workers and a pool of jobs. Each worker and each job has certain attributes that are valued by potential partners. The pairings of jobs and workers are such that neither workers nor jobs can do better ... (p.435)

In fact, of course, these perfect market situations do not exist. The possibility of substitutions both in respect of workers and of jobs is in many fields of employment very high, so high as to give the process of selection and placement a ritualistic rather than realistic character.

Drawing upon several decades of research on occupational and social mobility, and the links that exist between achieved educational levels and types of occupation entered, the sociologists have poured scorn on the individualist ideology of vocational counselling. Carter (1966) showed that only a third of the boys and half of the girls in his sample got jobs of the kind they were asking for. Maizels (1979) found that only one-third of leavers obtained jobs that reflected their own aspirations. Commenting upon these, and other similar findings, Roberts (1977) argues:

To predict the type of work that a school leaver will obtain, the relevant information concerns not what he would ideally like to do, but his educational qualifications and to a lesser extent the occupational status of his parents, together with the local job opportunity structure (p.3).

On this reading aspirations were best understood "not as preliminaries to decisive occupational choices, but as products of anticipatory socialization" (p.5).

Even in terms of its predominating individualist ethos, career education has been criticised for its failure to take individual needs into account. On the basis of their study of the transition from school to work, Hill and Scharff (1976) found that:

Whether there is a person responsible for 'careers' within the school or not, we found no one in any of the schools who thought *systematically* about the connection of work and the psychological meanings of a given job or occupation with the stage of development, with opportunities for growth, and with inner needs and resources of an individual student (p.268).

The work of guidance counsellors has for a long time been regarded with suspicion, especially by those committed to comprehensive forms of secondary education and the abolition of streaming and tracking. In the words of P. Taylor and Musgrove (1969):

The spread of counselling in our schools is one of the most potentially sinister features of the contemporary educational scene. It can become a device for restoring a teacher despotism which other forces have eroded. As more children of limited ability stay on in English schools beyond the statutory leaving age, we can expect to see an army of counsellors employed to cool them out (p. 11).

There has been recently a considerable vogue in sociological analyses that trace the connection - or, in terms popularized by Bowles and Gintis (1976) the "correspondence" - between the regime and values experienced and imbibed in schools, and the attitudes and behaviour consistent with occupancy of particular statuses in the adult world. An emphasis upon such "correspondence" has become the hallmark of those who find the educational and social arrangement of a contemporary capitalist society repugnant, and who wish by democratic, extra-parliamentary or, in some cases, even violent means to overthrow existing structures in favour of what usually turns out to be vaguely conceived arrangements consistent with highly personal millenarian interpretations of Marxism.

It is a pity that the debate on these matters has now acquired, at least in some places, such a strongly ideological character. It is surely possible to demythologize the rhetoric of careers preparation, and to recognize the realities of working life in an industrialized and urbanized class society characterized by a division of labour, *without* becoming an exponent of revolutionary change. For some radicals, the fact that society is unable to offer to all its youth a personally enriching as well as materially rewarding occupational future is a matter of grave moral concern. For conservatives, the impracticability of meeting the likely aspirations and expectations generated by better quality education is seen as a threat to social stability and orderly reform. Both radicals *and* conservatives who make judgements upon these matters are for the most part drawn from that narrow spectrum of society which has indeed learned to entertain large expectations of personal fulfilment through work. Unfortunately for the radical, fortunately for the conservative, it seems that a large proportion of our young people have not. Instead they possess reasonably "realistic" expectations about what working life has to offer. In the words of a recent study:

> ... young men and women had feared the entry to work. They had expected callousness, cruelty, unreasonable demands, ogre-like gaffers and carping or mischievous colleagues. The reality was always better than the expectations even in the most unsatisfactory jobs. For the majority, once the initial phase was over - and that usually lasted a short period of at the most six months, but usually a few weeks or even days for some - the new employee role was felt to be preferable to the pupil role, despite the lack of thought put into the changeover by most employers.
>
> This meant that, in common with other research ... we found that young people did not describe their own transition from school to work in terms of implying crisis. Education was, as David Downes describes it "an irritant" (Bazalgette, 1978).

To espouse barricade eschatology (Bowers, 1978) or the utopian images of the neo-romantics is easy. Much easier than to tackle the problems of improving the quality of working life, relating schooling and employment without sacrifice of fundamental educational values and facilitating transition between the two in an existing and very real world. It is thus hardly surprising that so many educators have adopted Neo-Marxist and quasi-Romantic postures. In the meantime, for some people at least, there is work to be done.

Reference has already been made to charges concerning the ritualistic character of vocational guidance and counselling. These have been linked with the view that such counselling played very little part in influencing individual decisions. This has been challenged by Lambert (1978) who states on the basis of an analysis of data collected in connection with the National Child Development Study:

The ... assertion that 'there is no study of school leavers in Britain in which the Careers service, Careers teachers or any other body offering vocational guidance has emerged as a major influence' ... is not borne out by our findings. For the young people in the NCDS the predominant source of information regarding their likely first job was said to be 'at school, from a teacher or careers talk or film'. Our findings have however shown that the influence of such information on their choice was likely to be greater on those who were doing well at school (p.158-159).

Within the past few years, the notion of "Careers Education" which first gained prominence in the United States, has been widely applied elsewhere. Such application has received an impetus in the United Kingdom from the requirements in the 1973 Employment and Training Act that local education authorities should provide such a service in all their education institutions. The scope of Careers Education is a good deal wider than that of vocational guidance. It has been defined by Dawes (1977) in the following terms:

CEPs are primarily concerned to help young people determine the kind of life that they want, and in that context to consider which amongst the jobs realistically available to them offers the most likely and approximate fit to what they seek as a style of life and as a satisfying way of "making a living". To achieve this, CEPs must first help pupils to achieve a degree of accurate and full self-awareness, including a realistic sense of personal strengths and limitations, a capacity for accurate calculation of the probabilities of their achieving what they find attractive, and a shrewd knowledge of what they might do - well in advance of meeting selection processes - to prepare themselves for these processes (another anticipatory socialization function) (p.11).

Bazalgette (1978) has argued that the site of such work should not be *between* school and employment, but should encompass elements of both.

Since we know that unemployment is part of the post-school reality with which pupils must contend, then a Careers Education Programme must give due weight to this possibility. This has been recognised by Watts (1978) who suggests that some possible currricular objectives relating to the issue of unemployment would include *employability skills*, such as job search, job acquisition and job retention; *adaptability awareness*, to broaden the range of what is contemplated as possible; *survival skills*, which would encompass an awareness of the psychological effects of unemployment and a knowledge of what support services are available within the community; *contextual awareness* embodying an appreciation of why unemployment is a current reality; *leisure skills, alternative opportunity awareness* such as Manpower Services Commission programmes and educational openings and finally *opportunity creation skills*, not omitting the possibilities of self employ-ment, and individual entrepreneurship.

Many of these principles have been incorporated in the UK Schools Council Careers Education and Guidance Project. Based upon a concept of Careers Education that "involves presenting individuals with learning experiences which encourage them to make personal decisions and to act on these decisions so that they can gain an increasing measure of control over their own lives", the Project leaders have argued for 'work' as a subject of study within the school. They have sought to provide teaching materials that could be used in an integrated way in connection with, for example, Social Education, Economics, English and other subjects, whilst at the same time providing examples and situations which pupils might discuss amongst themselves and with their teachers. Hitherto, there has been a heavy emphasis in vocational work in schools on the informational content of what is provided. But if pupils are unwilling or unable to use and interpret such information, merely to go on adding to it serves little purpose. Trials were conducted in over three hundred schools, and involved more than a thousand teachers working with 150,000 children. The teaching packages are of an unconventional design, based upon a media-style presentation designed to appeal to a broad range of pupil interests. Since there are great variations in the way in which schools tackle career work, the adaptability of the materials has been stressed.

If it is to be useful and effective, careers education needs to develop what may be called both horizontal and vertical linkages. Horizontally with on the one hand the processes of vocational education and training that feature in the general and specialist curriculum of the school, and on the other with the 'in-work' training that is supplied by employers. Vertically, in respect of those different categories of clients that have been identified by OECD (1978) as:

(i)   those who will enter the labour force at the end of compulsory education;
(ii) those who will enter the labour force at the various levels of post compulsory education;
    a.   with an employment qualification;
    b.   without an immediately usable employment qualification;
(iii) those new entrants already in the labour force who have difficulty in finding employment;
(iv) established members of the labour force who are unemployed or who wish to change their employment or improve their qualification (p.21).

While, as has been emphasized, information is not in itself sufficient as a basis for adequate counselling, it is vitally necessary. There are certain inherent lags in the signalling system by means of which educational institutions respond to changes in the market for labour, and employers modify their recruitment and training policies and structures in response to variations in the quantity and quality of the output from the schools and colleges. It must be stressed that this is essentially a two-way process of mutual influence. A whole paper could be written on ways in which the channel capacity and message clarity of this system could be increased, and the "noise" that surrounds many of the messages that it carries reduced, but in the present context it must be sufficient to mention one or two modest steps that might be taken in this direction.

In the post-secondary sphere, institutions need freedom within their budgets to respond to needs for skilled development and manpower training that arise, often at relatively short notice, from industrial, economic and technological developments in their neighbourhoods. This requires the existence of a strong regional or local orientation on the part of some at least of the institutions concerned, discretion in the mounting of new programmes and the closing of old ones, and staffing strategies, including buying-in of sessional instructors and the carrying of a proportion of short-term appointments, that will facilitate rapid adaption. It is partly with this in mind that a Department of Education and Science working group in the United Kingdom has recently recommended that Polytechnics and other public sector institutions of higher education, should, like universities, be "programme funded" rather than having to seek approval on a course-by-course basis.

But forms of financial and course control that facilitate institutional adaption will not work if internal structure inhibits change and requires lengthy administrative and political bargaining delays before a new course can be offered. Where a departmental structure based upon strongly institutionalized disciplines or professional orientations exists, such difficulties can sometimes be acute. The existence of a number of fairly loose interdisciplinary groupings, centres, units and areas can facilitate change without threatening the basic disciplinary or professional structure.

The efficacy of the signalling system between education and the world of work can also depend a great deal on the existence of a complex network of individual contacts, based upon professional associations, community groups, regular mutual visits, one-off lectures and consultancies, lay representation on governing bodies and advisory committees down to the individual department or course-team, access to common literature and so on. Effective signalling depends on permeable boundaries.

Fortunately, the production and dissemination of high quality information in usable form is being facilitated by the application of computer technology, the introduction of video display facilities such as those of the UK "Viewdata" system, and the growth of community broadcasting and cheap reprographics. Viewdata offers the possibilities of colleges and employers providing frequently updated information about job opportunities and training students and workers through telephone-linked television sets. Eventually such sets may be found in most homes. In the immediate future they will be a facility provided by job centres, post offices and public libraries.

The theory and practice of careers education has of necessity had to be developed in a way that takes account of the reality of status and income differentials; highly imperfect markets for labour; selection mechanisms the rhetoric of which is that of meritocratic desert, but which are still powerfully influenced by ascription and chance; role requirements that demand early rather than late socialization, and an economic context affected by the vicissitudes of international trade, the uncertainties of technological innovation and implementation, and the hazards of political judgements concerning fiscal and monetary policy. At the same time, careers education has to accommodate as best it may to the imperatives of equality, openness, recurrency of opportunity and democratic participation by means of which educational decisions, both at system and individual level, are increasingly legitimated.

In this context there are great difficulties in matching the individualist and development imperatives of what may be called the careers education ideology and the 'realities' of the world of work. Peterson and Johnson (1977) undertook a content analysis of a selection of the Careers Education materials used in the United States schools, and were forced to conclude that the analysed materials are defective in supporting career education's goals of realistic student expectations'. In their judgement 'curriculum writers have tended to work only one side of the street and ... the resultant unbalanced concentration on an idealized view of work promotes naivete that sets the student up for eventual disillusionment and defeat' (p. 54).

Just as the local medical practice lacks status in comparison to the research laboratory in which the causes of particular diseases are investigated and explained, so the careers educator has to endure the charges of the sociologists and radical reformers that he is merely facilitating or marginally modifying for the individual the impact of highly determined group processes, which his lack of activist political commitment debars him from altering.

This has had its consequences for the resources and the status accorded to the academic study of vocational guidance and careers education, and the opportunities available within colleges and the universities for the training and further education of its practitioners. Few professors of education in the United Kingdom claim this as their principal speciality. To complicate matters still further, the fact that most clients of careers education in the past were those who found it hardest to secure satisfying and remunerative employment, and for whom the concept of a "career" was in practice least appropriate, does not help the image and status of the specialism. To maintain the medical analogy, while the discovery in the laboratory of a particular virus and of the means of immunizing whole populations against it is much more 'significant' than the efforts up to that point of individual GPs to alleviate the condition of persons suffering from that disease, the possibility of such a discovery does not cancel out the importance and relevance of the GPs' work. Indeed, even when the larger medical or societal change has occurred, the need for individual diagnosis, prescription and evaluation does not disappear, even if its context is very different from before.

It would be a pity if the search for underlying historical and social determinants, the building of 'critical theory', and a stress on creating the political base for structural reform were to divert attention from the needs of individuals for information and face-to-face counselling and advice. A market system, which does not depend upon early indenture to specified occupations or upon the direction of labour, inevitably has its casualties. Devising the means whereby their number can be minimised, and those who fall can be helped, is inevitably less glamorous than the 'barricade eschatology' that increasingly seems to characterize some branches of educational discourse. But it is important work, none the less.

Education and the Quality of Working Life

Lest we embrace too sharp a contrast between the work orientation of Victorian times and that of today, we might remind ourselves that over a hundred years ago the socialist Lafargue wrote:

> A strange delusion possesses the working classes of the nations where capitalist civilization holds its sway. This delusion drags in its train the individual and social woes which for two centuries have tortured sad humanity. This delusion is the love of work. The furious passion for work, pushed even to the exhaustion of the vital force of the individual and his progeny. Instead of opposing this mental aberration, the priests, the economists and the moralists have cast a sacred halo over work. Blind and finite men, they have wished to be wiser than their Gods; weak and contemptible men, they have presumed to rehabilitate what their God had cursed. I who do not profess to be a Christian, an economist or a moralist, I appeal for their judgement to that of their Gods; from the preachings of their religious, economic or free thought ethics to the frightful consequences of work in capitalist society (pp. 9-10).

This theme has a continuous history, especially in radical thought. Marxist rhetoric in particular stresses the hostile and alienating character of work in a capitalist society, in which, in the words of Behn (1974) "... Job experiences are not rewarding beyond pecuniary gains. Work is necessary in order to consume and consumption is the sphere of activity where people can express their 'freedom' and 'creativity' to the extent that they can afford to do so ..."

It is impracticable for me to offer adequate evidence in the present context for a view that lies behind much of the subsequent discussion in this section, namely that the experiences of work in an industrialized capitalist society and in an industrialized socialist society are not all that different. Indeed, Marx himself in his "critique of the Gotha Programme", distinguishes between the conditions of post-revolutionary socialism, where unequal individual endowments will produce inequality in productive capacity and therefore unequal reward, and the position under the eventual 'higher stage' of genuine Communism, when such abundance has been achieved that individuals will receive according to their needs (Bell 1976 p. 262). Many radical humanists, recognizing the realities of employment under "State Socialism", lack any historical or currently extant model of an economic system and work relationship that accords with their own values and ideas. China for long had a claim to their allegiance, which it has recently begun to lose. As 'socio-technical' theorists of organizations have argued, the pattern of relationships in the work place is largely influenced by the nature of the technology employed. In this respect, motor car factories are very different places from steel works, coal-mines from hotels. The kinds of adult socialization that go on in these work settings, the nature of the everyday consciousness of the employee, have more to do with the kind of work he or she is doing than with the form of ownership and control. I do not want to argue that the latter is of no importance. There is, in fact, some interesting empirical evidence about the effects of employee ownership on productivity, profitability, morale and work satisfaction. In the light of all this, I do not find it particularly profitable to draw sharp contrasts between a subjective experience of work in, on the one hand, the UK, the USA and Australia, and on the other, the Soviet Union, Cuba or Albania. What is likely to matter much more than the particular political system of the society in which a person is employed is the level of industrialization and organization of the enterprise in those societies.

This said, what do we know about the criteria that people have concerning quality of working life, and to what extent can education help to satisfy these criteria? There is now an extensive literature on this subject: for a useful cross section, see Davis and Cherns (1975) Campbell (1976). Walton (1975) lists eight criteria:

(a)   Adequate and fair compensation.

(b)   Safe and healthy working conditions.
(c)   Immediate opportunity to use and develop human capacities.
(d)   Opportunity for continued growth and security.
(e)   Social integration in the work organization.
(f)   Constitutionalism in the work organization.
(g)   Work and the total life space.
(h)   Social relevance of work in life.

It is the conventional wisdom (especially, as we have seen, among intellectuals and educators) that most people do not enjoy a high level of work satisfaction. There is certainly some evidence to show that work is not a 'central life interest' for more than a minority. To quote a useful survey of the relevant literature by Dubin *et al* (1975):

> In the first study of this topic, twenty four per cent of the industrial workers in the sample reported work as a central life interest. In studies made since that time, an even lower percentage of blue-collar workers in a variety of settings have been found to have a central life interest in work. For example, only 14 per cent of the lumber workers surveyed ... and only 12 per cent of the long distance truck drivers ... had a job oriented CLI. Several studies have shown clerical workers to differ widely in their CLI in work; 76 per cent of the Amana Society sampled ... 24 per cent of the Canadian retail sales clerks ... and 14 per cent of the British Bank clerks.

But if work is not a central life interest, this does not mean that the worker is necessarily dissatisfied. When Cantril and his associates asked 20,000 people in countries around the world to identify features of their lives in respect of which they had particular feelings of deficiency only 26 per cent expressed a wish for 'more interesting work; [a] more congenial job' against twice that number opting for 'more pay, larger income' and a full 53 per cent who chose a 'better education than I have'. This, of course, proves nothing. As the record of human behaviour under extreme circumstances testifies, we are capable of adapting ourselves to a wide variety of circumstances, not least those of the work place. The fact remains that levels of work satisfaction reported in surveys (as distinct from the individual statements selected by some authors to illustrate their theses) tend generally to indicate a greater measure of contentment than superficial observation by non-participants, or short participative visits by sociologists with return tickets might suggest. This phenomenon has been discussed in relation to what is called "tolerance theory". By a combination of processes, including task disassociation, a focus upon peer-group relations, accommodation to short-term substitute goals which structure an otherwise meaningless activity, people come to terms with the demands of their working environments.

For many people - perhaps for most - this process of adjustment and accommodation means that something is lost. Novelists and imaginative writers have done rather better than psychologists and sociologists in describing what has to be sacrificed. We are short of accounts that analyse the human costs and benefits of socialization within the work place. We need more studies such as that of Ihde (1975), who looks at the phenomenology of man-machine relations in terms of the extent to which the machine is an extension of personal capacity, a tool under conscious control, or itself the determinant and director of speed and response, a difference that can be represented as [(man-machine) —— world] or [man —— (machine-world)]. It has been argued by Blauner (1964) that the possibilities for higher levels of work satisfaction are greater in the higher automated factory, where workers feel themselves to be in charge of the machine rather than paced by it; evidence on this issue is not all in the same direction (Cotgrove 1976) and much work remains to be done, especially in relation to the specific problems that are presented by such factors as the employment history of the area concerned and the specifics of the technologies involved (See also Bensman and Lillienfeld 1973).

In some contemporary statements about occupational alienation, the author too readily assumes that, if they had been given free choice before the corrupting effects of work in an industrialized society eroded their capacities for response, his subjects would have freely chosen some other kind of work and given it central life interest, just as the author's own work is for him. But there is another side to this. Coser (1974) has written of those institutions which make "... total claims on their members and which attempt to encompass within their circle the whole personality. These might be called *greedy institutions* in so far as they seek exclusive and individual loyalty and they attempt to reduce the clashes of competing roles and status positions on those they wish to encompass within their boundaries ..." (p. 6).

The last decade has seen efforts in several countries to give workers a larger say in the policies and decisions of their enterprises. Attempts to institutionalize participation, often within the rhetoric of industrial democracy, generally represent the application of a consensus model, in which employees acquire certain rights in return for the acceptance of greater responsibility. It has been argued, however, that the "conflict model" represented by collective bargaining and the growth of trade union power is a more real form of democratic participation than the creation of works councils and the co-option of employees onto Boards of Directors. But here as elsewhere, the evidence on the desire for and effects of greater participation in the work place is not all in one direction. Alutto and Belasso (1972) have introduced the idea that employees can be "decisionally saturated", called upon to participate to a greater extent than they desire, as well as "decisionally deprived". In their work with teachers, they found that *over-participation* could give rise to as much dissatisfaction as lack of opportunity to participate. In fairness, however, it must be said that the direction of their findings suggested that far more teachers are "deprived" rather than 'saturated', and there is a long way to go before an appropriate equilibrium is secured (Taylor 1976). Long (1978), in a study of a medium-sized regional trucking firm that had been taken over by its own employees following a series of disastrous losses, distinguishes between *ownership* and *participation*, the former having no necessary connotations for the latter. In examining the effects of employee ownership, he found that "Creation of a joint pay-off relationship through employee ownership did appear to favourably influence integration, involvement, commitment and satisfaction, independently of the effects of increased participation". Profits were up, labour turnover was down.

The implication of what has been said so far in this section is that efforts to raise job satisfaction, increase participation and spread the benefits of ownership, *can* have positive effects on the quality of working life as experienced and reported upon by those immediately concerned, but that, as in all things, excessive and ill-judged enthusiasm in these matters can have unforeseen negative consequences. Futhermore, we need to be aware of the bias that particular methodologies can introduce into studies in this area. Simonds and Orife (1975) examined worker behaviour (rather than attitude) in relation to job enrichment and remuneration and found strong support "... for the view that pay increases are important to non-supervisory workers even at small differentiations. It indicated either indifference to job routineness or perhaps that while some of the workers may have preferred less routine jobs, a possibly equal number may have preferred more routine jobs" (p. 611).

What in this context can be said about the role that education might play in improving the quality of working life? The establishment of clear one-to-one relations between particular kinds of educational input and subsequent gains in worker satisfaction and personal fulfilment are not really what matters. Behind every teacher's efforts lies the simple faith that the more literate, numerate and socially aware the students, the wider the range of personal, social, and occupational skills at their command, the greater their confidence and capacity for coping with adversity, then the more likely they are to secure a sure foothold in the world and to work, to derive something of value from their work experience and to render better service to family and fellows. Most teachers are not politically aware in the sense of cultivating a capacity for what analysts of ethnic and age relations have called "resistance" (Hall and Jefferson 1976). They cannot predict the future circumstances of their students, they cannot control the extent to which external circumstances, nepotism and chance will determine subsequent occupational opportunities and destinations. It is precisely this uncertainty that in the past has been used to justify a general rather than a vocational education, a broad preparation for a variety of unpredictable subsequent conditions, rather than specific training for a task that in five, ten or twenty years may no longer exist. In the last decade however, the problems of unemployment, complaints by both employers and employees about the "irrelevance" of what is done in schools to subsequent adult experience, and a desire to minimize the disaffection of youth from education have come together to encourage interest in the identification of the skills and competencies of working life which might now be used as a basis for an educational programme that is both general and vocational in character. The OECD (1978) has secured at least a verbal integration of general and vocational in a sentence that is worth pondering:

> Education will be completely general only when it includes preparation for life at work as an inseparable part of preparation for adult life (p. 18).

In 1980 an inter-governmental conference took place in Paris to consider the list of competencies drawn up by the secretariat of OECD and circulated to member countries in March 1979. The Secretariat distinguished between three competency domains - intellectual, psycho-social and practical. Within the first of these, the two major headings are *reasoning* (recognizing why certain processes or actions precede or follow others in a work situation; identifying and defining problems correctly) and the *ability to learn*. The psycho-social domain includes *personal* and *social skills* (of communication, acceptance of supervision and control, ability to work with others and alone, the taking of initiative and the assumption of responsibility) *knowledge of the world of work*, and competencies in *surviving and developing in employment*. Finally, under the heading of practical competencies come *literacy* (reading, writing, speaking and listening, knowledge of another language) *numeracy, manual dexterity, elementary technology, competency in finding a job* and *health and safety*.

Whether the details of this list will survive the scrutiny that it will undoubtedly receive in the member countries of the Organization and at the conferences called to prepare a final version remains to be seen. Whilst there is nothing very original about such lists, they do represent an attempt to break down content and status barriers that still exist between vocational and general education, and to relate both to the lives that students will live as citizens and as workers, not excluding the possibility of periodic unemployment.

To translate such aims into curriculum, pedagogical practices and appropriate modes of assessment is a larger and more problematic task. There is much work to be done in bringing learning theory and instructional methods to bear on the problems of skill acquisition and social learning. There is no shortage of schemes based upon operationalized objectives, but most such schemes have a rather narrow focus, being concerned with the impact of a particular unit of instruction or course without paying too much attention to student charcteristics and situational factors. Given the importance of attitudes and motivation on the part of students whose attendance will be largely on a voluntary basis, a satisfactory pedagogic model for the integration of general and vocational education will need to be constructed within a broader framework and one which places due emphasis on the way in which previous school and work experience influences response to subsequent learning. In this respect the 'Mastery Learning' model of Bloom (1976) has the advantage of stressing the importance of cognitive and effective entry charcteristics in relation to the success of instruction and its outcomes.

In passing, it is worth noting that the claim that "most students can attain a high level of learning capability if instruction is approached sensitively and systematically, if students are helped when and where they have learning difficulties, if they are given sufficient time to achieve mastery, and if there is some clear criteria of what constitutes mastery" (p.4), if substantiated, has important policy implications. In Bloom's own words:

> If the schools can bring a large majority of students to the level of learning that was hitherto expected of only the most gifted and able students, it can no longer be with expectation that such students will go on to do advanced work in the subject. No field could possibly use so many 'gifted' students. More and more it will be necessary to ask whether the time and effort required to learn a subject to a high level can be justified for the particular students, the school, and the society. Thus, the increased ability to control and determine the school learning of our students places upon educators increased responsibility for providing a curriculum which is in the best interests of the students and the society (p.214).

When the amount of talent in society is a scarce resource, assumed to be determined by genetic inheritance or by environmental influences that are beyond the educator's control, the task of the schools is to identify, select and nurture such talent. But if Bloom is right, and if we now have the means to bring everyone up to the level of the best, the policy problem is far greater. There are resonances here of the old argument about 'over-educating', of producing so many people with high school diplomas and degrees that there will be no-one left to undertake the computer-age equivalents of hewing wood and drawing water. I raise this problem only quickly to drop it again, as beyond the scope of this chapter. But the possibilities that Bloom's claims raise, even if we dispute the likelihood that mastery learning can be successfully operationalized within existing or likely resource constraints, certainly need discussion.

So do ideas such as those of Cronbach and Snow (1977) who in connection with an analysis of what we have to learn from research done on learning interactions ("an interaction is said to be present when a situation has one effect on one kind of person and a different effect on another" p.3), argue that single rank, meritocratic selection has a strongly conservative influence, in that it takes out of academic programmes those who are less easily taught and thus removes the incentive for teachers and institutions to devise procedures for helping those with 'non-standard talents'. Whilst not sharing Bloom's assumptions about our capacity to generalise high levels of mastery, Cronbach and Snow:

> urge the social planner to be concerned not with running a fair competition but with running a talent-development operation that will bring everyone somewhere near his or her highest level of contribution (with due regard to the educational requirements of the society). The complex technical society needs a high percentage of persons in advanced occupations to maintain physical well being and promote cultural developments. It can use trained persons in large numbers, and it has almost no way to use untrained manpower. Any untrained segment is a source of social chaos and demoralization (p.8).

It is also worth noting that Cronbach and Snow's findings are not consistent with those of Bloom as far as eventual outcomes are concerned. "We once hoped that instructional methods might be found whose outcomes correlate very little with general ability. This does not appear to be a viable hope. Outcomes from extended instruction almost always correlate with pretested ability, unless a ceiling is artificially imposed." Those last few words are also thought-provoking in relation to the aspirations that some people have for greater equality of outcomes.

Conclusions: Policy and Practice

In this final section I want, somewhat telegraphically and dogmatically, to list a number of developments in the policy and practice of education/work relations that would be beneficial to individual students, to schools and to society.

First, efforts are needed to raise the average attainments of the school leaver by identifying those skills and forms of knowledge into which every future worker and citizen needs to be inducted as a basis of subsequent learning and responsible social participation; by devising means whereby teachers and schools can be accountable to their publics without sacrificing appropriate kinds of professional autonomy or engaging in practices that stress short-term gain at the expense of long-term educational benefit; by more careful initial selection of teachers, improved initial training, systematic induction and carefully devised and freely available in-service education and career development; by the identification and dissemination of good practices, and by the selection, evaluation and effective utilization of audio-visual and computer-based teaching aids.

Second, on the assumption that unemployment consequent upon the imperfections of the world economic order and the impact of technological change will be a continuing problem in many countries for the foreseeable future, we need to devise support systems and training programmes calculated to minimize the effect of such unemployment on social adjustment, willingness to seek work, openness to new educational opportunities, and ability to render public service.

Third, we must learn from the long debate that has gone on about continuing education, recurrent education, *education permanente*, lifelong education and community education and create such structures and means of financial support as will encourage adult workers to take full advantage of post-experience training and re-training opportunities, especially during periods of involuntary unemployment and as a preparation for retirement. The targets for such programmes and financial support schemes need to include the whole range from adult non-literates to highly qualified professionals who require to be kept abreast of new research findings in their respective fields. While such needs cannot be met with a single type of institution, however polytechnical in character, the plurality of organisations, institutions and training mechanisms that make up such a system needs a minimum level of co-ordination, sufficient to ensure that gaps are identified and filled, and wasteful duplication is avoided.

Fourth, in those countries where agencies outside ministries and Departments of Education have grown up - sometimes very rapidly - to provide a variety of education and training schemes to cope with unemployment and shortages of skill-training facilities, careful thought must be given to the costs and benefits of administrative and financial separation of responsibility, and to the possibilities of integrating such education and training within a single comprehensive service.

Fifth, attention needs to be given to ways in which what I have called the 'signalling system' requires modification in the light of the looseness of fit that characterizes levels of schooling and entry to particular occupations where academic, general and vocational education are integrated within a single school system or range of post-compulsory institutions. While we need to understand the macro-relations of family background, school achievement, occupational choice and career progress, such understanding, and the programmes of social and political reform to which it is linked are no substitute for the provision of appropriate careers education for individual students. If individual counselling and guidance is to be effective, it needs to penetrate both school and work place, and to be conceived as a continuously available service, not simply as a means of easing the transition from school to work.

Sixth, we have to reconceptualize the idea of work in environmentally conscious, industrialized societies, in a way that takes account of the likelihood of structural unemployment, minimizes effects of such unemployment on individual morale without at the same time eroding a commitment to service, and lends dignity and value to those who are the recipients of income transfers without destroying motivation and the will to labour. All these things are much easier said than done. But it is nonetheless important that they be said, and go on being said, for it is through the dissemination of ideas by the media, through debate, through discussion and conference that such ideas are refined and assimilated and their institutional implications worked out.

Seventh, academics and researchers need to play their part in mobilizing all those disciplines capable of contributing to a better understanding of the relations between education and work. At present, the discourse of economists, sociologists, specialists in instructional methods, enterprise managers, policy-makers and guidance specialists share very little awareness of a common problem. Examine the bibliographies in articles and books produced by authors from these various fields, and you find very little intercitation. This is particularly marked when comparing the writings of sociologists on the distribution of opportunity and life chances *vis-a-vis* subsequent employment, and those of psychologists and guidance specialists discussing ways in which individuals can be better prepared to face the demands of work. The result is the use of a lowest common denominator of theory, concept and reference, with a corresponding loss of rigour and explanatory power.

The complex interdependencies characteristic of technological societies tends to place great power in the hands of small groups of people, such as the boards of multi-national companies and the executive committees of trade unions. If such groups pursue their interests without sufficient regard to broader concerns and some perception of the general good, then life in democratic societies becomes very difficult. It is always possible to produce intellectual justifications for action in the pursuit of self interest. The businessman asserts the importance of market freedom; the union leader stresses the absence of equality. The power that is wielded in this way creates situations for which our political, moral and educational systems have yet to come to terms.

The growth of centralized *political* power in the nineteenth century has been followed in this century by the growth of *organizational* and *technical* power, the button - and the show-of-hands ballot, that can under certain circumstances threaten the constitutional and social stability of the nation state. Appeals for national unity and a recognition of the public interests sit uneasily with the demythologized, disenchanted sophistication of our age. Marx, Freud and the examples of totalitarianism we have seen in the modern world have combined to make us suspicious of claims to represent the general will. Self consciousness of our own darker motives has affected our interpretation of the motives of our fellow men and women.

How then can we develop attitudes, behaviour and structures that recognize our interdependence and the dangers of electronic and group power, that recognize the sterility of a confrontational stance between manager and workers and the actual and potential dangers of conceptualising labour relations in terms of confrontation and conflict rather than co-operation and consensus, *without* resorting to outdated and reactionary calls for "national unity" and the pious neglect of self-interest, in ways that will protect democracy as well as fostering flexibility in employment patterns and practices? That is one of the most demanding challenges that face us.

Unemployment and the Schools

17

by Ivan Snook

Various solutions are proposed to 'the problem of unemployment'. Among the most persistent are those which depend on a belief that schools can provide a solution to the problem. There are those who believe that schools are the cause of the problem and there are others who suggest that, whether or not they are causally related to the problem, schools can be (and must be) a central part of the solution. This tendency to blame the schools and to saddle them with solving the problem performs a useful political function. Whether it is fair or reasonable is another matter.

Schools as Part of the Problem

The argument that schools are the cause (or a contributory cause) of unemployment runs something like this: Schools have provided curricula unrelated to life; they have concentrated on the academic to the neglect of the practical; they have given youngsters aspirations beyond their capabilities and neglected the skills needed by the labour market. Hence schools are directly responsible for the growth of unemployment. It is a coherent thesis, but is there any evidence for it?

The first piece of evidence usually cited is the fact that most of the unemployed are unskilled, the implication being that if the schools had done their job, these people would be skilled - and employed.

The relationship between level of skills and incidence of unemployment is much more complicated than is normally recognised. In Britain, for example, Hawkins argues that there was once a connection between deficient skills and unemployment but that since 1980 "The composition of the unemployed has ... moved closer to the composition of the labour force itself" (Hawkins, 1984 p. 38). Hawkins believes, however, that there is still a relationship between level of skills and incidence of unemployment pointing to the fact that a survey of long-term unemployed in 1979 showed that only a minority had formal vocational or educational qualifications. Similarly, Thompson and Ruehl (1985 p. 11) produce the following figures to document the connection between 'social class' (as they put it) and unemployment:

Table 1	
Male Unemployment Rates In Britain: 1981	
	%
1. Professional	2.5
2. Managerial/Administration	3.3
3. (a) Skilled non-manual	4.4
(b) Skilled manual	9.6
4. Semi-skilled	9.6
5. Unskilled	15.0

Care must be taken not to draw the wrong conclusion from these data. Two points must be noted:

(1) People who are qualified for more skilled positions can (and do) take positions at less skilled levels (teachers become postal workers, nurses become aids, tradesmen become labourers and typists take house work jobs). Thus lower level unemployment is exaggerated and higher level minimised (imagine, for example, if every trained teacher and nurse doing some less skilled job were to be counted as unemployed). In addition, as Hawkins points out:

> In a market where many workers are chasing few vacancies, employers are likely to raise their recruitment standards so that the more marginal applicants are automatically rejected (1984 p. 38).

(2) Unemployment *rates* depend not only on the number of job-seekers but on the number of vacancies. Hawkins (p. 51) shows that between 1975 and 1982 the ratio of unemployed to vacancies in the 'craftpersons' category rose from 2:1 to 27:1 and during the same period the ratio among managerial/professional groups rose from 2:1 to 17:1.

So, even if there is the normally assumed correlation between the skills a person has and the likelihood of unemployment, it would be ridiculous to lay blame on the schools. If they are turning out 'too many' unskilled people it is equally true that they are turning out 'too many' skilled people as well. That is to say, they are turning out too many people - which in the employment sense is right: there are too few jobs for the number seeking them. If the schools were able to turn unskilled workers into craft persons or professionals they would not automatically become employed: they are more likely to become unemployed potters or lawyers.

But schools do not normally teach particular or vocational skills. They turn out people with rather general credentials. And here, the picture is even more confused. In April 1978, the Department of Labour carried out a survey of the 10,424 registered unemployed in a sample of New Zealand towns and cities, and concluded:

> Contrary to what is generally believed, the distribution of educational qualifications among the registered unemployed in the survey does not differ too greatly from that of the New Zealand labour force as a whole (*Labour and Employment Gazette*, 1979 p. 4).

As an example, 69.3% of the unemployed had no formal qualifications *but 69.2% of the workforce* had no such qualifications either. Similarly 3.9% of the unemployed were 'highly qualified' (i.e. had tertiary qualifications); 4.0% of the workforce have such qualifications. On the basis of these data it can be said that, compared to other similarly placed persons, a person with a tertiary qualification is just as likely to be unemployed as a person with no qualification at all. This suggestion is supported by Susan Shipley's findings in Palmerston North, although her sample is too small to justify firm generalisations (1982 p. 103). Thus, for example, 44% of the females employed full-time, and 50% of the unemployed females seeking full-time work had no school qualifications. At the other extremes 5.2% of the males employed full-time and 6.7% of the unemployed males seeking full-time work had passed Bursary or University Scholarship. Overall, 17.7% of the employed and 15% of the unemployed had University Entrance or Sixth Form Certificate.

Such figures must be used with care for they are possibly confounded by the extreme youthfulness of the unemployed. It is possible that the young unemployed are better educated than older people and hence distort the spread of qualifications (though Hawkins did not find this to be the case in Britain).

To sum up: the evidence linking unemployment with deficient skills and insufficiently credentialled people is less decisive than is often assumed. If education were causally related to unemployment there would be a serious mismatch between the jobs available and the skills which the unemployed lack. Such a situation is possible and on a very limited scale sometimes occurs, particularly in a developing nation where schooling has not caught up with rapid social change. It is not, however, the situation in advanced countries during the past fifteen years. The figures cited earlier indicate that at all levels of skill, the number of jobs available has decreased in relation to those qualified to occupy them. In New Zealand there has actually been a substantial decline in the number of jobs available while at the same time a notable increase in the available work force.

For these reasons the verdict of Watts must stand: Unemployment is not an educational problem. It is essentially due to economic forces, and political responses to these forces (Watts, 1984 iv). Later on, a tempering sentence from Watts will be given and its significance for schooling discussed. For the present, however, the point being made is this: schools are in no way the cause of unemployment.

Schools as Part of the Solution

It may be, however, as some argue, that schools can be part of the cure. The feverish clamour inside and outside schools to provide 'transition education', 'careers education', 'vocational guidance' and 'work experience' seems to presume that schools can help eliminate or mitigate unemployment. Several different arguments are brought forward for this.

1. The first is based on the conviction that the school can make a difference by providing young people with sets of skills. This belief is clearly associated with the mistaken belief discussed earlier. There is, however, more direct evidence to reinforce how mistaken it is. Studies overseas have shown clearly that whether or not vocational skills are taught in school is of little relevance to whether a person is employed or not. The Carnegie Report, for example, concluded that in the U.S.A.:

> High school curriculum is clearly NOT a dominant factor in the unemployment of young men and women after they leave high school (Grasso and Shea, 1979 p. 100)

In Britain, Collins on the basis of his study concluded:

> Vocational education in the schools for manual positions is virtually irrelevant to job fate (Collins, 1979 p. 16).

Thurlow points out that there is in the U.S.A. a surplus of almost all labour skills; thus there is no need for training people for occupational skills (1979 p. 35). This point is accentuated by Collins who reports that 84% of businesses in the San Francisco Bay area are able to retrain their employees within three months (Collins,

1979 p. 17). He adds, 'Nearly any skill can be learned on the job, but many skills cannot be learned off the job' (p. 136). School-work of a direct vocational sort is useless or unnecessary.

The same point has to be made to those who stress careers education and job-seeking skills and those who imply that defects of character or the school's neglect of moral attitudes are at the root of unemployment. No amount of careers guidance, job skills, or character training will create a single job. If jobs are short (as they are) they will not be affected by these programmes.

Of course, programmes can improve the chances of a particular person (though even this claim is dubious since programmes are often such that those selected are already more likely to get jobs). This, of course, is not a negligible achievement but schools which adopt this approach should be aware of what they are doing (and not doing).

Schools which claim that unemployment is not a problem for them should not assume the superiority of their curriculum or staff. They are more likely reflecting the class background of their students. Oxenham has drawn attention to studies of employers in Mexico and Sri Lanka who were asked what differences they detected in employees of different educational levels:

> Not only was there scarcely a mention of 'higher productivity' or some equivalent phrase, but there was not mention of superior occupational skills ... On the other hand, 30 per cent (the largest single group but still a minority) stated that the really significant difference lay in *presentation* - that is bearing, personal presence and manner, or 'image'. But is *presentation* a product of schooling or social class? (Oxenham, 1984 p. 67).

Similarly, according to Oxenham, studies in Indonesia, Panama, the Philippines and Botswana suggest that 'the greater the competition for employment, the greater the importance of social connections in addition to social background and education' (Ibid p. 70). It is likely that even in 'egalitarian' New Zealand, the 'Old Boy network', never without its influence, will become more powerful as credentials become inflated and, because of the demise of national assessment, difficult to standardise.

2. There are those who accept the thrust of the foregoing arguments and who argue that the schools should cease trying to educate for employment and, instead, educate for unemployment. This boils down usually to 'education for leisure'. To some extent schools have always tried to do this by their emphasis on the broader activities of life: literature, history, music, science, physical education, art and the like are presumed to improve the quality of a person's life and hence be relevant to her 'leisure' if not to her job. To this extent, the position is valid but I believe that

this is not the correct response to the challenge of unemployment. For one thing, unemployment is not leisure; leisure is defined by contrast to employment and, at least in contemporary society, disappears with it. Thus 'education for leisure' reflects a cynical neglect of the social situation of the unemployed.

School pupils have always been more realistic than their teachers. They have been well aware of the close connection between school and the labour market and hence have not responded well to their teachers' talk about the 'intrinsic' value of certain subjects. It is hard to see them being more favourably disposed if these subjects are put in the context of unemployment and 'leisure'. This context may well increase their resistance especially as the 'school's' view of worthwhile activities seems to conflict with that of most people and so to highlight the gap between a monolithic 'school' and a culturally diverse community.

There may, of course, be a valuable insight in the notion of 'education for leisure' but it should not be too readily adopted as the justification of the curriculum. It so easily degenerates into an unthinking conservatism and prevents school people from really facing the challenge of unemployment and, more centrally, the challenge of schooling in the modern world.

It is time to add a codicil to the quotation I cited earlier in the paper. Watts, it will be recalled, concluded that:

> Unemployment is not an educational problem. It is essentially due to economic forces, and political responses to these forces.

He adds -

> It is, however, a problem for education since it challenges many of the assumptions built into the structure of our educational system (Watts, 1984 iv).

Unemployment is not caused by schools and cannot be solved by schools but there is a lesson to be learned from unemployment which is significant for education today and would remain significant even if some unlikely economic change were to eliminate unemployment tomorrow. It is, at this stage, important to remind ourselves that even in times of full employment

- employers are very unhappy with the products of schooling
- most of what is done at school has little relevance to real life
- many kids don't like school.

Strategies to resolve unemployment provide a clue to solving these three problems. Vocational courses, as I have argued, do not have any effect on unemployment and overall do not help individuals very much. But they are not worthless because, overwhelmingly, they are popular among the young people who do them. This, I suspect, is because they are (1) active rather than passive, requiring students to carry out certain tasks rather than to absorb information from the teacher. (2) Related to aims and plans which the student - however mistakenly - has. Thus, the courses seem directly relevant to subjective plans the young people have. (3) Interesting to the student since they relate to, extend, and coordinate knowledge which the learner already has or is acquiring.

As we know, employers frequently complain about the *general* educational skills of their employees, their attitude to work, authority, customers and the absence of traits such as honesty, reliability, self-reliance. Such criticisms are reasonable enough. The traits they draw attention to are not restricted to employment in a modern enterprise but to life in a modern interdependent society. Schools have always stressed traits such as perseverance, concern and cooperation and have to some extent produced people with these traits. Increasingly, however, teachers are realising what theorists have suggested for so long: that such traits cannot be imparted by formal direct teaching (as many conservatives seem to believe). They have to be acquired by engagement in activities in which these attitudes are naturally embedded. A student, for example, who is working on a computer project and finds she cannot solve a programming problem can be encouraged to ask someone who understands computers. She is learning not only about computers but also about cooperation - from the activity and not from a moralising lecture. Similarly, the student who helps her less fit colleague up a steep slope on a camping trip is 'learning to care' in the only way it can be learned.

Thus, unemployment does bring us back to fundamentals which are not new at all but are frequently overlooked in times of full employment when schools *seem to be doing their job* and hence are not challenged. The assumptions underlying schooling need to be challenged but in times of economic growth only political activists and academic theorists get around to such challenges - and few listen to them for schools are carrying out (or appear to be carrying out) their main function of preparation for the labour market. Economic down-turns and unemployment disturb the complacency and frequently call forth inappropriate and counter-productive strategies. I have argued that we must neither sink into complacency nor adopt simple-minded solutions. Rather, teachers, administrators and planners should accept the challenge and examine critically the structures of the educational system. The challenge is to take the mental disturbance that unemployment brings to schooling and to use it to develop courses which excite and challenge the young as they prepare for life in the widest sense. If unemployment forces us to do this it will have brought some good along with so much that is bad.

Vocational Skills Training In Transition Education
Successful Practice In New Zealand?

18

by Wanda Korndörffer

This chapter will analyse the structural conditions which constitute the multi-faceted social context within which the practice of transition education is conducted, and explore the nature of the 'success' that such conditions permit. I will demonstrate that transition education needs to be understood as a specific 'coping' response to a specifically capitalist crisis - the collapse of the youth labour market - and that transition education tutors and students construct a way of living within the discourse and reality of that crisis. The discussion will draw on substantive field work studies carried out in a New Zealand Polytechnic.

Transition Education - Response to a Capitalist Crisis

State-sponsored training programmes for young people in secondary schools and technical institutes were a direct response to the collapse of the youth labour market in New Zealand. As a form of educational intervention, such training programmes were legitimated on the grounds that they provide skills for young people which effectively increase their opportunities for access to the labour market (Task Force on Youth Training, 1982). This legitimation was derived from a set of theoretical assumptions about the nature of the labour market and its relationship to the state and to education. An examination of the role and effects of such training programmes, as a state-initiated educational intervention, may usefully begin, therefore, with an examination of the theoretical adequacy of the assumptions upon which such an intervention is legitimated.

If the market place for labour power is one of free and open competition then it seems to follow that those who are unable to sell their labour must be lacking some qualities that the successful sellers possess. At one level this appraisal of the labour market is accurate and supports a perspective based on the necessity for investment in human capital, particularly through vocational training and education. However, such an 'obvious' analysis of the labour market operates to obscure the relations of control, competition, alienation and class division that underlie the buying and selling of labour. There is an arena of common sense ideas and practices surrounding unemployment, the demands of the labour market and the role of schools in producing employable youth which excludes, by its very common sense nature, any penetration of the labour market in a capitalist economy that might challenge those ideas and practices. As Codd (1984, p.12) claims, "common sense knowledge structures mass consciousness in ways which mask and mystify the existing power relations and social arrangements" and various discourses interact with common sense perceptions of reality to produce a general, if fragmented, consent to the social order.

The discourses produced within this arena rest on a set of unacknowledged contradictions, the major one being that, although there are measurably insufficient jobs being created to absorb the potential workforce, the unemployed are still held to account for their lack of employment. While capital sheds labour in the restructuring crisis, the process of leaving school and selling one's labour power on the market is seen as an individualised process of 'fit' - it is the individual who cannot get a job and it is therefore the individual who is 'unemployable' and lacks the skills that effective training could provide that would 'fit' the person into employment. Unemployment thus becomes a temporary condition based on individual pathology, rather than a permanent structural feature of the process of capital production and accumulation that devolves unequally on different sectors in society. The production of temporary and modifiable pre-employment programmes emphasises both the short-term nature of the problem and the adaptability of the solution to 'individual needs', and the legitimating discourse that surrounds the programmes coheres with the common sense notions about unemployment - namely that individuals are unemployed because they are deficient in some way and that, therefore, they need skills and attitude training to enable them to become productive and disciplined workers that are acceptable to employers. However:

> If it is the case, as the preponderance of evidence suggests, that most of the work places for which vocational students are being prepared do not require significant amounts of skill, understanding of the technology involved in the production process, nor innovation on the part of the worker, then specific cognitive and manual skills training seems, at best, superfluous. Especially if the requisite skills can be quickly acquired on the job, then it seems clear that the "investment" both by the state and the student in curricula to develop such skills may be wasted (Violas, 1981, p.148).

According to Edgley (1978, p.21) industrial skills "require no particular intelligence, can be learned in four or five weeks or less, and are properly exercised without conscious attention" and that these properties are rapidly becoming the attributes of clerical, sales and service skills. There is substantial support for this claim, although there are cogent arguments that 'deskilling' is a more complex process in practice across firms and across industries than Braverman (1974), for example, admits in theory (Wood, 1982). Cohen (1984, p.105) asserts that "the emphasis given to 'skilling' in both the secondary school curriculum and the 16-19 training provision, is primarily about the inculcation of social discipline". Marks (1983, p.119), writing in the New Zealand context, demonstrates clearly that, even if workers did *need* a higher level of skill for present production, the "average skill levels, as measured by educational attainment, increased slightly between 1976 and 1981". (It should be noted, however, that rises in the levels of education do not necessarily reflect rises in the skill levels of work [Freeman-Moir, 1980, p.24.])

The problem for the state, in so far as it acts in the interests of capital, is not one of sufficient investment in human capital to produce a necessary level of skill in workers, nor is it one of equity. The problem is centrally one of how to maintain a cultural apprenticeship for young people, that is, how to maintain a 'work ethic' and a set of common sense cultural attitudes towards work, when work in its traditional sense is not available (Willis, 1984). Finn and Frith state that:

> the real key to the importance of policies concerning youth lies in the necessity of ensuring both the reproduction of the labour force over time and the stable recruitment of the young to their role as the next generation of workers and parents. And here working class youth represents a 'weak link'; for the potential labour force must be prepared not only for entry to work, but also for wage labour within the antagonistic social relations of capitalism; this is the kernel of the problem of the transition from school to work (1981, p.59).

The 'problem' of transition only comes to the fore, therefore, when there is a crisis in production that dislocates the smooth, though fragile, transition from school to work; when the framework of adult identity that work provides in our society is fractured. And this is not just any work, but wage labour within a particular set of social relations, the wage labour that underpins the production of profit. One of the ways in which the state attempts to deal with this problem is through the creation of training programmes and transition education aimed specifically at the pool of young unemployed (or potentially unemployed), programmes that are overt substitutes for the lost cultural apprenticeships of employment. By providing courses which say to young people that their unemployment results from their own lack of social and vocational skills, it is possible for the state to maintain a commitment to waged labour and to the social relations of production in these young people. Such a response serves the ideological function of blaming young people for their continued unemployment, i.e. blaming the victim. As Stafford has pointed out:

> Criticising the personal characteristics of young people ensures that responsibility and, more seriously, the blame for unemployment can be diffused and deflected away from the state and transferred onto young people themselves (1981, p.57).

In addition, transition education is not a homogeneous process for young people within the social relations of capitalist production: it is differentiated along class lines in its starting points, the experience of transition itself and in its destinations (Clarke and Willis, 1984, p.7). The provision of training programmes and transition education not only reinforces the notion that the market for labour is freely competitive and fair (i.e. that all that unemployed young people lack are skills which can be provided through transition education). It also reinforces the common sense distinction between mental and manual labour, a division that is central to the production of capital, by replicating the hierarchical ordering of the labour market; a differentiation of knowledge and access to knowledge, which reflects the deskilling and alienating aspects of the labour market for those in subordinate sectors, is inherent in the structures of transition education programmes. Education in this way can be a process whereby capital indirectly attempts both to reproduce an individually competitive (yet hierarchically ordered) workforce that will 'fit' the needs of the labour market and, at the same time, to control workers by promoting skill and knowledge divisions among them (Wilson, 1979, pp.8-13). And transition education is a part of that process that reinforces common sense explanations for such division and renders invisible the conflict between capital and labour in the market. The crisis of youth unemployment is not that of 'skills', 'qualifications' or 'adaptability' - it is a crisis in the reproduction of the 'work ethic', 'work habits' and 'disciplined attitudes' in young people and it is this crisis that the state attempts to resolve at the ideological level by the provision of transition education programmes (Hextall, 1980). Such programmes facilitate keeping school leavers in a holding pattern until work is available, reproduce youth into the existing social relations of production, maintain a work ethic in young people through periods of unemployment and place the blame for their unemployment on young people themselves.

Transition Education in Practice

Concomitant with the current restructuring of the labour market is an attempted restructuring of youth itself and, particularly, unemployed youth. Instead of being offered credentialled skills training, young people are to become 'adaptable', 'flexible' and 'redeployable' in their approaches to the labour market, their possession of skills and their ability to maintain themselves physically and psychologically through periods of unemployment. Watts (1983, p.74) refers to this process as 'training for stock': if training does not create jobs, presumably it attempts to create appropriately skilled workers who will be available if and when the economy picks up sufficiently to need them. This form of training, however, is not in specific technical skills, but in normative attitudes, motivation and social competence within a framework which suggests that routine tasks are more difficult than they really are (Dickinson and Erben, 1982).

This context presents those who teach vocational skills in programmes for unemployed youth with three major structural constraints: (i) a contracting and segmented labour market; (ii) deskilling; and (iii) credentialling. The first constraint impinges on these programmes in that there is a contradiction in offering specific skills training for unskilled or semi-skilled work when insufficient jobs are available at the conclusion of that training. The second constraint presents the problem of *what* skills should be offered in the programmes when the jobs that are available are being restructured and deskilled - work is atomised and homogenised to such an extent that little training is needed for employment in the sector of the labour market at which these courses are aimed. The third constraint confronts those who work in the programmes with the fact that, in a contracting labour market, employers use 'real' credentials (usually academic credentials) to select and sort young people into work. They use such credentials not only as an indication of other general behavioural and attitudinal qualities in young people (Maguire and Ashton, 1981, pp.34-35), but also as a device to cut down on the sheer numbers of job applicants (Berg, 1970). As Freeman-Moir (1980, p.29) has pointed out, the "growing supply of educated labour determines the upgrading of requirements in industry as much as the changing content of jobs". Vocational skills training courses for unemployed young people cannot compete with this demand for credentialled labour (Grubb and Lazerson, 1981, p.99).

How those who work in transition education cope with these constraints may now be discussed with concrete reference to my New Zealand research. In 1982, six ten-week Young Persons Training Programme (YPTP) courses, with an average of fourteen students per course, were implemented in one particular New Zealand technical institute. These courses became the subject of a participant-observation case study that addressed both the discourse and the practice of transition education. While the study referred to below was carried out in 1982 within a particular form of transition education which has now been superseded, the inferences drawn from the data have relevance for recent transition education practices such as the implementation of the ACCESS scheme.

The basis and form of the provision of the Young Persons Training Programme (YPTP) have been described elsewhere (Korndörffer, 1985 and 1986). Briefly, these government-funded and facilitated programmes aimed to "provide training for young job-seekers who clearly need some form of vocational training (whether in social or occupational skills) before they can be referred to an employer for placement" (Department of Labour, 1979). The provision of YPTP was premised on the notion that, even with a high rate of youth unemployment, it was possible for regional offices of the Department of Labour to discover or predict specific areas of labour shortages (for example, foodhandling or farm labour) - the YPTP courses would then provide the skills that young people needed to take up positions in these areas. Trade union demands, however, limited the skills offered on the courses to a sub-apprenticeship level. The courses offered during the period of the study were Foodhandling Skills (2 courses), Receptionist and Typing Skills, General Office Skills, Retailing Skills and Warehousing Skills. Two major components made up the basis of the courses: work skills, and social and life skills.

At this point it is obvious that the very basis of the provision of the courses was contradictory: if possible job opportunities were at an unskilled (sub-apprenticeship) level, then those positions that came onto the market would be filled readily by young people from a long queue of unskilled unemployed looking for work - there was no need for courses to teach 'skills' in this vocational sense. And, if the work was either not available at the end of a course or could be learned easily with one week's on-the-job training, what was the point in offering skills courses at all?

While tutors in the YPTP courses in this study did their best to provide comprehensive, ten-week skills training (in the theory and practice of warehousing, for example), some found the process difficult to justify. In order to justify ten-week skills training for unskilled (or, at most, semi-skilled) work, they held up high standards for students. The tutors needed to convince themselves and the students that these standards were necessary. To this end, they applied quite deliberate role-modelling theory and techniques in that they believed that, if the students were treated as workers and if they were expected to have high standards in their approach to work, then they would respond with high standards and *be* workers in the sense of having disciplined, work-oriented attitudes. These techniques failed consistently with the students and this failure led to frustration for the work skills tutors as the courses proceeded.

These tutors undoubtedly wanted to provide young people with genuine skills that would enable them to gain employment - the structural constraints and inherent contradictions of the courses, however, ensured that they did in fact prepare the young people 'for the social order' (Gleeson, 1983, p.2). The difficulties for the work skills tutors in providing a real skills training meant that they focused on the production of work attitudes in class. If, however, the basic intentions of the YPTP courses and the work skills tutors were to instill an observable work ethic in these students, they failed to a remarkable degree. Tutors became more and more frustrated during each course as the students resisted this pressure to conform to what they saw as the social relations of a schooling that they had escaped and the work skills component of the courses provided the clearest examples of the difficulties faced by tutors who worked to do a job within social relations that mystified their ability to do it.

The students, in general, *did* subscribe to a traditional work ethic, but it was one that they saw as being realised in work, not in training. They simply did not see why they should produce work attitudes in a non-work environment and expected that they would be given an explicit course of instruction in work skills not a generalised attitudinal training. Gaskell and Lazerson (1980-81, p.91) discovered in their study of the transition of working class young people from school to work that the experience of work, no matter how routine, boring or supervised, was quite different from the experience of school for these young people: "Accomplishing an externally defined if routine task and getting rewarded for it is a public definition of competence. It provides a public identity that compares favorably to the identity of the non-worker, whether student, housewife, or welfare recipient". Work is perceived to be the source of an independent, adult identity and it is this that the structures of schooling (whether secondary schooling, tertiary education or transition training programmes) cannot reproduce. Male and female students on the YPTP courses valued work skills training equally - getting a job (and work skills training was seen as a preliminary to this) was the central focus of both sexes' lives. An alternative domestic role, for example, was either an unconsidered or an unappealing choice for most of the female students. While the great majority of students of both sexes wanted a 'normal' future (in terms of marriage and a family), they saw the gaining of employment as an essential prerequisite for this future. In other words, both male and female students gained their social identity from paid work. (Sex-role stereotyping typical of that present in the structures of the labour market was evident in the selection of students onto courses - for example, thirteen of the fourteen Warehousing Skills students were male, and all of the students on the Receptionist and Typing Skills and Retail Skills courses were female - but there was little difference between male and female students in their responses to their position in the labour market.)

These YPTP students *knew* that the training programme was not 'real work' no matter how insistent the work skills tutors and the Department of Labour officers were that it be treated as a real job. The division of the day itself in these courses into 'morning = work skills' and 'afternoon = social and life skills' - a division that the students recognised explicitly as a separation of the real world of work from the impractical world of theory - reinforced a message that there is a rigid boundary between work and non-work, between the employed and the dole-bludger. Work skills tutors supported these beliefs with their implicit and explicit attitudes that having a steady job was the only conceivable way of living (Hilgendorf and Welchman, 1982, p.28). This student knowledge triggered many of their absences, their unpunctuality and their refusal to produce work attitudes and discipline in the classroom (or even, for example, at the work experience restaurant *when they were with the tutor* - when they were doing paid work in the restaurant at night they produced very appropriate attitudes and were good workers). Contrary to Hearn's thesis that disillusionment with work may apply most frequently and most directly to the unskilled and the unqualified (1981, p.14), these students were not disillusioned with work. These young people looked forward to waged employment and were willing workers, but they resisted returning to the authoritarian structures of school - their resistance took the form of a marked absenteeism. Many of these students on YPTP were adult in every sense of the word and resented feeling as if they were back at school, being treated like 'kids' by the work skills tutors - i.e. they felt that they were not trusted, that they were patronised and that they had to 'shut up and put up'. The work skills tutors blamed the students for the structural difficulties inherent in teaching in these courses (i.e. those difficulties that related to a contracting labour market, deskilling and credentialling). The students responded to the denigratory remarks and the authoritarian discipline of the work skills tutors (which arose from the contradictions of their teaching situation) with both absenteeism and delinquency (in the sense that they often refused to produce work attitudes and work discipline in class and in that they were disruptive and committed petty acts of vandalism such as writing on the bottoms of their chairs).

These students were quite capable of tugging their forelocks while raising two fingers behind their backs (Newby, 1977), i.e. producing deferential behaviour as part of a more complicated game of manipulation. In general, however, students were very straightforward in their responses within the courses and they genuinely respected and deferred to the superior knowledge of work processes and the work place that they assumed was possessed by the work skills tutors - they were sensitive to the fact, therefore, that, for much of the time that they spent with the work skills tutors, this respect was not reciprocated.

The students, in the main, were prepared to work hard in the work skills course components at anything that they perceived as 'real' work, e.g. copytyping, preparing a lunch for tutors and students, speedtyping, office routines skills (e.g.

filing, banking, memos, etc.), visits to restaurant kitchens or warehouses - work that was seen to be directly related to a 'real' job. While the students' lack of literacy skills sometimes frustrated their note-taking, they approved of taking down lengthy notes or lists from the blackboard. They saw note-taking as 'real' work, work that they 'should' be doing in the course, work that was seen to be directly related to a 'real' job, work that would get them a job (in this they were similar to the '4M' girls in Jones' 1987 study of Pacific Island girls' knowledge of school). During these periods, the students accepted the authoritarian social relations that the work skills tutors attempted to impose within the classroom because they perceived the tutors as having something that they wanted - specific knowledge that would enable them to get a job. While the students had rejected the authoritarian relations and attitude training of the secondary school, they were prepared to accept these, to a degree, within any situation that they perceived as 'real work' (Dent, 1978). As a result, the work skills tutors tended to give them more and more note-taking to do as the course wore on. The students would then complain that the work skills parts of the courses were too theory oriented and did not have enough work experience or work practice built into them; that there was too much talk and not enough cooking or warehousing or office work. The ideal structuring of the course in their terms (and it mirrored that of the work skills tutors) would be one where work skills theory (i.e. extensive note-taking) took up the whole of the morning period and work skills practice (in a real kitchen or office or warehouse or shop) took up the whole of the afternoon period. Apart from the Foodhandling students, who had a very limited access to a restaurant kitchen for some practical work, students did not do their work skills training in either a real or an artificial work situation. There were obvious practical difficulties in providing such a situation, in providing a 'training' warehouse, for example, or a 'training' shop. (This would not have been impossible: Frith [1980, p.31] refers to a factory process workshop on a training programme for young unemployed people in Coventry, where students worked all day on a production line making electrical goods that were, on completion, dismantled into their separate components and sent back to the beginning of the line.) In order to provide them with some experience of the realities of the workplace, the students went out of the course onto work experience on an employer's premises for one to two days per week for the last half of the course.

The work experience on employers' premises was variable and based on expediency. Both work skills and social and life skills tutors attempted to match students with suitable work placements, i.e. they attempted to get the students work experience in a specific area (for example, one student wanted to do his work experience in the morgue and this was arranged for him) or in an area that they hoped would be interesting for the student. Good matching was important: if the students disliked their work experience they were liable to simply walk out or to create such a bad impression with the employer that no further work placements would be possible in that firm; if employers disliked the students they were sent, this reflected badly on the course itself and it jeopardised future work placements and the job opportunities of other students. Finding good work placements (and following up on these, resolving any problems that arose, etc.) took considerable skill and energy on the part of all the tutors. However, it was difficult in the main to find any work placements at all: often, it was a matter of sending students out to whatever job was available (i.e. to whichever employer had been persuaded that having a student on work experience would be in their interest), crossing fingers and hoping for the best. The work experience in the courses often had a delayed starting date because of the difficulty of finding suitable placements.

Jamieson and Lightfoot (1981) claim that work experience placements are often dominated by administrative rather than curricular considerations (for example, finding enough placements) and this was the dominant constraint on the provision of work experience in these courses. However, even if the tutors had been able to be more selective as to work placements, it is unlikely that the students' experience of these would have been different. (Williamson, 1983, p.87, demonstrates that, even where work experience placements are made carefully and are viewed as appropriate by trainees, their reactions to the experience are varied.) The nature of their work experiences in the unskilled sector of the labour market in itself conditioned the YPTP student responses.

The students regarded the social and life skills training provisions of the courses as a waste of their time in that, in the main, they came onto the courses to learn *work* skills that would give them a job (Korndörffer, 1987). They wanted specific skills that would enable them to get a specific job, not generalisable social skills that were seen as irrelevant to the urgent task of gaining employment. The students wanted what the skills training programme appeared to offer: the chance of a regular, secure job and the skills to gain and retain such employment. They were critical of any course content that did not appear to be aimed at those ends. However, Barry (c.1984, p.8) and Reid (1983) discovered that the main demands that New Zealand employers make of potential employees are dependability, willingness to 'fit in', predictability and willingness to stay on the job; that these *social* skills are the marketable skills that employers refer to; that employers prefer to teach the required specific job skills themselves. The paradox of these training courses for the students, then, was that the *real* skills they needed for employment were those that they devalued and, in many cases, rejected - the social and life skills - rather than the specific work skills which employers prefer to teach on the job.

Who needs transition education?

While employers can be encouraged or persuaded by subsidies to take on young people, by definition capitalists cannot be forced to employ the young within a free enterprise labour market, governed by cycles of demand and supply, within which individuals enter into fairly and freely negotiated wage contracts (Finn, 1982, p.48). It is this reality, the reality of the youth labour market, that underpins the provision of transition education. Gleeson (1983, p.2) claims that there is developing in England a dual system of training for young people: there are those who receive 'real training for real jobs' and those who receive 'social and life skills' for the dole. He suggests (1984, p.98) that the emergence of youth training has little to do with technical changes in production or with providing the necessary skills for improved efficiency - rather, it is concerned with "regulating youth labour markets and with establishing training as a substitute for employment". In New Zealand this 'educational apartheid' is particularly obvious in technical institutes where training programmes for young unemployed people have been implemented - real courses with real certification for real jobs are offered to apprentices, secretarial and nursing students; ersatz skills training courses, with no certification beyond a certificate of attendance, and with little promise of future employment, are offered to unemployed youth. Moore (1983, p.26) puts the problem of providing young unemployed people with 'skills training' succinctly: young people "are not least preferred [in the labour market] because of anything they lack but because of what they are". The only way in which they could become more attractive to employers is if they could be employed on youth rates, i.e. become cheaper to employ. However, there has always been strong opposition by organised labour to differential rates of pay according to age and there are few awards in New Zealand that contain youth rates. The issues, then, in the provision of work skills in training programmes for unemployed youth, are not simply about the transition from school to work, but also about "the nature and quality of work, about deskilling, low pay and the recomposition of labour" (Markall and Gregory, 1982, p.63).

In transition education 'success' cannot be discussed without taking seriously the obvious question, 'Success for whom?'. For the state the very taken-for-granted acceptance of *transition* education rather than *continued* education is a success; for the colleges and tutors 'success' is more problematic and contested; for the students 'success' is getting a job - and on that criteria many find vocational skills training in transition education courses distinctly unsuccessful.

Contributors

Jan Branson is Senior Lecturer in the Centre for the Study of Innovation in Education, School of Education, La Trobe University, Bundoora, Victoria, Australia.

Noam Chomsky is Professor in the Department of Linguistics and Philosophy, Massachusetts Institute of Technology, Cambridge, Massachusetts, USA

Harold Entwistle is Professor in the Department of Education, Concordia University, Montreal, Quebec, Canada.

Adrian Furnham is Lecturer in the Department of Psychology, University College London, England.

Wanda Korndörffer is Junior Lecturer in the Department of Education, Massey University, Palmerston North, New Zealand.

Gary McCulloch is Lecturer in the Department of Education, University of Auckland, New Zealand.

Robert R. Sherman is Professor in Foundations of Education, College of Education, University of Florida, Gainesville, Florida, USA

Ian Shirley is Professor in the Department of Social Policy and Social Work, Massey University, Palmerston North, New Zealand.

Ivan Snook is Professor in the Department of Education, Massey University, Palmerston North, New Zealand.

William Taylor is Vice Chancellor, University of Hull, Hull, England.

Jim Walker is Senior Lecturer in the Department of Social and Policy Studies in Education, University of Sydney, New South Wales, Australia.

Douglas Weir is Director of the Vocational Initiatives Unit, Department of Education, University of Glasgow, Glasgow, Scotland.

Arthur G. Wirth is Professor of Education, Graduate Institute of Education, Washington University in St Louis, Missouri, USA.

Colin Wringe is Lecturer in the Department of Education at the University of Keele, Staffordshire, England.

Bibliography

Alutto, J. and Belasso, J. (1972) A typology for participation in organisational decision making. *Administrative Sciences Quarterly* 17

Anderson, D., Saltet, M. and Vervoorn, A. (1980) *Schools to Grow In: An Evaluation of Secondary Colleges.* Australian National University Press: Canberra.

Anderson, N. (1964) *Dimensions of Work: The Sociology of a Work Culture.* McKay: New York.

Apple, M. (1982) *Education and Power.* Routledge Kegan Paul: London.

Arendt, H. (1958) *The Human Condition.* University of Chicago Press.

Armstrong, P., Glyn, A. and Harrison, J. (1984) *Capitalism Since World War II.* Fontana: London.

Attfield, R. (1984) Work and the human essence. *Journal of Applied Philosophy* 1: 141-150.

Ball, S. and Lacey, C. (1980) Subject disciplines as the opportunity for group action: a measured critique of subject subcultures. In P. Woods (1980c) op. cit.

Ball, S. (ed.)(1984) *Comprehensive Schooling: A Reader.* Falmer Press: London.

Banks, M., Clegg, C., Jackson, P., Kemp, N., Stafford, E. and Wall, T. (1980) The use of the General Health Questionnaire as an indicator of mental health in occupational studies. *Journal of Occupational Psychology* 53: 187-194.

Banks, M. and Jackson, P. (1982) Unemployment and risk of minor psychiatric disorder in young people: cross-sectional and longitudinal evidence. *Psychological Medicine* 12: 789-798.

Banks, O. (1955) *Parity and Prestige in English Secondary Education.* Routledge Kegan Paul: London.

Barker, T. (1982) The economic consequences of monetarism: a Keynesian view of the British economy 1980-1990. Economics Reprint No. 48, University of Cambridge. Reprinted from *Cambridge Journal of Economics* 4, 4 (December 1980). Academic Press: London.

Barlow, M. (1967) *History of Industrial Education in the United States.* Charles A. Bennett and Co.: Peoria, Ill.

Barnett, C. (1979) Technology, education, and industrial and economic strength. *Journal of the Royal Society of Arts* 5271: February.

Barnett, C. (1986) *The Audit of War: The Illusion and Reality of Britain as a Great Power.* Macmillan: London.

Baron, P. (1957) *The Political Economy of Growth.* Modern Readers: New York.

Barrett, M. (1980) *Women's Oppression Today: Problems in Marxist Feminist Analysis.* Verso: London.

Barrett, M. (1987) The concept of difference. *Feminist Review* 26: Summer.

Barrett, M. and McIntosh, M. (1982) *The Anti-Social Family.* Verso: London.

Barry, A. (c.1984) *Aspects of Employment Training Programme for Disadvantaged Youth: A Comparative Approach.* Working Paper No. 23, Department of Sociology, University of Waikato.

Bates, I. et al. (ed.) (1985) *Schooling for the Dole?: The New Vocationalism.* Macmillan: London.

Baxter, J. (1975) The chronic job changer: a study of youth unemployment. *Social and Economic Administration* 9: 184-206.

Bazalgette, J. (1978) *School Life and Work Life*. Hutchinson: London.

Behn, W. (1974) School is bad: work is worse. *School Review* 83.

Bell, D. (1973) *The Coming of Post-Industrial Society*. Basic Books: New York.

Bell, D. (1976) *The Cultural Contradictions of Capitalism*. Heinemann: London.

Bensman, J. and Lillienfeld, R. (1973) *Craft and Consciousness: Occupational Technique and the Development of Work Images*. Wiley: New York.

Berg, I. (1970) *Education and Jobs: The Great Training Robbery*. Penguin: London.

Bernstein, B. (1975) *Class, Codes and Control Vol. 3: Towards a Theory of Educational Transmissions*. Routledge Kegan Paul: London.

Bernstein, B. (1977) *Class, Codes and Control Vol. 3: Towards a Theory of Educational Transmissions* (second edition) Routledge Kegan Paul: London.

Best, F. (1973) *The Future of Work*. Prentice Hall: New Jersey.

Bisseret, N. (1979) *Education, Class Language and Ideology*. Routledge Kegan Paul: London.

Blackburn, J. (1986) Policy response to the case studies. In Fensham et al. op. cit.

Blake, W. (1934) *The Poetical Works of William Blake*. Oxford University Press.

Blauner, R. (1964) *Alienation and Freedom: The Factory Worker and His Industry*. University of Chicago Press.

Bloom, B.S. (1976) *Human Characteristics and School Leaving*. McGraw Hill: New York.

Boomer, G. (ed.) (1982) *Negotiating the Curriculum: A Teacher-Student Partnership*. Ashton Scholastic: Sydney.

Borus, M. (1982) Willingness to work among youth. *Journal of Human Resources* 27: 581-593.

Bourdieu, P. (1977a) *Outline of a Theory of Practice*. Cambridge University Press.

Bourdieu, P. (1977b) Cultural reproduction and social reproduction. In *Power and Ideology in Education* edited by J. Karabel and A. Halsey, Oxford University Press.

Bourdieu, P. and Passeron, J. (1977) *Reproduction in Education, Society and Culture*. Sage Publications: London.

Bowers, C. (1978) Educational critics and technocratic consciousness. *Teachers College Record* 80, 2.

Bowles, S. and Gintis, H. (1976) *Schooling in Capitalist America*. Basic Books: New York.

Branson, J. and Miller, D. (1977) Feminism and class struggle. *Arena* 47 & 48.

Branson, J. and Miller, D. (1979) Class, sex and education. In *Capitalist Society: Culture, Ideology and the Reproduction of Inequalities in Australia*. Longman-Sorrett: Melbourne.

Braverman, H. (1974) *Labor and Monopoly Capital: The Degradation of Work in the Twentieth Century*. Monthly Review Press: New York.

Brenner, J. and Ramas, M. (1984) Rethinking women's oppression. *New Left Review* 144: 33-71.

Burton, C. (1985) *Subordination: Feminism and Social Theory*. Allen and Unwin: Melbourne.

Caldwell, B. and Spinks, J. (1986) *Policy-Making and Planning for School Effectiveness*. Education Department of Tasmania: Hobart.

Callaghan, J. (1976) Ruskin College speech. *Times Educational Supplement*, 22 October.

Callahan, R. (1962) *Education and the Cult of Efficiency*. University of Chicago Press.

Campbell, A. (1976) *The Quality of American Life: Perceptions, Evaluations and Satisfactions*. Russell Sage Foudation: New York.

Carr, W. and Kemmis, S. (1983) *Becoming Critical: Knowing Through Action Research*. Deakin University Press.

Carter, M. (1966) *Home, School and Work*. Pergamon: London.

Chomsky, N. (1969a) *At War with Asia*. Pantheon: New York.

Chomsky, N. (1969b) *American Power and the New Mandarins*. Pantheon: New York.

Chomsky, N. (1971) *Problems of Knowledge and Freedom*. Pantheon: New York.

Cixous, H. and Clement, C. (1986) *The Newly Born Women*. University of Minnesota Press.

Clarke, J. and Willis, P. (1984) Introduction. In Bates et al. op cit.

Clifford, H. (1961) *Exploring New England*. Follett: Chicago.

Codd, J. (1984) *Philosophy, Common Sense and Action in Educational Administration*. Deakin University Press.

Coffield, F. (1984) Learning to live with unemployment: what future for education in a world without jobs. unpublished paper, University of Durham.

Cohen, G. and Nixon, J. (1981) Employment policies for youth in Britain and the U.S.A. *Journal of Social Policy* 10: 331-351.

Cohen, P. (1984) Against the New Vocationalism. In Bates et al. op. cit.

Collins, R. (1979) *The Credential Society: An Historical Sociology of Education and Stratification*. Academic Press: New York.

Connell. R. (1985) *Teachers' Work*. Allen and Unwin: Sydney.

Corson, D. (1985) *The Lexical Bar*. Pergamon Press: Oxford.

Corson, D. (1985a) Education for work: reflections towards a theory of vocational education. *International Review of Education* 31: 286-302.

Corson, D. (1985b) Quality of judgment and deciding rightness: ethics and educational administration. *Journal of Educational Administration* XXIII: 122-130.

Corson, D. (1986) Policy in social context: a collapse of holistic planning in education. *Journal of Education Policy* 1: 5-20.

Corson, D. (1987) *Oral Language Across the Curriculum*. Multilingual Matters: Bristol and Philadelphia.

Corson, D. (1988) *Language Policy Across the Curriculum*. Multilingual Matters: Bristol (in press).

Corson, D., Merrington, P. and Wenn, M. (1986) School boundaries: setting classifications and frames to educational knowledge. *Theory into Practice in Tasmania*. 2, 2: 2-8.

Corson, D., Cowling, R. and Wenn, M. (1986) Utilitarianism: the principal's principle? *Theory into Practice in Tasmania*. 2, 3: 1-10.

Coser, L. (1974) *Greedy Institutions*. Free Press: New York.

Cotgrove, S. (1976) Technology and work. In *The Future of Work* edited by D. Elliott, The Open University Press.

Cronbach, L. and Snow, R. (1977) *Aptitudes and Instructional Methods*. Irvington: New York.

Curriculum Development Centre (CDC) (1980) *A Core Curriculum for Australian Schools*. Canberra.

Dahrendorf, R. (1975) *The New Liberty*. Routledge Kegan Paul: London.

Dale, R. (ed.) (1985) *Education, Training and Employment: Towards a New Vocationalism?* Pergamon Press: Oxford.

Dale, R., Esland, G. and MacDonald, M. (eds) (1976) *Schooling and Capitalism: A Sociological Reader*. Routledge Kegan Paul: London.

Darcy, J. (1978) Education about unemployment: a reflective element. *Oxford Review of Education* 4: 289-294.

Davis, L. and Cherns, A. (eds) (1975) *The Quality of Working Life: Vols 1 and 2*. Free Press: New York.

Dawes, P. (1977) Are careers education programmes in secondary schools a waste of time? *British Journal of Guidance and Counselling* 3.

Dayton, C. (1981) The young person's job search: insights from a study. *Journal of Counselling Psychology* 28: 321-333.

Dent, L. (1978) Unemployment: some implications for education. *Radical Education Dossier*. February: 4-8.

Department of Education and Science (DES) (1977) *Education in Schools*. HMSO: London.

Department of Education and Science (DES) (1979) *Local Authority Arrangements for the School Curriculum*. HMSO: London.

Department of Labour (1979) Volume 3, Circular No. 170. Wellington.

Dewey, J. (1915) Education vs. trade training: Dr Dewey's reply. *The New Republic* 3: 15 May.

Dewey, J. (1916a) Comment. *The New Republic* 3: 5 May.

Dewey, J. (1916b) *Democracy and Education*. Macmillan: New York.

Dewey, J. (1940) Learning to earn. *Education Today* Putnam: New York.

Dewey, J. (1944) Challenges to liberal thought. *Fortune* 30: (August).

Dewey, J. (1946) Learning to earn. *Education Today*. Putnam: New York.

Dewey, J. (1950) *Reconstruction in Philosophy*. The American Library: New York (1960 edition)

Dickinson, H. and Erben, M. (1982) Technical culture and technical education in France: a consideration of the work of Claude Grignon and its relevance to British further education curricula. *British Journal of Sociology of Education* 3: 145-159.

Dobb, M. (1973) *Theories of Value and Distribution Since Adam Smith: Ideology and Economic Theory*. Cambridge University Press.

Donovan, A. and Oddy, M. (1982) Psychological aspects of unemployment: an investigation into the social and emotional adjustment of school leavers. *Journal of Adolescence* 5: 15-30.

Dowling, P. and O'Brien, G. (1981) The effects of employment, unemployment and further education upon the work values of school leavers. *Australian Journal of Psychology* 33: 185-195.

Dowling, P. and O'Brien, G. (1983) The work values of unemployed and employed youth: a reply to Rump. *Australian Journal of Psychology* 35: 91-96.

Drost, W. (1967) *David Snedden and Education for Social Efficiency*. University of Wisconsin Press.

Dubin, R. (1975) Central life interest and organization commitment of blue collar and clerical workers. *Administrative Sciences Quarterly* 20, 3.

Duchen, C. (1986) *Feminism in France from May '68 to Mitterand*. Routledge Kegan Paul: London.

Duchen, C. (ed.) (1987) *French Connections: Voices from the Women's Movement in France*. Hutchinson: London.

Dworkin, R. (1983) In defense of equality. *Social Philosophy and Policy* 1: 24-40.

Edgley, R. (1978) Education for industry. *Radical Philosophy*. 19: 18-23.

Eisenstein, Z. (ed.) (1979) *Capitalist Patriarchy and the Case for Socialist Feminism*. Monthly Review Press: New York.

Entwistle, H. (1970) *Education, Work and Leisure*. Routledge Kegan Paul: London.

Entwistle, H. (1978) *Class, Culture and Education*. Methuen: London.

Escheté, A. (1974) Contractarianism and the scope of justice. *Ethics* 85: 38-49.

Feather, N. (1982) Unemployment and its psychological correlates: a study of depressive symptoms, self esteem, Protestant ethic values, attributional style and apathy. *Australian Journal of Psychology* 34: 309-323.

Feather, N. and Davenport, P. (1981) Unemployment and depressive effect: a motivational and attributional analysis. *Journal of Personality and Social Psychology* 41: 422-436.

Fensham, P., Power, C., Tripp, D. and Kemmis, S. (eds) (1986) *Alienation from Schooling*. Routledge Kegan Paul: London.

Finn, D. (1982) Whose needs? Schooling and the 'needs' of industry. In *Youth Unemployment and State Intervention* edited by T. Rees and P. Atkinson, Routledge Direct Editions: London.

Finn, D. and Frith, S. (1981) Education and the labour market. In *The State and the Politics of Education* Part 2, Block 1, Open University Press.

Fish, F. (1910) The vocational and industrial school. *NEA Proceedings*.

Fleming, D. and Lavercombe, S. (1982) Talking about unemployment with school-leavers. *British Journal of Guidance and Counselling* 10: 22-33.

Fowler, B., Littlewood, B. and Madigan, R. (1976) Immigrant school-leavers and the search for work. *Sociology* 18: 336-351.

Frank, A. (1980) *Crisis: In the World Economy*. Heinemann: London.

Freeman-Moir, J. (1980) Education and the reproduction of labour power. Paper presented at NZARE Conference, Massey University, November.

Friedman, M. (1962) *Capitalism and Freedom*. Chicago University Press.

Friedman, M. (1975) Unemployment versus inflation? Occasional Papers No. 44, Institute of Economic

Affairs: London.

Friedman, M. (1980) cited in *Controlling the Economic Future* by M. Stewart, Wheatsheaf: London.

Frith, S. (1980) Education, training and the labour process. In *Blind Alley* edited by M. Cole and B. Skelton. Hesketh: Ormskirk.

Furnham, A. (1982a) Explanations for unemployment in Britain. *European Journal of Social Psychology* 12: 335-352.

Furnham, A. (1982b) The Protestant work ethic and attitudes towards unemployment. *Journal of Occupational Psychology* 55: 277-286.

Furnham, A. (1983) Attitudes to the unemployed receiving social security. *Human Relations* 36: 135-150.

Furnham, A. (1984) Getting a job: school-leavers' perceptions of employment prospects. *British Journal of Educational Psychology* 54: 293-305.

Furnham, A. and Gunter, B. (1984) Just world beliefs and attitudes towards the poor. *British Journal of Social Psychology* 23: 265-269.

Galbraith, J. (1973) *Economics and the Public Purpose*. Houghton Mifflin: Boston.

Gallop, J. (1982) *The Daughter's Seduction: Feminism and Psychoanalysis*. Cornell University Press.

Galtung, J. (1977) *The New International Economic Order*. Seminar Presentation, Massey University, June.

Gamble, G. (1986) The free or the good. In *The Ideology of the New Right* edited by R. Levitas, Polity Press: Cambridge.

Game, A. and Pringle, R. (1983) *Gender at Work*. Allen and Unwin: London.

Gaskell, J. and Lazerson, M. (1980-81) Between school and work: perspectives of working class youth. *Interchange* 11: 80-96.

Giddings, F. (1896) *Principles of Sociology*. Macmillan: New York.

Gilligan, C. (1982) *In a Different Voice: Psychological Theory and Women's Development*. Harvard University Press.

Gleeson, D. (1983) Further education, tripartism and the labour market. In *Youth Training and the Search for Work* edited by D. Gleeson, Routledge Kegan Paul: London.

Gleeson, D. (1984) Someone else's children: the new vocationalism in further education and training. In *Social Crisis and Educational Research* edited by L. Barton and S. Walker, Croom Helm: London.

Gleeson, D. (ed.) (1987) *TVEI and Secondary Education*. Open University Press.

Godfrey, M. (1986) *Global Unemployment: The New Challenge to Economic Theory*. Wheatsheaf Books: London.

Gough, I. (1979) *The Political Economy of the Welfare State*. Macmillan: London.

Grasso, J. and Shea, J. (1979) *Vocational Education and Training: Impact on Youth*. A technical report from the Carnegie Council on Policy Studies in Higher Education.

Greenberger, E., Steiner, L. and Vaux, A. (1981) Adolescents who work: health and behaviour consequences of job stress. *Developmental Psychology* 17: 691-703.

Greenfield, T. (1978) Reflections on organisation theory and the truths of irreconcilable realities. *Educational Administration Quarterly* 14: 1-23.

Griggs, C. (1983) *The Trades Union Congress and the Struggle for Education*. Falmer Press: London.

Grubb, W. and Lazerson, M. (1981) Vocational solutions to youth problems: the persistent frustrations of the American experience. *Educational Analysis* 3: 91-103.

Grubb, W. (1985) The convergence of educational systems and the role of vocationalism. *Comparative Education Review* 29: 526-548.

Grumet, M. (1981) Restitution and reconstruction of educational experience: an autobiographical method for curriculum theory. In *Re-Thinking Curriculum Studies* edited by M. Lawn and L. Barton, Croom Helm: London.

Gurney, R. (1980a) The effects of unemployment on the psychosocial development of school-leavers. *Journal of Occupational Psychology* 53: 205-213.

Gurney, R. (1980b) Does unemployment affect the self-esteem of school-leavers. *Australian Journal of Psychology* 32: 175-182.

Gurney, R. (1981) Leaving school facing unemployment and making attributions about the causes of unemployment. *Journal of Vocational Behaviour* 18: 79-91.

Habermas, J. (1971) *Knowledge and Human Interests* (translated by J. Shapiro) Beacon Press: Boston.

Habermas, J. (1975) Legitimation Crisis. (translated by T. McCarthy) Beacon Press: Boston.

Habermas, J. (1985) *The Theory of Communicative Action : Volume 1, Reasoning and the Rationalisation of Society* (translated by T. McCarthy) Heineman: London.

Hall, S. and Jefferson, T. (eds) (1976) *Resistance through Rituals: Youth Sub-Culture in Post-War Britain*. Hutchinson: London.

Hargreaves, D. (1980) The occupational culture of teachers. In P. Woodsh 1980c op. cit.

Hargreaves, D. (1981) Unemployment, leisure and education. *Oxford Review of Education* 7: 197-210.

Hargreaves, D. (1982) *The Challenge for the Comprehensive School*. Routledge Kegan Paul: London.

Harman, G. (1980) Exploring politics in education: some barriers and some theoretical considerations. In *Politics in Education*. The Australian College of Education : Brisbane.

Harman, G. (1982) Policy making and the policy process in education. In *Canadian and Comparative Educational Administration* edited by R. Farquhar and I. Housego, University of British Columbia.

Harris, K. (1977) Peters on schooling. *Educational Philosophy and Theory*, 9: 33-48.

Harvey, J., Ickes, W. and Kidd, R. (eds) (1975) *New Directions in Attribution Research: Vol. 2*. Erlbaum Press: Hillsdale, New Jersey.

Hawkins, K. (1984) *Unemployment*. Penguin Books: London.

Hayek, F. (1949) *Individualism and Economic Order*. Routledge Kegan Paul: London.

Hearn, J. (1981) Crisis, taboos and careers guidance. *British Journal of Guidance and Counselling* 9: 12-23.

Heimberg, R., Cunningham, J., Stanley, J. and Blacenburg, R. (1982) Social skills training to prepare unemployed youth for the job interview. *Behaviour Modification* 6: 299-322.

Herbst, P. (1973) Work, labour and university education. In *The Philosophy of Education*, edited by R. Peters, Oxford University Press.

Hextall, I. (1980) Up against the wall: restructuring state education. In *Blind Alley* edited by M. Cole and B. Skelton, Hesketh: Ormskirk.

Hilgendorf, L. and Welchman, R. (1982) Organizational and social issues in the transfer and use of learning. Learning at Work Development Project: Working Paper No. 7 (mimeo) Tavistock Institute of Human Relations: London.

Hill, J. and Scharff, D. (1976) *Between Two Worlds: Aspects of the Transition from School to Work*. Careers Consultants Ltd: London.

Hirst, P. (1965) Liberal education and the nature of knowledge. In *Philosophical Analysis and Education*, edited by R. Archambault, Routledge Kegan Paul: London.

Hollandsworth, J. Glazeski, R. and Dressel, M. (1978) Use of social skills training in the treatment of extreme anxiety and deficient verbal skills in the job interview setting. *Journal of Applied Behaviour Analysis* 11: 259-269.

Hollandsworth, J., Kazelskis, R., Stevens, J. and Dressel, M. (1979) Relative contributions of verbal articulative and non-verbal communication to employment decisions in the job interview setting. *Personnel Psychology* 32: 359-367.

Holt, J. (1979) *Instead of Education*. Penguin: London.

Holt, M. (ed.) (1987) *Skills and Vocationalism: The Easy Answer*. Open University Press.

Hood, E. Lindsay, W. and Brooks, N. (1982) Interview training with adolescents. *Behaviour Research and Therapy* 20: 581-592.

Hu, T. (1980) *Studies of the Cost-Efficiency and Cost-Effectiveness of Vocational Education*. National Centre for Research in Vocational Education: Ohio State University.

Humboldt, W. von (1969) *The Limits of State Action*, edited by J. Burrow. Cambridge University Press.

Hunt, E. (1980) A radical critique of welfare economics. In *Growth, Profits and Property: Essays in the Revival of Political Economy*, edited by E. Nell, Cambridge University Press.

Ihde, D. (1975) A phenomenology of man-machine relations. In *Work, Technology and Education* edited by W. Feinberg and H. Rosemont, Urbana: Illinois.

Illich, I. (1971) *Deschooling Society*. Penguin Books: London.

Illich, I. et al. (1972) *After Deschooling What?* Penguin Books: London.

Irigaray. L. (1985) *Speculum of the Other Woman*. Cornell University Press.

Jackson, P., Stafford, E., Banks, M. and Warr, P. (1983) Unemployment and psychological distress in young people: the moderating role of employment commitment. *Journal of Applied Psychology* 68: 525-535.

Jamieson, I. and Lightfoot, M. (1981) Learning about work. *Educational Analysis* 3: 37-51.

Jessop, B. (1987) The political economy of Thatcherism. Seminar presented at Massey University, September.

Jones, A. (1987) "At school I've got the chance I've got": some Pacific Island girls' knowledge about school and work. In Korndorffer (1987) op. cit.

Kaldor, N. (1982) Monetarism and UK monetary policy. Economics Reprint No. 50, University of Cambridge. Reprinted from *Cambridge Journal of Economics* 4, 4 (December 1980) Academic Press: London.

Kalecki, M. (1971) *Selected Essays on the Dynamics of the Capitalist Economy*. Cambridge University Press.

Keane, J. and Owens, J. (1986) *After Full Employment*. Hutchinson: London.

Kelly, A.V. (1986) *Knowledge and Curriculum Planning*. Harper and Row: London.

Keynes, J. (1926) *The End of Laissez-Faire*. Hogarth: London.

Keynes, J. (1936) *The General Theory of Employment, Interest and Money*. Macmillan: London.

Kilpatrick, W. (1963) *Philosophy of Education*. Macmillan: New York.

Kohn, C. and Drummond, D. (1963) *The World Today*. McGraw Hill: New York.

Korndörffer, W. (1985) Young Persons Training Programmes and the ideology of common sense. In *Political Issues in New Zealand Education*, edited by J. Codd, R. Nash and R. Harker, The Dunmore Press: Palmerston North.

Korndörffer, W. (1986) Labouring to learn: the other purposes of Young Persons Training Programmes (YPTP). *New Zealand Journal of Educational Studies* 20: 59-64.

Korndörffer, W. (ed.) (1987) *Transition: Perspectives on School to Work in New Zealand*. The Dunmore Press: Palmerston North.

Kuhn, A. and Wolpe, A. (eds) (1978) *Feminism and Materialism*. Routledge Kegan Paul: London.

Labour and Employment Gazette 29: 1 March 1979.

Lafargue, P. (1883) *The Right to be Lazy and Other Studies*. (Paris) reprinted (1973) by Gordon Press: New York

Lambert, L. (1978) Careers guidance and choosing a job. *British Journal of Guidance and Counselling* 6, 2.

Lavercombe, S. and Fleming, D. (1981) Attitudes and duration of unemployment among sixteen-year-old school-leavers. *British Journal of Guidance and Counselling* 9: 36-45.

Lawton, D. (1981) *An Introduction to Teaching and Learning*. Hodder and Stoughton: London.

Lawton, D. (1983) *Curriculum Studies and Educational Planning*. Hodder and Stoughton: London.

LeVine, R.A. and White, M.I. (1986) *Human Conditions: The Cultural Basis of Educational Developments*. Routledge and Kegan Paul: London.

Long, R. (1978) The effects of employee ownership on organizational identification, employee job attitudes and organizational performance. *Human Relations* 31, 1.

Maclure, S. (1985) Hands up for the enterprise culture? *Times Education Supplement*. 8 February.

Maguire, M. and Ashton, D. (1981) Employers' perceptions and use of educational qualifications. *Educational Analysis* 3, 2.

Main, B. and Raffe, D. (1983) The transition from school to work in 1980/81: a dynamic account. *British Educational Research Journal* 9: 57-70.

Maizels, E. (1979) *Adolescent Needs and the Transition from School to Work.* Athlone: London.

Makeham, P. (1980) *Youth Unemployment: An Examination of Evidence on Youth Unemployment Using National Statistics.* Department of Employment: London.

Malinvaud, E. (1984) *Mass Unemployment.* Blackwell: Oxford.

Malos, E. (ed.) (1980) *The Politics of Housework.* Allison and Busby: London.

Manpower Services Commission (MSC) (1977) *Young People and Work.* HMSO: London.

Manpower Services Commission (MSC) (1984) *Core Skills in YTS.* HMSO: Sheffield.

March, J. and March, J. (1978) Performance sampling in social matches. *Administrative Sciences Quarterly* 23, 3.

Markall, G. and Gregory, D. (1982) Who cares? The MSC interventions: full of Easter promise. In *Youth Unemployment and State Intervention,* edited by T. Rees and P. Atkinson, Routledge Direct Editions: London.

Marks, P. (1983) The slowdown in labour productivity growth rates in New Zealand in the 1970s. In *Studies in the Labour Market,* edited by B. Easton, New Zealand Institute for Economic Research: Wellington.

Marland, S. (1971a) Criticism, communication and change. *College and University Journal* 10: 17-19.

Marland, S. (1971b) Educating for the real world. *Business Education Forum* 26: 3-5.

Marland, S. (1971c) Career education. *Today's Education* 60: 22-25.

Martin, J. (1984) Philosophy, gender and education. In *Women and Education* edited by S. Acker, J. Megarry, S. Nisbet and E. Hoyle, Kogan Page: London.

Marx, K. (1963) Economic and social manuscript. In *Karl Marx: Early Writings,* edited and translated by T. Bottomore, C.A.Watts: London.

Marx, K. (1970) The eighteenth brumaire of Louis Bonaparte. In *Selected Works of Karl Marx and Friedrich Engels.* Progress Publishers: New York.

Mauss, M. (1967) *The Gift.* Norton and Coy: London.

McGregor, D. (1960) *The Human Side of Enterprise.* McGraw Hill: New York.

McCulloch, G. (1984) Views of the alternative road: the Crowther concept. In *The Alternative Road,* edited by D.Layton, University of Leeds.

McCulloch, G. (1985) Pioneers of an 'Alternative Road'? The Association of Heads of Technical Schools, 1951-1964. In *Social History of the Secondary Curriculum,* edited by I. Goodson, Falmer Press: London.

McCulloch, G. (1986) Policy, politics and education: the TVEI. *Journal of Education Policy* 1: 35-52.

Millar, C. (1961) *Foundations of Guidance.* Harper and Row: New York.

Miller, D. and Branson, J. (1987) Pierre Bourdieu. In *Creating Culture,* edited by D. Austin, Allen and Unwin: Melbourne.

Miller, K. (1973) Educational and vocational guidance. In *Educational Research in Britain* 3, edited by J. Butcher and H. Pont, University of London Press.

Millham, S., Bullock, R. and Hosey, K. (1978) Juvenile unemployment: a concept due for recycling? *Journal of Adolescence* 1: 11-24.

Mills, C. (1970) *The Sociological Imagination.* Pelican: London.

Mills, C. (1973) In *The Future of Work,* edited by F. Best op. cit.

Ministry of Education (1963) *Half Our Future.* HMSO: London.

Mitchell, J. (1984) *Women - The Longest Revolution: Essays in Feminism, Literature and Psychoanalysis.* Virago: London.

Moi, T. (1985) *Sexual/Textual Politics.* Methuen: London.

Moi, T. (ed.) (1986) *The Kristeva Reader.* Blackwell: London.

Moore, R. (1983) Further education pedagogy and production. In D. Gleeson (1987) op. cit.

Moran, P. (1988) *Female Youth Culture in an Inner City School* (Occasional Paper No. 17) University of Sydney Faculty of Education.

Musgrave, P. (1986) Some methodological, substantive and theoretical aspects. In Fensham, et al. op. cit.

Newby, H. (1977) *The Deferential Worker: A Study of Farm Workers in East Anglia.* Penguin Books: London.

New Zealand Education Department (1987) *The Curriculum Review.* Wellington.

Nystrom, D. and Hennessy, J. (1985) Cost differential analysis: providing data for added cost funding. *Journal of Industrial Teacher Education.* 53-61.

Oakeshott, M. (1971) Education: the engagement and its frustration. *Proceedings of the Philosophy of Education Society, 5.*

O'Connor, J. (1973) *Fiscal Crisis of the State.* St Martin's Press: New York.

O'Connor, R. (1969) *Pacific Destiny.* Little, Brown and Co.: Boston.

OECD (1977) *Structural Determinants of Employment and Unemployment.* Paris.

OECD (1978) *Education Committee: Draft Report on Future Policies for Vocational Education and Training.* Paris.

OECD (1985) *Education and Training after Basic Schooling.* Paris.

Offe, C. (1984) *Contradictions of the Welfare State.* Hutchinson: London.

Ontario Ministry of Education (1984) *Ontario Schools.* Toronto.

Ostriker, A. (ed.) (1977) *William Blake: The Complete Poems.* Penguin Books: London.

Oxenham, J. (1984) Employers, jobs and qualifications. In *Education versus Qualifications*, edited by J. Oxenham, Allen and Unwin: Hemel Hempstead.

Parker, S. (1971) *The Future of Work and Leisure.* Paladin Books: London.

Parkin, F. (1979) *Marxism and Class Theory: A Bourgeois Critique.* Tavistock: London.

Parsons, T. (1960) *Structure and Process in Modern Societies.* Free Press of Glencoe: Illinois.

Peters, R. (1966) *Ethics and Education.* Allen and Unwin: London.

Peters, R. (1970) Education and the educated man. *Proceedings of the Philosophy of Education Society of Great Britain.* IV: 5-20.

Peters, R. (1973) Aims of education: a conceptual enquiry. In *The Philosophy of Education* edited by R.S. Peters, London: Oxford University Press.

Peters, R. (1977) *Education and the Education of Teachers.* Routledge Kegan Paul: London.

Peterson, R. and Johnson, J. (1977) *The Work Ethic in Career Education Materials.* Far West Laboratory for Education Research and Development: San Francisco

Poole, M. (1983) *Youth: Expectations and Transitions.* Routledge Kegan Paul: London.

Popper, K. (1961) *The Poverty of Historicism.* Routledge Kegan Paul: London

Popper, K. (1963) *Conjectures and Refutations: The Growth of Scientific Knowledge.* Routledge Kegan Paul: London.

Popper, K. (1972) *Objective Knowledge: An Evolutionary Approach.* Clarendon Press: Oxford.

Popper, K. (1976) *An Intellectual Autobiography: Unended Quest.* Fontana Collins: London

Postman, N. and Weingartner, C. (1971) *Teaching as a Subversive Activity.* Penguin Books: London.

Poulantzas, N. (1973) *Political Power and Social Classes.* New Left Books: London.

Prebble, T. and Stewart, D. (1981) *School Development: Strategies for Effective Management.* The Dunmore Press: Palmerston North.

Presthus, R. (1962) *The Organisational Society.* Random House: New York.

Pring, R. (1976) *Knowledge and Schooling.* Open Books: London.

Pring, R. (1986) Curriculum for ages 14-18: "The New Vocationalism" In *Melbourne Studies in Education*, edited by I. Palmer, Melbourne University Press.

Prosser, C. and Quigley, T. (1950) *Vocational Education in Democracy.* American Technical Society: Chicago.

Psacharopoulos, G. (1987) To vocationalize or not to vocationalize? That is the curriculum question. *International Review of Education* XXXIII: 187-211.

Raelin, J. (1981) A comparative study of later work experience among full-time, part-time and unemployed male youth. *Journal of Vocational Behaviour* 19: 315-327.

Raffe, D. (1983) Employment instability among less qualified young workers. *British Journal of Guidance and Counselling* 11: 21-34.

Rawls, J. (1972) *A Theory of Justice.* Oxford University Press.

Reid, M. (1983) *The Role of Skills Specification in Easing the Transition from School to Work: A Pilot Study.* Department of Education, University of Canterbury.

Reynolds, J. and Skilbeck, M. (1976) *Culture and the Classroom.* Open Books: London.

Roberts, K. (1977) The social conditions, consequences and limitations of careers guidance. *British Journal of Guidance Counselling* 5.

Roberts, K., Duggan, J. and Noble, M. (1982) Out-of-school youth in high unemployment areas: an empirical investigation. *British Journal of Guidance and Counselling* 10: 1-11.

Rose, J. (1986) *Sexuality in the Field of Vision.* Verso: London.

Rugguro, M. and Steinberg, L. (1981) The empirical study of teenage work. *Journal of Vocational Behaviour* 19: 163-174.

Rump, E. (1983) A comment on Dowling and O'Brien's "Employed" and "Unemployed" group. *Australian Journal of Psychology* 35: 89-90.

Russell, B. (1919) *Proposed Roads to Freedom: Anarchy, Socialism and Syndicalism.* Holt and Co.: New York.

Schools Board of Tasmania (1986) *Handbook for Syllabus Development.* Hobart, April.

Schwartz, R. (ed.) (1970) The politicking over Marland. *Nation's Schools* 86, 5.

Schwartz, R. (ed.) (1971a) Marland asks realignment of federal education priorities. *Nation's Schools* 87, 4.

Schwartz, R. (ed.) (1971b) Quoting Marland. *American Education* 7: 3-4.

Schwartz, R. (ed.) (1971c) Career education. *Nation's Schools* 88, 6.

Sherman, R. (1974) Vocational education and democracy. *Studies in Philosophy and Education* 8: 205-223.

Shipley, S. (1982) *Women's Employment and Unemployment.* SROW Research Report, Massey University.

Shirley, I. (ed.) (1982) *Development Tracks.* The Dunmore Press: Palmerston North.

Simonds, R. and Orife, J. (1975) Worker behaviour versus enrichment theory. *Administrative Sciences Quarterly* 20, 4.

Skilbeck, M. (1984) *School-Based Curriculum Development.* Harper and Row: London.

Smith-Hughes Act of 1917. *U.S. Statutes at Large* XXXIX: 1.

Snedden, D. (1908) Differences among varying groups of children should be recognized. *NEA Proceedings.* 29 June-30 July.

Snedden, D. (1915) Comment. *The New Republic* 3: 5 May.

Snedden, D. (1924) Education for a world of team players and team workers. *School and Society* 20: 1 November.

Southgate, B. (1987) History lessons. *The Times Higher Education Supplement.* 4 September: 13.

Spivak, G. (1987) *In Other Worlds: Essays in Cultural Politics.* Methuen: London.

Stafford, A. (1981) Learning not to labour. *Capital and Class* 15: 55-66.

Stafford, E. (1982) The impact of the Youth Opportunities Programme on young people's employment prospects and psychological well-being. *British Journal of Guidance and Counselling* 10: 12-21.

Stafford, E. and Jackson, P. (1981) Job choice or job allocation? Work allocations and job seeking in an area of high unemployment. unpublished.

Stirling, A. (1982) Preparing school leavers for unemployment. *Bulletin of the British Psychological Society* 35: 421-422.

Tanham, G. and Duncanson, D. (1969) Some dilemmas of counterinsurgency. *Foreign Affairs* 48: 113-122.

Task Force on Youth Training (1982) *Training and Employment for Youth: Options for Action.* A

Discussion Document (mimeo) Wellington.

Taylor, I. (1987) Law and order, moral order - the shifting rhetorics of the Thatcher government. In *The Socialist Register,* edited by R. Miliband and L. Panitch.

Taylor, P. and Musgrove, F. (1969) *Society and the Teacher's Role.* Routledge Kegan Paul: London.

Taylor, W. (1976) Participation. *Australian Council for Educational Research Bulletin* 6.

Tessler, R. and Sushelsky, L. (1978) Effects of eye contact and social status on the perception of a job applicant in an employment interviewing situation. *Journal of Vocational Behaviour* 13: 338-347.

Therborn, G. (1986) *Why Some Peoples are More Unemployed than Others: The Strange Paradox of Growth and Unemployment.* Verso: London.

Thompson, G. and Ruehl, S. (1985) *Unemployment.* Block 6. Units 22 and 23, Open University Press.

Thurlow, L. (1979) Technological unemployment and occupational education. In *Educating for Careers: Policy Issues in a Time of Change.* Pennsylvania State University Press.

Times Education Supplement (TES) (1984) The power and the pendulum. 14 September.

Treasury (1986) *Notes on Education.* The Treasury: Wellington.

Uberoi, J. (1978) *Science and Culture.* Oxford University Press.

UNESCO (1984) *The Concept of Endogenous Development.* Paris.

United Nations (1979) *Evaluation of the World Trade and Economic Situation and Consideration of Issues, Policies and Appropriate Measures to Facilitate Structural Changes in the International Economy.* Geneva.

Violas, P. (1981) Reflections on theories of human capital, skills training and vocational education. *Educational Theory* 31: 137-151.

Walby, S. (1987) *Patriarchy at Work.* Polity Press: London.

Walker, J. (1987a) Greeks versus Aussies: male youth culture, school and work in the inner city. *Youth Studies Bulletin* 6: 6-11.

Walker, J. (1987b) School sport, ethnicity and nationality: dimensions of male youth culture in an inner city school. *The Australian Journal of Education* 31, 3.

Walker, J. (1987c) *Educative Leadership for Curriculum Development.* ACT Schools Authority: Canberra.

Walker, J. (1987d) Knowledge, culture and the curriculum. In *Educating Teachers: Changing the Nature of Professional Knowledge,* edited by W. Smyth, Falmer Press: London.

Walker, J. (1988a) The way men act: gender formation in the school context. *British Journal of Sociology of Education* 9, 1.

Walker, J. (1988b) *Louts and Legends: Male Youth Culture in an Inner City School.* Allen and Unwin: Sydney.

Walker, J. (1988c) *Learning Cultures: Teaching and Curriculum in an Inner City School.* Allen and Unwin: Sydney.

Wallerstein, I. (1979) *The Capitalist World Economy.* Cambridge University Press.

Walton, R. (1975) Criteria for quality of working life. In Davis and Cherns op. cit.

Warnock, M. (1977) *Schools of Thought.* Faber: London.

Warr, P., Jackson, P. and Banks, M. (1982) Duration of unemployment and psychological well-being in young men and women. *Current Psychological Research* 2: 207-214.

Watts, A. (1978) The implications of school-leavers' unemployment for careers education in schools. *Journal of Curriculum Studies* 3: 233-250.

Watts, A. (ed.) (1983) *Work Experience and Schools.* Heinemann: London.

Watts, A. (1984) *Education, Unemployment and the Future of Work.* Open University Press.

Weekly Reader (1971) Fourth Grade Edition, January.

Weisberg, A. (1983) What research has to say about vocational education in the high schools. *Phi Delta Kappa* 33: 335-339.

Wenn, M. (1986) School Councils in Tasmanian Secondary Schools. unpublished MEd thesis, University of Tasmania.

Whitehead, A. (1962) *The Aims of Education*. Benn: London.
Whitfield, G. (1957) The grammar school through half a century. *British Journal of Educational Studies* 5, 2.
Wilkes, C. and Shirley, I. (eds) (1984) In the Public Interest: Work, Health and Housing in New *Zealand*. Benton/Ross: Auckland.
Williams, R. (1958) *Culture and Society 1780-1950*. Chatto and Windus: London.
Williamson, H. (1983) WEEP - Exploitation or advantage? In *In Place of Work: Policy and Provision for the Young Unemployed*, edited by R. Fiddy, Falmer Press: Lewes, Sussex.
Willis, P. (1977) *Learning to Labour*. Saxon House: London.
Willis, P. (1984) Conclusion: theory and practice. In Bates op. cit.
Wilson, B. (1979) Education and work: a reappraisal of the contribution of schooling to placement on the job market. Paper presented at SAANZ Conference (mimeo) Canberra College of Advenced Education.
Wirth, A. (1966) *John Dewey as Educator*. Wiley and Sons: New York.
Wirth, A. (1974) Philosophical issues in the vocational-liberal studies controversy (1900-1917): John Dewey vs. the social efficiency philosophers. *Studies in Philosophy and Education* 8: 169-182.
Wirth, A. (1977) Issues affecting education and work in the eighties: efficiency versus industrial democracy. *Teacher's College Record* 79: 55-67.
Wirth, A. (1981) Exploring linkages between Dewey's educational philosophy and industrial reorganization. *Economic and Industrial Democracy* 2: 121-140.
Wolpe, A. (1978) Education and the sexual division of labour. In *Feminism and Materialism*, edited by A. Kuhn and A. Wolpe, Routledge Kegan Paul: London.
Wood, S. (ed.) (1982) *The Degradation of Work? Skill, Deskilling and the Labour Process*. Hutchinson: London.
Woods, P. (1980a) *Sociology and the School: An Interactionist Viewpoint*. Routledge Kegan Paul: London.
Woods, P. (1980b) *Pupil Strategies: Explorations in the Sociology of the School*. Croom Helm: London.
Woods, P. (ed.) (1980c) *Teacher Strategies: Explorations in the Sociology of the School*. Croom Helm: London.
Woods, P. (1984) Negotiating the demands of schoolwork. In *Life in School: The Sociology of Pupil Culture* edited by M. Hammersley and P. Woods, Open University Press.
Wright, E. (1979) *Class Crisis and the State*. Verso: London.
Yates, L. (1987a) Curriculum theory and non-sexist education: a discussion of curriculum theory, feminist theory, and Victorian education policy and practice 1975-1985. unpublished PhD thesis, La Trobe University.
Yates, L. (1987b) Australian research on gender and education 1975-1985. In *Australian Education: A Review of Recent Research*, edited by J. Keeves, Allen and Unwin: Sydney.
Young, D. (1984a) Coping with change: the New Training Initiative. *Journal of the Royal Society of Arts*. 5335: June.
Young, D. (1984b) Presentation of certificates for Education for Capability Initiative. *Journal of the Royal Society of Arts*. 5335: June.
Zaretsky, E. (1976) *Capitalism and the Family*. Harper and Row: New York.

Index